THE O.J. FILES:
EVIDENTIARY ISSUES IN A TACTICAL CONTEXT

By

Gerald F. Uelmen
Professor of Law, Santa Clara University School of Law

AMERICAN CASEBOOK SERIES®

**WEST
GROUP**

ST. PAUL, MINN., 1998

COPYRIGHT © 1998 By WEST GROUP
                610 Opperman Drive
                P.O. Box 64526
                St. Paul, MN 55164–0526
                1–800–328–9352

ISBN 0–314–22921–3

*TEXT IS PRINTED ON 10% POST
CONSUMER RECYCLED PAPER*

For Nancy, Amy and Matt:

*Children who love wisdom
make their father glad.*
Prov. 29:3

*

Introduction

Whatever opinion we may have of the criminal trial of *People v. O.J. Simpson,* or the follow-up civil trial of *Rufo v. Simpson,* (and rare indeed is the person who has *no* opinion), we must recognize the unique educational opportunity the cases present for teachers and students of the law of evidence. The spectrum of evidentiary issues litigated in the cases touched nearly every issue covered in a typical law school evidence course. The factual setting in which these questions arose are widely known and understood. A full transcript of the trial proceedings and most of the pleadings are readily available on line. Thus, the cases offer an unprecedented setting for the teaching of evidence with actual examples from real-life litigation with which students will have some familiarity. More important, the tactical context in which the questions were litigated, and their impact upon the ultimate outcome, can be fully considered. Too often, evidence is learned in a fragmentary manner, with students never appreciating the tactical context in which issues are actually litigated in a trial.

Judge Lance Ito was frequently criticized for the painstaking time and attention he devoted to evidentiary rulings in the criminal trial, and the frequent interruptions that bench conferences required. The pundits often lacked any appreciation of the critical nature of the evidentiary issues being discussed, however. After thirty years of litigating evidentiary issues in both trials and appeals, and twenty five years of teaching evidence and trial practice, I can personally attest that very few cases will offer better examples of careful preparation and presentation of evidentiary issues by highly skilled lawyers on both sides. Students may be heartened to discover, however, that even in these cases, arguments were overlooked, issues were missed, and erroneous rulings were made.

The eighteen issues included in these materials were selected to supplement and enliven a law school evidence course in several possible ways. Each issue identifies the item of evidence or proposed jury instruction which was actually presented in the criminal or civil trial, or both. The tactical considerations surrounding the presentation of the issue are then briefly described. Excerpts from the actual arguments presented by each side are then offered, drawn from the pleadings and transcripts. The judges' rulings are presented, followed by comments and questions, frequently drawing on post-trial published commentaries.

The material will provide ample fodder for lively classroom discussion. The arguments presented can be critiqued or expanded, treating the judges' rulings as tentative ones. Students can be asked to reformulate the arguments using the Federal Rules of Evidence or the Evidence Code of their state. (The judges' rulings were all made pursuant to the California Evidence Code). Students can be assigned to brief and/or argue an appellate challenge to the judges' rulings.

Students may be surprised to discover how frequently the rulings in the criminal and civil trial differed, or how often the lawyers trying the two cases pursued different tactical options. In some instances, the differences were attributable to actual changes in the California law of evidence between the two trials. The differences will provide excellent opportunities to convey to students the unpredictable vagaries of litigation that so frequently influence the results.

Underlying any of these exercises will be strong opinions and judgments about the final outcome of the cases. Students should be encouraged to analyze those opinions and judgments, and their impact upon the positions they favor. This may present the most significant educational opportunity of all, by replicating the passion of zealous advocates.

Acknowledgements

This book contains the work product of a remarkable collection of talented lawyers, including F. Lee Bailey, Phillip A. Baker, Robert C. Baker, Robert D. Blasier, Melissa S. Bluestein, Marcia Clark, George Clarke, Johnnie Cochran, Jr., Chris Darden, Alan Dershowitz, Nathan Dershowitz, Carl Douglas, Hank Goldberg, Scott Gordon, Rockne Harmon, William Hodgman, Daniel P. Leonard, Cheri Lewis, Lisa Kahn, Brian Kelberg, Peter Neufeld, Daniel Petrocelli, Barry Scheck and Robert Shapiro, as well as my own. Those are just the names on the pleadings or counsel who made the arguments that are quoted. There were many more working behind the scenes. We don't have to admire each other to recognize the craft and skill reflected in these pages. And each of us knows the pundits could never put themselves in our shoes.

I especially want to thank Robert D. Blasier for guiding me through all the transcripts he downloaded onto my Thinkpad, Phillip A. Baker for so promptly responding to some cries for help, and Barry Scheck and Judge Lance Ito for reading the manuscript. Professor Miguel Mendez, whose *California Evidence* was on Judge Ito's bench throughout the criminal trial, offered some practical and much appreciated advice and encouragement, as did Professor Roger Park. My Research Assistant David Bozanich and the students in my Fall, 1997 course in Evidence at Santa Clara caught most of my mistakes, although I'm certain a few remain.

Permission is gratefully acknowledged for reprinting selections from the following copyrighted sources:

OUTRAGE: The Five Reasons Why O.J. Simpson Got Away With Murder by Vincent Bugliosi. Coyright © 1996 by Vincent Bugliosi. Reprinted by permission of W.W. Norton & Company, Inc.

WITHOUT A DOUBT by Marcia Clark with Teresa Carpenter. Copyright © Lykart Limited, 1997. Reprinted by permission of Viking Penguin Press.

MADAM FOREMAN: A Rush to Judgment? by Armanda Cooley, Carrie Bess, and Marsha Rubin-Jackson as told to Tom Brynes with Mike Walker. Copyright © 1995 by Dove Audio, Inc. Reprinted by permission of Dove Books.

REASONABLE DOUBTS by Alan Dershowitz. Copyright © 1996 by Alan Dershowitz. Reprinted by permission of Simon & Schuster.

THE PROSECUTION RESPONDS by Hank M. Goldberg. Copyright © 1996 by Hank M. Goldberg. Reprinted by permission of Birch Lane Press.

THE SEARCH FOR JUSTICE by Robert L. Shapiro with Larkin Warren. Copyright © 1996 by Robert L. Shapiro. Reprinted by permission of Warner Books, Inc.

LESSONS FROM THE TRIAL by Gerald F. Uelmen. Copyright © 1996 by Gerald F. Uelmen. Reprinted by permission of Andrews & McMeel.

GERALD F. UELMEN

Santa Clara, California
October 1, 1997

Table of Contents

	Page
INTRODUCTION	v
ACKNOWLEDGEMENTS	vii

Chapter I. Relevance, Conditional Relevance and Preliminary Facts **1**

A. Autopsy Photos 1
   1. The Evidence 1
   2. The Tactical Context 4
   3. Defense Argument 5
   4. Prosecution Argument 7
   5. Judges' Rulings 10
   6. Comments and Questions 11
B. The "Dream" Testimony 12
   1. The Evidence 12
   2. The Tactical Context 13
   3. Prosecution Argument 13
   4. Defense Argument 18
   5. Judges' Rulings 20
   6. Comments and Questions 21
C. The Bronco Chain of Custody 26
   1. The Evidence 26
   2. The Tactical Context 27
   3. Defense Argument 27
   4. Prosecution Argument 29
   5. Judges' Rulings 33
   6. Comments and Questions 35
D. Jury Instructions Re: Blood Evidence 36
   1. Proposed Jury Instruction 36
   2. The Tactical Context 37
   3. Defense Argument 38
   4. Prosecution Argument 38
   5. Judges' Rulings 39
   6. Comments and Questions 39

Chapter II. Character Evidence **40**

A. Prior Spousal Abuse by Simpson 40
   1. The Evidence 40

Page

A. Prior Spousal Abuse by Simpson—Continued
  2. The Tactical Context 42
  3. Defense Argument 43
    a. Evidence of Prior Specific Instances of Conduct Is Not Admissible to Show Propensity. 43
    b. Evidence of Prior Specific Instances of Conduct Is Not Admissible to Show Identity. 44
    c. Evidence of Prior Specific Instances of Conduct Is Not Admissible to Show Motive or Intent. 45
    d. Evidence of Prior Specific Instances of Conduct Is Not Admissible to Show a Common Plan or Scheme. 45
    e. The Admission of Prior Instances of Conduct Would Violate Defendant's State and Federal Constitutional Rights. 46
    f. The Prejudicial Impact of Evidence of Prior Specific Instances of Conduct Outweighs Its Probative Value. 46
    g. Out of Court Statements by Nicole Brown Simpson Expressing Fear of Defendant Are Inadmissible Hearsay. 47
  4. Prosecution Argument 47
    a. Introduction. 47
    b. Without Resort to Traditional Evidence Code Section 1101(b) Analysis, Where a Defendant Is Charged with a Violent Crime and Has or Had a Previous Relationship With a Victim, Evidence Demonstrating Jealousy, Quarrels, Hostility, or Aggression Between Defendant and Victim Is Admissible to Prove Motive, and thus, the Perpetrator's Identity and Intent. 48
    c. The Rule of *Haston* Is Inapplicable in Relationship Violence Cases. 50
    d. Applying Traditional Evidence Code Section 1101(b) Analysis, the Evidence Regarding the Relationship Between Victim and Defendant Is Admissible. 50
    e. The Evidence Proffered Is Highly Probative and Not Excludable Under Evidence Code Section 352. 52
  5. Defense Reply Argument 53
    a. Introduction. 53
    b. *People v. Zack* Establishes No "Special Rule" Permitting Evidence of Prior Abuse. 53
    c. Prior Acts Are Not Relevant to Show Motive, Identity, Intent or Common Plan. 54

Page

A. Prior Spousal Abuse by Simpson—Continued
    d. Probative Value of the Evidence of Prior Acts Is Outweighed by the Risks of Undue Consumption of Time and Undue Prejudice. 56
  6. Judges' Ruling 56
  7. Comments and Questions 58
B. Prior Police Misconduct by Fuhrman 62
  1. The Evidence 62
  2. Tactical Context 66
  3. Defense Argument 66
    a. Introduction. 66
    b. The Evidence of Prior Misconduct Is Admissible Under California Evidence Code Section 1101(b). 67
    c. Evidence of Prior Instances of Police Misconduct Is Relevant to Show Habit and Custom. 69
    d. The Probative Value of the Evidence Substantially Outweighs Any Prejudicial Impact or Risk of Undue Consumption of Time. 70
    e. The Jury Must Assess the Credibility of Detective Fuhrman's Statements. 71
  4. Prosecution Argument 72
    a. The Proffered Allegations of Misconduct Are Temporally Remote. 72
    b. The Defense Has Proffered No Evidence to Demonstrate the Statements Made by Mark Fuhrman Describing Acts of Misconduct Have Any Basis in Fact. 72
    c. The Proffered Evidence Does Not Qualify for Admission Under California Evidence Code Section 1101(b). 73
    d. The Proffered Evidence Does Not Constitute Admissible Evidence of Habit or Custom. 75
    e. The Court Should Exercise Its Discretion Under Evidence Code Section 352 to Exclude the Proffered Materials. 75
  5. Judges' Rulings 77
  6. Comments and Questions 79

Chapter III. Hearsay and Exceptions **82**

A. The "911" Tapes 82
  1. The Evidence 82
  2. The Tactical Context 89
  3. Defense Argument 89
    a. The "911" Tapes Are Not Admissible as "Spontaneous Statements." 89

Page

A. The "911" Tapes—Continued
   b. Many Statements Contained on the 911 Tape Are
      Inadmissible Opinions. ----------------------------- 91
   c. The Admission of the 911 Tapes Would Violate the
      Defendant's Constitutional Rights to Confront
      and Cross Examine the Witnesses Against Him.   92
   4. Prosecution Argument ----------------------------- 92
   5. Judges' Rulings ------------------------------------ 97
   6. Comments and Questions -------------------------- 98
B. Nicole's Statements in Police Reports ------------------- 98
   1. The Evidence --------------------------------------- 98
   2. The Tactical Context ------------------------------- 99
   3. Defense Argument ---------------------------------- 99
      a. The Statement to Sgt. Lally Is Not Admissible to
         Show "State of Mind." ---------------------------- 99
      b. The Statement to Sgt. Lally Is Not Admissible Un-
         der the Hearsay Exception for Official Records or
         Business Records. -------------------------------- 100
      c. The Statement to Sgt. Lally Is Not Admissible as a
         "Spontaneous Statement." ------------------------ 101
   4. Prosecution Argument ----------------------------- 102
   5. Judges' Rulings ------------------------------------ 103
   6. Comments and Questions -------------------------- 105
C. O.J.'s Statement to Police Detectives ------------------- 106
   1. The Evidence --------------------------------------- 106
   2. The Tactical Context ------------------------------- 119
   3. Defense Argument ---------------------------------- 121
   4. Prosecution Argument ----------------------------- 124
   5. Judges' Rulings ------------------------------------ 125
   6. Comments and Questions -------------------------- 130
D. Former Testimony of Thano Peratis --------------------- 132
   1. The Evidence --------------------------------------- 132
   2. The Tactical Context ------------------------------- 134
   3. Defense Argument ---------------------------------- 135
   4. Prosecution Argument ----------------------------- 136
   5. Judges' Rulings ------------------------------------ 137
   6. Comments and Questions -------------------------- 138

Chapter IV. Cross–Examination, Impeachment and
   Rehabilitation of Witnesses -------------------------- 140

A. Cross–Examination of Fuhrman Re: Racial Bias ------------- 140
   1. The Evidence --------------------------------------- 140
   2. The Tactical Context ------------------------------- 142
   3. Prosecution Argument ----------------------------- 142
      a. The Defense Attack on Detective Mark Fuhrman. ----- 143

Page

A. Cross–Examination of Fuhrman Re: Racial Bias—
    Continued
    b. Mere Evidence of Motive or Opportunity Is Insuffi-
       cient to Warrant the Introduction of Evidence
       That a Third Party Is Culpable, Even if Such
       Evidence Was Credible. 145
    c. The Evidence Should Be Excluded Under Evidence
       Code Section 352. 146
  4. Defense Argument 148
    a. Relevance of the Credibility of Detective Mark
       Fuhrman. 149
    b. Inaccurate Factual Assumptions in the People's Mo-
       tion. 150
    c. Rules of Evidence Regarding the Motive of Third
       Parties to Commit the Crime Are Inapplicable. 151
    d. The Motion Is Premature. 152
    e. The Probative Value of Evidence Challenging the
       Credibility of Detective Fuhrman Outweighs Any
       Prejudicial Impact. 152
  5. Oral Argument 153
  6. Judge's Ruling 160
  7. Comments and Questions 163
B. Impeachment of Fuhrman by McKinney Tapes 165
  1. The Evidence 165
  2. The Tactical Context 166
  3. Defense Argument 167
  4. Prosecution Argument 168
  5. Judge's Ruling 169
  6. Comments and Questions 170
C. Threats and Prior Errors by the Coroner 172
  1. The Evidence 172
  2. The Tactical Context 173
  3. Prosecution Argument 174
  4. Defense Argument 179
  5. Judges' Rulings 184
  6. Comments and Questions 184

Chapter V. Expert Witnesses 186

A. Luminol Test Results 186
  1. The Evidence 186
  2. The Tactical Context 186
  3. Defense Argument 186
  4. The Prosecution Argument 190
  5. Judges' Rulings 192
  6. Comments and Questions 193
B. Waiver of Kelly–Frye Hearing 193
  1. The Proffer 193

Page

B. Waiver of *Kelly–Frye* Hearing—Continued
  2. The Tactical Context -- 194
  3. Defense Argument -- 196
  4. Prosecution Argument -- 200
  5. Judge's Ruling -- 203
  6. Comments and Questions -- 203

Chapter VI. Privileges -- **204**

A. Jury Instructions Re: Invocation of the Fifth Amendment
    by Fuhrman -- 204
  1. Proposed Instruction -- 204
  2. The Tactical Context -- 206
  3. Prosecution Argument -- 207
  4. Judges' Ruling -- 211
  5. Defense Argument -- 212
  6. Final Ruling of the Court -------------------------------------- 218
  7. Comments and Questions -- 219
B. Invocation of Clergyman–Penitent Privilege by Rosie Grier 221
  1. The Evidence --- 221
  2. Tactical Context -- 222
  3. Prosecution Argument -- 223
  4. Defense Argument -- 226
  5. Judge's Ruling -- 230
  6. Comments and Questions -- 233
C. Attorney–Client Privilege and Polygraph Evidence ----------- 234
  1. The Evidence --- 234
  2. The Tactical Context -- 235
  3. Examination of O.J. Simpson ---------------------------------- 237
  4. Reconsideration of Ruling ------------------------------------- 245
  5. Instructions to Jury -- 247
  6. Motion for Mistrial --- 248
    a. Reference to Taking a Purported Polygraph Exami-
       nation. -- 248
    b. Admission of the Purported Polygraph Test Violated
       the Attorney–Client Privilege. -------------------------- 251
  7. Comments and Questions -- 253

THE O.J. FILES:
EVIDENTIARY ISSUES IN A TACTICAL CONTEXT

*

Chapter I

RELEVANCE, CONDITIONAL RELEVANCE AND PRELIMINARY FACTS

A. AUTOPSY PHOTOS

1. THE EVIDENCE

The prosecution proposed to present 26 of 61 photos taken during the coroner's autopsy of Ronald Goldman, and 33 of 61 photos taken during the coroner's autopsy of Nicole Brown Simpson. A formal offer of proof described each photo in detail and the reason it was offered. The offer is reproduced here for five of the photographs:

Photo No.	Description	Proposed Relevancy
G1	Clothed body of Ronald Goldman as received at the Coroner's Office on June 13, 1994. (Upper two-thirds of body including head).	This photograph, in conjunction with photograph number G2, shows the condition of the body of Ronald Goldman at the time it was received at the Coroner's Office. These two photographs are relevant to establish the chain-of-custody with respect to clothing and body appearance. In addition, the condition of the pants, in particular the bleeding on the left pant leg, is relevant to correlate with a left thigh stab wound received by Mr. Goldman. The nature of the bleeding down the length of the pant leg is relevant to help establish the relative position of Mr. Goldman at the time he received that thigh wound and the relative time during the course of the lethal assault when the thigh wound was received.

G5   This photograph depicts the left flank wound to the abdominal aorta as well as two abrasions (one over the left shoulder and one on the radial aspect of the left hand at the wrist level) which are not described by Dr. Golden in his original protocol or addendum. The photograph also shows areas of lividity.

This photograph is the only photograph which depicts the unaddressed abrasions to the left shoulder and radial aspect of the left hand/wrist. It also demonstrates the presence of lividity, a factor that will be discussed in the estimation of time of death. This photo also shows the relative position on the body where the left flank injury was received.

G37   Photograph G37 shows two semi-parallel superficial incise wounds to the neck, anterior portion, and a stabbing/cutting wound to the left side of the neck. In addition, a non-fatal, superficial stab wound or cutting wound to the right upper chest at the lateral border of the right clavicle is shown. This photograph also depicts a small superficial cut above the two semi-parallel incise wounds and a small abrasion below the two semi-parallel incise wounds.

This photograph is relevant to the issues of premeditation and deliberation, malice and the nature of circumstances surrounding the lethal assault on Mr. Goldman. In addition, the small superficial cut above the incise wounds and the small abrasion below the incise wounds are neither addressed or diagrammed in Dr. Golden's original protocol or addressed in his addendum.

B1   Clothed body of Nicole Brown Simpson as received at the Coroner's Office on June 13, 1994. (Upper two-thirds of body including head).

This photograph, in conjunction with photograph number B2, shows the condition of the body of Nicole Brown Simpson at time it was received at the Coroner's Office. These two photographs are relevant to establish the chain-of-custody with respect to the clothing and body appearance. In addition, at the preliminary hearing, Dr. Golden was cross-examined concerning the failure to take a sexual assault kit in this case. Photographs B1 and B2 are relevant to establish the bases on which a judgment was made that there was no evidence to suggest Nicole Brown Simpson had been sexually assaulted as part of the assault which led to her death.

B13   This photograph depicts the face and neck areas. The photograph depicts an area of lividity to the left side of the face, consistent with the position in which the body was found as depicted in crime scene photos. The photograph also depicts the left lateral end of the major stab/incise wound to the neck, in particular depicting the pointed end to that wound. The photograph also depicts the relative anatomical positions between that major stab/incise wound to the neck and a

This photograph is relevant to the issues of premeditation and deliberation, malice and the nature and extent of any struggle between Nicole Brown Simpson and the perpetrator of the lethal knife assault. The appearance of lividity on the left side of the face is relevant to establish that the area of pinkish contusion ecchymosis to the right side of the back is not a product of lividity but rather a product of blunt force trauma. This photograph is also the only photograph to docuseries of four stab wounds to the left side of the neck. ment the relative anatomical positions between the major stab/incise wound to the right side of the neck and the four stab wounds to the left side of the neck, three of which share a common area of injury to the left carotid artery and left jugular vein. In addition, this photograph clearly demonstrates the upward angle of the major stab/incise wound as it goes from the left and mid-portions of the neck to the area just below the right earlobe. The angle of that stab/incise wound is relevant to establishing the position of the perpetrator with respect to Nicole Brown Simpson at the time the stab/incise wound was inflicted. This further goes to the issues of premeditation and deliberation and malice.

In response to the Offer of Proof, Judge Ito requested the defense to list specific objections to each item offered. The defense then proffered the following objections to the photographs listed above:

G1   The photographs of the clothed and unclothed body of Ronald Goldman are especially gruesome. No wounds appear in this photograph that are not more clearly depicted in other photographs. The chain of custody of clothing is simply not in issue in the case. To the extent the pattern of blood flow on the jeans is relevant, it can be shown through oral testimony, physical evidence (the jeans themselves) or by a cropped photograph showing just the jeans.

G5   While this photo may be the only depiction of abrasions to the left shoulder and left wrist, these abrasions have no particular relevancy that requires graphic presentation in photos. They are not knife wounds. If lividity requires demonstration, it can be shown through photograph G7.

G37   This photograph may become relevant if the defense challenges Dr. Golden's failure to address the abrasions depicted. But the mere possibility that such a challenge may be made does not entitle the prosecution to utilize otherwise inadmissible evidence to anticipate it. In addition, this gruesome portrayal of the neck wounds misrepresents the nature of the wounds by distending the neck to open and expose the wound interior. The photograph can also be cropped to eliminate irrelevant facial features.

B1   The clothed and unclothed full body photographs of Nicole Brown Simpson are especially gruesome. No wounds appear in these photographs that are not more clearly depicted in other photographs. The chain of custody of her clothing is simply not an issue in the case. There is no contention by anyone that there was a sexual assault in this case. While Dr. Golden may explain his failure to take a sexual assault kit in this case by the fact that the panties were intact, the photographs are not necessary to corroborate that explanation. The defense is not contending that a sexual assault kit was warranted by the condition of the panties. To the contrary, the defense contention is that a sexual assault kit would have yielded useful information about the time of death if there was evidence of recent sexual intercourse, and the protocol calls for a sexual assault kit whenever it could yield useful information.

B13　　This photograph is especially gruesome and inflammatory. The neck is artificially distended to enlarge and exaggerate the size of the wound. Everything the People wish to demonstrate regarding the nature of the neck wound can be illustrated by Photograph B10, so this photograph is duplicative. Premeditation, deliberation and malice are not demonstrated by these wounds, and are not in issue in the case. The struggle between Nicole Brown Simpson and the perpetrator is conceded, not in issue, and is amply demonstrated by other evidence. While this photograph may become relevant if the defense challenges Dr. Golden's failure to address the conditions depicted, in the absence of such a challenge the photograph should be excluded.

2.　THE TACTICAL CONTEXT

The medical examiner who conducted the autopsies, Dr. Irwin Golden, had been subjected to a vigorous cross-examination at the Preliminary Hearing, and the prosecution was anxious to anticipate and foreclose attacks on his testimony. They filed a separate *in limine* motion to limit his cross examination. See Chapter IV(C) *infra*, "Threats and Prior Errors by the Coroner." For the defense, attacking the competence of the coroner was a vital part of the strategy to suggest the scientific evidence in the case could not be trusted. Thus, the prosecution hoped to utilize the autopsy photos to illustrate back-up expert testimony by others, and perhaps to even avoid having to call Dr. Golden as a witness at all, although this tactical agenda was never revealed in litigating the admissibility of the autopsy photos.

While ordinarily a motion to exclude autopsy photos would be filed by the defense, in the *Simpson* criminal trial, the prosecution filed a "Motion to Admit" the photos in advance of formally offering them, explaining they needed an advance ruling as to which photos could be admitted in order to complete "exhibit boards" which would be utilized during the testimony of the coroner.

3. DEFENSE ARGUMENT

The People request an advance ruling on the admissibility of selected crime scene and autopsy photographs, to expedite the preparation of exhibit boards prior to the testimony of the medical examiner. Such a ruling requires the court to carefully weigh the probative value of each photograph and balance it against the substantial danger of undue prejudice, of confusing the issues, or or misleading the jury. California Evidence Code Section 352.[1]

The defense respectfully suggests that the proper determination of probative value and danger of prejudice requires the court to examine all of the available crime scene and autopsy photographs, not just the ones selected by the People. The availability of alternative photographs which may be less prejudicial than those selected by the People would establish that there is no compelling evidentiary need to subject jurors to highly inflammatory photographs that may have been selected for their shock value rather than for legitimate evidentiary purposes. Thus, at the hearing of this motion, the defense requests that the Court be supplied with not only the selected photographs, but all available photographs. This will also facilitate a determination by the defense whether it wishes to itself offer any photographs in evidence that have not been selected by the People. While the defense was given the opportunity to review autopsy photographs, we were not supplied with our own set of these photographs. The defense would also respectfully suggest that the review of photographs by the Court and counsel be conducted in chambers.

California appellate rulings have carefully delineated the appropriate exercise of judicial discretion in ruling on the admissibility of photographs of this nature. The mere offering of a plausible theory of relevance or materiality cannot justify the admission of such photographs. The court is required to *weigh* the probative value, which means the evidence must be placed in the context of other available evidence to determine whether it is truly necessary, or is simply cumulative. In *People v. Ford,* 60 Cal. 2d 772, 801 (1964), the Supreme Court found it unnecessary to even view the

---

1. California Evidence Code, Section 352 provides:

"The court in its discretion may exclude evidence if its probative value is substantially outweighed by the proba-bility that its admission will (a) necessitate undue consumption of time or (b) create substantial danger of undue prejudice, of confusing the issues, or of misleading the jury."

photographs to determine they were improperly admitted, because the trial court failed to engage in this essential weighing process.

Similarly, the Court in *People v. Smith,* 33 Cal. App.3d 51 (1973) noted that the kind of justifications offered by the prosecution in this case, (*e.g.,* "to show malice"), are routinely offered by prosecutors in every case. Such justifications must be carefully evaluated in terms of whether an issue is actually in dispute, and whether other less inflammatory sources are available to prove the same point.

It is indeed ironic that the People argue that the incompetence of the medical examiner creates the need for admission of the gruesome photographs. In *People v. Carrera,* 49 Cal.3d 291 (1989), the need for the medical expert to use photographs was created by the death of the doctor who actually performed the autopsy. Here, the doctor who performed the autopsy remains available, but we are told that the failure to describe wounds in his initial report, or the incompleteness of such descriptions, created the need for "multi-page addendum reports" which provide "amendments and additions to the original protocol," based on a "review of the photographs." Obviously, if the admissibility of otherwise inadmissible photographs can be justified by the incompetence of the medical examiner, there will be little incentive for prosecuting authorities to address the institutional problems of lack of supervision and training in the the coroner's office.

Ultimately, the admissibility of the photographs must be determined by their probative value to the jury as the finders of fact with reference to issues that are actually in dispute, rather than their value to the coroner in correcting his mistakes. The Court in *People v. Burns,* 109 Cal. App.2d 524, 541–42 (1952) articulated the appropriate standard:

> "In view of the fact that no question was raised as to these bruises and abrasions, and the fact that a view of them was of no particular value to the jury, it is obvious that the only purpose of exhibiting them was to inflame the jury's emotions against the defendant.... Surely, there is a line between admitting a photograph which is of some help to the jury in solving the facts of the case and one which is of no value other than to inflame the minds of the jurors. That line was crossed in this case."

The required weighing of probative value and potential prejudice requires careful assessment of each proffered photograph in the context of all available evidence and testimony, and the issues actually in dispute, as well as its probable impact upon the emotions of the jurors.

4. PROSECUTION ARGUMENT

First, unlike the discretion exercised by the prosecution in carefully selecting from the vast number of available autopsy photographs only the required minimum number of photographs to fully, fairly and accurately depict the injuries, fatal and non-fatal, received by Nicole Brown Simpson and Ronald Goldman in the course of their murders, defense counsel has objected to every single photograph. Unlike the defense, which has failed to offer a single controlling case authority to support their novel position that because the defense perceives "the only issue (that) the jury must resolve in this case (is) whether the prosecution has proven beyond a reasonable doubt that O.J. Simpson was the perpetrator of the murders of Nicole Brown Simpson and Ronald Goldman," the prosecution should be precluded from using any of these photographs, the People have provided recent, controlling and compelling authority from the California Supreme Court and California Courts of Appeal that the photographs proffered for use with the jury are relevant and probative to prove (1) the existence of malice; (2) premeditation and deliberation; (3) the fact that one physically superior perpetrator murdered both the 5'9", 170 pound Ronald Goldman and the 5'5", 129 pound Nicole Brown Simpson; (4) that one knife was responsible for all sharp force injuries received by both murder victims; (5) that these murders were the product of a rage attack as testified to by Detective Lange and not drug related, Columbian "necklace" or "necktie" murders, as posited by Mr. Cochran in his opening statement and his cross-examination of Detective Lange and other police officers; (6) the extent of bleeding resulting from the multiple sharp force injuries received by both murder victims, which, among other things, is relevant to establish the fact of a single killer who could not have left the scene of the murders without leaving visible bloody shoe prints; and (7) the nature and extent of the struggle with each murder victim, which, among other things, establishes not only the circumstances of the murders of Nicole Brown Simpson and Ronald Goldman, but the source for the defendant's finger injury, and, *a fortiori*, the source of the blood drops on the Bundy walkway next to the bloody shoe prints as having been left by the murderer, O.J. Simpson.

In addition, the photographs are admissible to assist the jury in their understanding and evaluation of the forensic pathology testimony presented at trial. See *People v. Wilson*, 3 Cal.4th 926, 938 (1992) and *People v. Crittenden*, 9 Cal.4th 83, 131–36 (1994).

Defense counsel contend that the autopsy photos are of no value in identifying the perpetrator of these murders. Nothing could be further from the truth. In establishing the murders as born of rage, a juror would undoubtedly look to whether the defendant's previous evidence of domestic violence against his former wife, Nicole Brown Simpson, evidence reflecting his jealousy and possessory attitude towards her, would motivate such an emotional response, especially given the evidence already heard by the jury describing the earlier events which occurred on June 12, 1994. Further, in establishing that one knife could be responsible for all sharp force injuries as these photographs do (with testimony of a qualified, forensic pathologist identifying the relevant features of each wound's appearance in the appropriate photograph), defense counsel's contention is shown to be fallacious. If evidence that one knife could be responsible for all of the sharp force injuries received by both murder victims is accepted by this jury, then undoubtedly, the jury will want to consider what single individual, possessing the requisite physical strength and agility, along with the appropriate motive, would have committed these rage murders, leaving at the scene of those murders bloody shoe prints, size 12, and blood drops which, based upon appropriate D.N.A. analysis, match the defendant, O.J. Simpson. These simply are two aspects of the autopsy photographs which will serve, along with consideration of all other evidence, to establish that the defendant was in fact the murderer of his ex-wife and Mr. Goldman.

Although the defense claims that the existence of malice is not in issue, ... the law clearly requires that the prosecution prove beyond a reasonable doubt the existence of all elements of murder, including express malice and premeditation and deliberation for first degree murder.

... In a recent case from the United States Supreme Court, a defendant convicted of the murder of a child contended that the trial court erred when it allowed the prosecution to admit evidence of battered child syndrome. The defendant contended that "because no claim was made at trial that (the child) died accidentally, the battered child syndrome evidence was irrelevant and violative of due process." In rejecting the defendant's contention, the High Court held "the prosecution's burden to prove every element of the crime is not relieved by a defendant's tactical decision not to contest an essential element of the offense." *Estelle v. McGuire,* 112 S. Ct. 475, 481 (1991).

Defense counsel object to the admission of all photographs on the grounds that their prejudicial impact outweighs their probative value. As this Court is well aware, before relevant evidence may be excluded under Section 352, that section gives the Court discretion to "exclude evidence if its probative value is *substantially outweighed* by the probability that its admission will ... create *substantial* danger of undue prejudice." Counsel's failure to acknowledge that Section 352 requires a showing that the prejudice *"substantially outweighs"* the probative value is understandable given the significant probative value of these photographs. Counsel's failure to acknowledge the true test under Section 352 is akin to evidence suggesting consciousness of guilt on the part of a defendant. Counsel's failure is consciousness of recognition that these photographs are properly admitted for all the reasons expressed by the prosecution.

Counsel's suggestion that the number and extent of the wounds can be illustrated by alternative means ... not only flies in the face of human experience ("a single picture is worth a thousand words") and scientific reality (photographs fairly and accurately depicting the actual wounds and injuries received cannot in any realistic way be equated with the rather inexact and crude drawings and charts prepared by Dr. Golden), but flies in the face of Mr. Shapiro's own representations on May 9, 1995, when he acknowledged that photographs are the best documentation of the actual injuries. Although counsel's effort to exclude these photographs from the jury's view and consideration is understandable given their significance to the broad array of issues identified, the law is clear that the prosecution, which has the burden of proof in this case, is not to be relegated to what counsel deem to be "alternative means" which clearly lack the force and weight of the evidence proffered.

Counsel allege that the real reason the People seek to utilize the photographs is to anticipate and explain potential challenges to mistakes by the coroner in his reports and addendums. Simply put, defense counsel are dead wrong. The "real reason" the People seek to introduce these photographs is to provide this jury with the fullest, fairest and most accurate evidence concerning the forensic pathology aspect of the case. By doing so, the prosecution hopes to facilitate the jury's search for the truth, which is, after all, what this, and any other criminal trial, is intended to be. (See *Izazaga v. Superior Court,* 54 Cal.3d 356 (1991)).

As the Court is well aware, it was defense counsel which raised Dr. Golden's "incompetency" in Mr. Cochran's opening statement. It was defense counsel which reiterated the contention of that "incompetency" when Dean Uelmen successfully urged this Court to permit the defense to question Dr. Golden about mistakes he made in two other cases in 1990. It is defense counsel which seeks to obtain a tactical advantage by first precluding the prosecution from giving the jury the full facts presented by these photographs and the circumstances of the autopsy findings and then, on cross-examination, raising the issue of Dr. Golden's "incompetency", thus suggesting to the jury that the prosecution intentionally withheld evidence of Dr. Golden's mistakes in an effort to cover up those mistakes. Efforts to seek such a tactical advantage are the antithesis of a search for the truth.

In summary, defense counsel has launched an all out assault to keep this jury from seeing the best evidence of what this defendant did when he murdered his former wife and her friend, thereby seeking to deprive this jury of some of the most significant evidence available for its consideration not only on the issue of the identity of the murderer, but whether these two murders are murders of the first or second degree. It bears repeating the recent observation made by the Court of Appeal in *People v. Thompson,* 7 Cal.App.4th 1966, 1973–74 (1992):

We have two observations. First, we subscribe to Justice Gardner's wise perception:

"(1) murder is seldom pretty, and pictures, testimony and physical evidence in such a case are always unpleasant; and (2) many attorneys tend to underestimate the stability of the jury. A juror is not some kind of a dithering nincompoop, brought in from never-never land and exposed to the harsh realities of life for the first time in a jury box. There is nothing magic about being a member of the bench or bar which makes these individuals capable of dispassionately evaluating gruesome testimony which, it is often contended, will throw jurors into a paroxysm of hysteria. Jurors are our peers, often as well educated, as well balanced, as stable, as experienced in the realities of life as the holders of law degrees. The average juror is well able to stomach the unpleasantness of exposure to the facts of a murder without being unduly influenced. The supposed influence on jurors of allegedly gruesome or inflammatory pictures exists more in the imagination of judges and lawyers than in reality." (Citation omitted).

"Second, a defendant has no right to transform the facts of a gruesome real-life murder into an anesthetized exercise where only the defendant, not the victim, appears human. Jurors are not, and should not be, computers for whom a victim is just an 'element' to be proved, a 'component' of a crime. A cardboard victim plus a flesh-and-blood defendant are likely to equal an unjust verdict."

5. JUDGES' RULINGS

All proffered autopsy photos were admitted in evidence at both the criminal and the civil trial.

6. COMMENTS AND QUESTIONS

(a) Ordinarily, prosecutors like to open a homicide case with the coroner as the first witness. Marcia Clark explains why the coroner and his autopsy photos did not lead the evidentiary line-up in the trial of *People v. O.J. Simpson*:

> "A common procedure in murder cases is to call the coroner as the first witness. It's easy to understand why prosecutors do this. Calling the coroner places the victims' bodies squarely in the jury's line of sight. You can't say it any more bluntly: 'Two people have been murdered, folks. That's why we're here.' If ever a jury needed a reminder of that, it was in this case, where so much of the attention had been riveted upon the defendant.

> But this wasn't a standard case. We simply could not afford to lead with Dr. Golden. Even before preliminary hearings back in July, we'd realized that the deputy medical examiner's report was riddled with errors.... So we went to our fallback position. We had Golden's report redone under the direction of his boss, the chief medical examiner, Dr. Lakshmanan Sathyavagiswaran. Dr. Lucky, as we called him, would have to use Golden's memory and the police photos to splice together some description of the wounds. But at the time, the redone report was a work in progress. Dr. Lucky wasn't ready to go to the top of the lineup. He wouldn't have the original report completely redone; we'd have to start our case by admitting a whole lot of Golden's original mistakes. Not a strong opening gambit."

Marcia Clark, *Without a Doubt,* pp.279–281 (Viking Penguin, 1997).

(b) Would the tactical decision to use the testimony of a substitute medical examiner strengthen or weaken the prosecution's arguments for the admissibility of the photographs? This decision had apparently already been made at the time the admissibility of the photographs was argued. If so, why would the prosecution conceal it?

(c) Assuming their admissibility, consider how the photographs could be most effectively presented to the jury. Would their "shock value" erode with a longer exposure? The direct testimony of the coroner consumed over two weeks of trial time, with a very tedious presentation and analysis of all the wounds inflicted on the victims. In what was hailed as one of the most brilliant tactical maneuvers of the trial, Robert Shapiro concluded his cross-examination of the coroner in less than an hour:

> "Shapiro, on cross examination, spotlighted the fact that eight days of direct examination was far more speculation than

substance when he asked this good question: 'Isn't it true, Doctor, that after eight days of testimony, there's only four facts you can testify to with a reasonable degree of medical certainty: that the deaths were homicides, that the fatal injuries were stab wounds, that the victims bled to death, and that they were killed between 9:00 and shortly after midnight?' Though the doctor gave a long, defensive answer, the essence of it was that this was true."

V. Bugliosi, *Outrage: The Five Reasons Why O.J. Simpson Got Away With Murder,* pp.124–25 (W.W. Norton Co. 1996). At the civil trial, the plaintiffs presented the expert testimony of the pathologist in less than one day.

(d) Would it make any difference if the defense offered to stipulate that the wounds were all inflicted by the same knife, or even that the murder was a first degree murder? At the close of the criminal trial, the defense objected to the jury being instructed that second degree murder was a lesser-included offense. In a decision rendered two years after the *Simpson* criminal trial, the California Supreme Court rejected a lower court's reversal of a murder conviction because grisly crime-scene photos were admitted despite a defendant's offer to stipulate the murder was premeditated:

"The defense's offer to stipulate as to the fact or manner of the shootings did not negate the relevance of the photograph. 'The prosecutor "was not obliged to prove these details solely from the testimony of live witnesses' or to accept antiseptic stipulations in lieu of photographic evidence.' " *People v. Scheid,* 16 Cal.4th 1, 16 (1997).

(e) The jurors had a very strong reaction to the autopsy photos. Amanda Cooley, the jury foreman, wrote: "The autopsy photos were terrible. That was enough to send everybody out to lunch. Afterward, we had nightmares about them. I couldn't sleep." Juror Marsha Rubin-Jackson added, "I was doing okay with the crime scene photos. But the autopsy photos were bad, and they showed them just before lunch." Cooley, Bess & Rubin–Jackson, *Madam Foreman: A Rush to Judgment?,* at pp. 124–25 (Dove Books, 1995).

B. THE "DREAM" TESTIMONY

1. THE EVIDENCE

Witness Ronald Shipp told prosecutors for the first time in late January, 1995, while being interviewed to prepare the presentation of his trial testimony, that he had a bedroom conversation with O.J. Simpson on June 13, 1994, the evening of the day he returned from

Chicago, as O.J. was preparing for bed. He described the conversation as follows:

> [O.J. said] "I was interviewed by detectives and they asked me to take a lie detector test."
>
> I replied, "Well, what did you say?"
>
> And he kind of chuckled, and he says, "Hey, to be truthful, Ron, Man, I've had a lot of dreams about killing her." And he says, "I really don't know about taking that thing."
>
> He did not say he wouldn't take it. He says, "I really don't know about taking it."

The prosecution delivered a copy of this statement to the defense the following day. Shipp was called to testify one week later, on February 1, 1995.

2. THE TACTICAL CONTEXT

The defense did not want the jury to hear that the defendant was reluctant to take a lie detector test. On the other hand, the testimony that he said he "dreamed" about killing his ex-wife would take on a whole different cast if taken out of the context of the discussion of a lie-detector test. To some extent, the underlying relevance of the "dream" itself was given short shrift in the arguments. The admissibility of the evidence was not fully briefed in *in limine* motions, but was orally argued out of the presence of the jury just prior to calling Ron Shipp to the witness stand.

The defense asked for more time to research the issues before Shipp was called.

3. PROSECUTION ARGUMENT

Mr. Goldberg: Your honor, apparently the defense has been aware of the statement since January 22nd, and obviously if there were any issues as to legal admissibility, there was plenty of time to research those to address those today.

... I would first like to start out with a discussion of the relevancy of the statement because I think counsel seems to be suggesting under 352 it is not admissible, and any discussion probably should start with an issue of why is it probative, why is it relevant? And then I will get into the issue of the polygraph aspect of the statement in the second part of my response.

As to the probative value of the statement, your honor has already ruled in the context of domestic violence evidence that the prosecution is entitled to put on evidence ... for the purposes of showing the defendant's mental state and showing his intention at or around the time of the murder.

The Court: Yes, the controverted statement, though, is the very next day, so I mean, we are out of the category of domestic violence, wouldn't you say?

Mr. Goldberg: I just want to tie it all in as to why it is relevant in the context of all of the evidence that the court has allowed. The purpose of that evidence is to allow the jury to infer something circumstantially about what the defendant was thinking at or around the time of the murder, what his mental state and his motivations were.... The chain of inference is that we can determine from his conduct what his intention, what his mental state must have been.

The evidence pertaining to Mr. Shipp differs in only one respect and that is that instead of being circumstantial evidence of his intent and his mental state, it is direct evidence, because it is him saying this is what I have been thinking and from the context of the statement it was over a period of time. Now, the distinction between direct and circumstantial evidence isn't directly important. What I would suggest to the court is important is the way that the respective sides have asked the jury and this court to interpret the circumstantial evidence, because what we have said is, "look, what this evidence shows is that the defendant had an obsession with Nicole Simpson, and that it was an obsession that led to her murder." I guess we could term it a fatal obsession.

Isn't that precisely what the statement to Mr. Shipp is saying? "I have been dreaming about killing my wife." Isn't that powerful evidence of that fatal obsession, except that instead of coming in the form of circumstantial evidence, it is coming in the form of direct evidence?

The defense, on the other hand, has a different interpretation of the domestic violence evidence. They say, no, it is not really evidence that shows the defendant's state of mind in terms of a fatal obsession. What it really shows is a cycle of benevolence, and they are entitled to make that argument, your honor. We are not saying that is improper. That is a proper jury argument. But when they are allowed to stand before the jury and say that all that the circumstantial evidence that the prosecution has introduced simply shows a cycle of benevolence and we have direct evidence which conclusively shows that that isn't true—

The Court: Mr. Goldberg, let's sort of leap ahead to what really concerns me. I agree that it is an interesting statement, and were I in your shoes, I would probably want to get it before the jury. What concerns me about this is two things: One, the 351.1 prohibition of any mention of polygraph or lie detector which is included in the context of this statement;[2] And secondly, whether or not it is fair or somehow fundamentally misleading to the trier of fact to pluck this sentence out of the context in which it was said, which is beginning and ending with comments about polygraphs. So is it fair to pluck this out? That is the concern that I have.

Mr. Goldberg: ... The reason that I made some comments about relevancy is that in our state under our constitution, Article 1, Section 28,[3] we do have a right to truth in evidence in this state, and there are only certain specified exceptions to that right, and those exceptions are that a statement can be excluded if it is privileged, which this isn't, if it is hearsay, which this isn't, if it is 352, which this isn't, if it is protected by the rape shield law that is codified in 1103 and 782, which this isn't, or if it is taken in violation of the federal constitution, which this isn't. And that is what the constitution of our state says, it shall be admitted. This is highly relevant evidence and it doesn't come under any of the exceptions and therefore should be admitted....

Therefore, the issue becomes, your honor, are we somehow going to, contrary to the clear policy of the right to truth in evidence provision, exclude highly probative evidence, evidence which really seems to blow a hole in the defense theory of the cycle of benevolence, simply because contained within that statement are other materials which your honor is rightfully concerned about and which are inadmissible?

Clearly, the law does not lead us to what in our view would be an absurd conclusion. ... Starting with Evidence Code Section 356,[4] ... what the statute stands for is the very common sense

---

2. California Evidence Code Section 351.1 provides:

"(a) Notwithstanding any other provision of law, the results of a polygraph examination, the opinion of a polygraph examiner, or any reference to an offer to take, failure to take or taking of a polygraph examination, shall not be admitted into evidence in any criminal proceeding, including pretrial and post conviction motions and hearings,or in any trial or hearing of a juvenile for a criminal offense, whether heard in juvenile or adult court, unless all parties stipulate to the admission of such results.

(b) Nothing in this section is intended to exclude from evidence statements made during a polygraph examination which are otherwise admissible."

3. Section 28(d) of Article I of the California constitution, added by an Ini-

tiative measure known as "Proposition 8" in 1982, provides as follows:

"*Right to Truth in Evidence.* Except as provided by statute hereinafter enacted by two-thirds vote of the membership of the membership in each house of the Legislature, relevant evidence shall not be excluded in any criminal proceeding.... Nothing in this section shall affect any existing statutory rule of evidence relating to privilege or hearsay, or Evidence Code Sections 352, 782 or 1103."

The exclusion of polygraphs in Section 351.1 was enacted by the legislature by a two-thirds margin in 1983. Calif. Stats. 1983, c. 202, § 1, eff. July 12, 1983.

4. California Evidence Code Section 356 provides:

"Where part of an act, declaration, conversation, or writing is given in evi-

proposition that when you put in part of the statement and the other side can demonstrate that it is necessary to put in another part of that statement, to put it in context, that can be allowed, and there are a number of cases that interpret 356 in that way.

. . . One being *People v. Breaux,* 1 Cal.4th 281, and what it says of Evidence Code Section 356 is:

"The section permits introduction only if statements on the same subject or which are necessary for the understanding of the statement already introduced. The other conversation referred to in the Evidence Code Section 356 must have some bearing upon or connection with the admissions or declaration in evidence."

So in other words, when we needed to put something in context, then we can use Evidence Code Section 356 to do that. I think the case of *People v. Pride,* 3 Cal.4th 195, is more instructive for your honor. There what happened is the defendant gave a very lengthy tape-recorded interview to the police that occurred over a course of approximately two hours, and instead of producing the tape recording, the prosecution called the detective to the stand and they asked him about only one tiny little snippet of that conversation. That was the statement to the effect that the defendant accounted for his whereabouts and those whereabouts were false, so the prosecution simply wanted to prove that in a couple sentences of that lengthy interview he had made a false statement. And the defense says, "well, we want to put in the whole thing. We want to put in the whole thing to show that maybe the defendant's state of mind was such that he was confused or wasn't really focusing in on what the detective was asking him. We want to put it in to show that he was giving an estimation or approximation in accounting for his whereabouts, as opposed to a definitive type statement." The trial court there did not allow it in and what the California Supreme Court held was that it was properly excluded because they reviewed the tape themselves and they found that it would have been an abuse of discretion to admit the rest of the tape because it does not support the defendant's theory that there was psychological coercion, it did not help to explain or account for the statement, and in fact the tape amply supported the prosecution's theory that the defendant gave a positive accounting for his time which turned out to be false. So they held that if the court had admitted it, it would have been an error. So I think that very, very strongly supports what the prosecution is asking the court to do here.

---

dence by one party, the whole on the same subject may be inquired into by an adverse party; when a letter is read, the answer may be given; and when a detached act, declaration, conversation, or writing is given in evidence, any other act, declaration, conversation, or writing which is necessary to made it understood may also be given in evidence."

Now, let's take a look back at the defendant's statement to Mr. Shipp. The quote being, "Hey, to be truthful, Ron, Man, I've had a lot of dreams about killing her." In and of itself the statement is perfectly understandable. It is perfectly clear. It is the defendant saying I have dreamed about killing this woman. It is very simple, very straightforward. What is the statement that immediately preceded that? "I was interviewed by the detective and they asked me to take a lie detector test," and then he chuckles. How does that possibly put any different spin on the statement? It doesn't explain the statement, qualify the statement, retract the statement. It doesn't do anything to make the statement more understandable.

How does the fact that he says I was offered to take a lie detector test either contribute or detract from the statement that he was dreaming about killing his wife? Does it make it more likely that he was dreaming about killing his wife or less likely? I would submit to you that it is logically entirely irrelevant and this is a statement which stands alone, which is perfectly comprehensible, perfectly understandable in and of itself. And that if you subtract the parts about the polygraph test, you don't lose anything at all.

I think the defense will have difficulty articulating why you did lose something. But even if they can, then I would ask the court to refer back to *People v. Pride,* where the defense threw out some theories there as well as to why they needed the entire tape and the court reviewed it, made its own determination, and said no, I don't buy that, that doesn't explain, qualify or in any way detract from the statement, and it was upheld by the California Supreme Court.

The Court: But we have sort of the inverse situation here, where they don't want the context because of the discussion of polygraph and the negative implication that can be drawn from that by the trier of fact, not fully aware of the nature and circumstances of the admissibility of the polygraph evidence.

Mr. Goldberg: Well, then it sounds like if that is the case, we are all in agreement. If we are saying all we want is the statement, and they are saying all we want is the statement, where is the disagreement?

The Court: Well, I will hear what their position is in a second. I'm just asking you since it is the inverse situation.

Mr. Goldberg: Yes, I think that what they are trying to do is ... say that we want the statement kind of because maybe if we do that the court will throw the whole thing out, the baby with the bathwater. It is very analogous to the situation that your honor has undoubtedly confronted in the context of *Aranda* issues, where the prosecution wants to introduce the statement of the defendant which implicates the co-defendant, and we say, "well, your honor, just redact out the stuff that refers to the co-defendant so we could have a joint trial of these two defendants." The attempt is always going to be foiled by saying, "we have to put in the statement that refers to the co-defendant in order to place into proper context our client's statement." And in reality what I think is happening is an effort to put in something that really doesn't logically help them for the purposes of getting a severance, yet the courts have over and over again redacted those statements under *Aranda,* and said no, you can't put in your client's statements which implicate the co-defendant because they aren't logically necessary here.

The other analogy I give the court is in the context of a defendant's confession where he, in a lengthy tape-recorded statement, discusses things that are clearly inadmissible, for example, sometimes defendants will talk about their prior criminal history, what they were doing in state prison, things that clearly don't come in, and those are redacted out all the time.

And I don't think the defense can be heard to say, "well, those are prejudicial to us so we don't want them to be heard by the jury, therefore you have to throw out the whole statement."

I mean, I understand the defense here is in a tactical bind. They don't want the statement about the polygraph to come in, but apparently they also want to argue that it should come in in order to get the whole statement removed, and I just don't think that is a consistent position.

4. DEFENSE ARGUMENT

Mr. Douglas: Let me begin by saying categorically that we deny that the conversation ever took place or that the statements were ever made. The court must understand that as a predicate, so that the court can appreciate the seriousness with which I will then have to cross-examine the witness about the entire conversation.... As the court understands, as a former defense attorney, I am going to examine this witness about everything, given the context of that conversation, ... and I am going to try to demonstrate that he is lying when he says that Mr. Simpson told him that there was a dream about killing his wife.

But, your honor, we have a problem, a problem that the *Pride* case, a problem that the other case does not address, and that is Evidence Code Section 351.1. I'm not going to waive that code section's applicability to this case, but in no sense does the law allow any discussion or reference concerning polygraphs to be admitted. Yet in the statement where I must attempt to challenge the authenticity and the accuracy, there is a chuckle. Query: what does that chuckle mean? Does that chuckle mean that Mr. Simpson is taking a flip sense of the whole concept of a polygraph? Does that chuckle presage the joke that was made by the questioned language, such that the jury can understand that the questioned language was given in terms of a joke, because the speaker has a general flippant, joking sense of polygraphs in general?

I am unable to challenge that, I am unable to put this statement, which I say never occurred, in any kind of a context, and that is unfair. That denies me due process rights. That denies me confrontation clause rights. That violates Mr. Simpson's rights under both the California and federal constitution.

And that is not just a technicality, your honor. That goes to the very essence of what a fair trial is all about. I cannot challenge a statement that I say never occurred, a statement where there is, even from the mouths of the witness, information that might suggest that the statement was not offered in total seriousness, in true appreciation for the value of that statement.

And there is another problem which runs into 352. I am informed, although I have not spoken to anyone professionally, that whenever there are statements of dreams or questions of dreams, it is not necessarily indicative of the state of mind of the speaker. It does not necessarily mean that if he dreamt something it is relevant to an issue in the case that he killed her. There is a misconception that Mr. Goldberg apparently holds as well, that there is some probative nexus between someone saying that I dreamt about something, assuming for the sake of my statement that the statement was made, and that it means something that is relevant to the trier of fact.

Therefore, there is going to be a great deal of scientific testimony that I will have to try to obtain, to put on people that will be able to talk about dreams and particularly in the context when this man is told that very day that a woman with whom he had been involved for seventeen years had just died.... He is told on the telephone that this happens and he rushes back and he is consumed with all this grief and all of this uncertainty and all of this emotion and he is tired because he didn't sleep going to Chicago and didn't sleep coming back and there are these family members that are also grieving with him.

There is an entire context, your honor, that it would be unfair to require that we simply examine under a microscope six or seven different words without appreciating the entire context in which it is offered. I argue, your honor, that on this level the answer is clear: when you must balance the obligations of the people and their interests in getting this evidence in against the possible danger of unfair prejudice, and the potential for consuming undue time, against the inability for me to vigorously contest the very context in which the statement is weighed, the results are clear and you should rule in favor of not allowing the statement to come in.

. . .

The Court: I don't suppose either side has found cases that deal with admissibility of dreams?

Mr. Goldberg: . . . Quite frankly, we didn't even research that, your honor, because it seemed like our thought process was much the same as the court's and we were more concerned about the issue of the polygraph and redacting that out. The issue of relevance always turns about a jury using their collective life experience and their common sense for the purposes of interpreting evidence. Counsel made the exact same argument about the domestic violence evidence, your honor. "Well, just because you hit someone, it doesn't necessarily mean that you are later going to kill them." . . . But what we are always asking the jury to do, with any kind of circumstantial evidence, is use common sense, life experience, and that is all we are going to be asking them to do here.

Mr. Douglas: There is clearly a mine field that we will be delicately walking around and between if we get into this particular area, and we are going to be opening the door. In this instance it is important to remember that on June 15, 1994, Robert Shapiro sent a letter to [Detective] Vannatter asking and offering a polygraph, so long as the results were stipulated and admissible by stipulation. Therefore, your honor, I cannot simply rest on seven certain words, "I've had a lot of dreams about killing Nicole," and then move on to my next topic, because before those words were uttered there was a chuckle and that chuckle does have significance, because it might even arguably place into some question the seriousness of the statements that follow.

5. JUDGES' RULINGS

Judge Ito ruled that the reference to the polygraph should be redacted, but the statement about the dreams would be admitted. The witness was instructed accordingly, and the evidence about the dreams was admitted in the following form:

By Mr. Darden:

Q When we left off, Mr. Shipp, I believe you told us that the defendant told you that the police told him that they had found a bloody glove, is that correct?

A That's correct.

Q And they also said they found a watchcap or something somewhere?

A   They said they found a watchcap on the property.

Q   Did you and the defendant discuss things unrelated to Nicole Brown's death?

A   Unrelated to her death?

Q   Unrelated.

A   Not at this time.

Q   Did you know that defendant had gone down to the LAPD headquarters that day?

A   Yes, I did.

Q   Well, did he ask you any questions, any questions about the investigation?

A   After he told me about what they found at his house, he asked me how long does it take DNA to come back.

Q   And at that time, did you know the correct answer to that question?

A   I did not know the correct answer, but what I did say, I just off the cuff say two months.

Q   And what did he say in response to your indication that it takes two months to come back?

A   He kind of jokingly just said, you know, "to be honest, Shipp—" that's what he called me, Shipp. He said, "I've had some dreams of killing her."

Q   Did he say how many dreams he had had of killing her?

A   No, he did not.

Q   Did he say it was more than one?

A   He just said dreams, plural.

At the civil trial, Ron Shipp was never called as a witness. On cross-examination of O.J. Simpson, however, he was questioned about both the polygraph and his alleged conversation with Ron Shipp. See Chapter VI(C), *infra*.

6. COMMENTS AND QUESTIONS

(a) Consider how you would go about cross-examining Ron Shipp based on the testimony that was actually admitted. Would you inquire about the basis for his conclusion that the statement was made "jokingly"?

(b) Although Shipp did not tell the prosecution about the alleged "dream" statement until January, 1995, the information appeared in a tabloid book published within a month of the murders, entitled "Raging Heart" by Sheila Weller. Shipp admitted he was the source of the information published by Ms. Weller. Anticipating that this would be the subject of cross-examination, Chris Darden elicited the prior statement to Weller on direct examination.

(c) Many commentators questioned why the prosecution offered the "dream" evidence, suggesting its admission may have injected reversible error into the record:

> "Quite apart from why the prosecution would even want to present extremely weak dream evidence when it had a Himilayan mountain of other very solid evidence against Simpson, the decided weight of authority in the United States is against the admissibility of such evidence, since the medical profession has not yet been able to establish, through empirical studies, an unmistakable connection between dreams and actual conduct. Yet Ito nonetheless allowed this evidence to be heard by the jury, undoubtedly bringing a smile to the face of Alan Dershowitz, who felt that if there was an eventual conviction, Ito's incorrect ruling in allowing the jury to hear the dream evidence would be one of the stronger grounds on appeal seeking a reversal of the conviction."

V. Bugliosi, *Outrage: The Five Reasons Why O.J. Simpson Got Away With Murder,* p. 74 (W.W. Norton Co., 1996).

(d) Marcia Clark suggests a theory of admissibility that was never even argued during the trial:

> "What we wanted to show was Simpson's general mind-set on the day after the murders. Here you have him to suggesting to [Detectives] Tom [Lange] and Phil [Vanatter] in the police statement that he and Nicole were totally cool about their failed reconciliation. A few hours later he's telling Ron Shipp that he's had dreams of *killing* her."

Marcia Clark, *Without A Doubt,* p. 287 (Viking Penguin, 1997). Would the dream testimony be admissible to contradict Simpson's statement to the police that same afternoon? [Simpson's statement to the police was never offered in evidence by the prosecution].

(e) Alan Dershowitz may not have been smiling as broadly as Bugliosi believed. After including the "dream testimony" on his list of Judge Ito's rulings he believed were erroneous, Professor Dershowitz concluded:

> "... I was never optimistic about winning a reversal in the Simpson case if the jury convicted. The issues were strong, but appellate judges are human beings who watch the same television, read the same newspapers, and listen to the same gossip as others of their background, race, social class and gender.

The judges who would have decided this appeal come largely from the group of Americans who believed most strongly in Simpson's guilt. Moreover, this was a lengthy and expensive trial that would have been even more difficult to retry. The appellate judges would almost certainly have found several of Judge Ito's rulings erroneous.... But I suspect that the appeals court would have found these errors 'harmless.' That is, they would have concluded that any jury would have convicted Simpson even if Judge Ito had ruled correctly."

A. Dershowitz, *Reasonable Doubts,* p. 194–95 (Simon & Schuster, 1996). To what extent is it appropriate for prosecutors to seek the admission of evidence they believe an appellate court might find erroneous but are confident the error would be deemed "harmless"? If an appellate court accepts the reliability of DNA evidence, is it conceivable they would ever find that *any* error was reversible in a case where the evidence includes a DNA match?

(f) Prosecutor Hank M. Goldberg suggests that the decision to seek admission of the "dream" testimony may not have been given a great deal of thought by the prosecution team. He was assigned to brief the issue the morning the testimony was to be presented:

"Marcia said, 'Hank, if you can get this in, I'll buy you dinner.'

I asked, 'why me?'

'Ito likes you,' Marcia replied.

... After Marcia made the assignment, I quickly walked back to my office to write out an argument. I had plenty of time, about thirty minutes, before I had to present it.

... As I stood at the podium and began to answer Juge Ito's question, Marcia passed me a note. 'A dream is a wish your heart makes.—Walt Disney.' I had to make a conscious effort not to laugh."

H. M. Goldberg, *The Prosecution Responds,* pp. 48–49 (Birch Lane Press, 1996).

(g) The defense strategy to deal with the "dream" evidence was a direct attack on the credibility of Ron Shipp. Several of O.J. Simpson's family members disputed Shipp's claim that he spent time alone with O.J. at the time the alleged "dream" statement was made. Apparently, the jurors simply rejected Shipp's testimony:

Jury Foreman Armanda Cooley: "I felt Ron basically saw an opportunity where he could make money, and I felt that he was lying about that dream. His testimony was that O.J. said he had a dream in which he killed Nicole. My question to Ron is, 'If he's your best friend for twenty-something years, basically, I

would not have let it just lie there. I would have asked
questions regarding that dream. Like, what do you mean you
had a dream about killing your wife? What exactly happened in
that dream? I would have tried to get some details. Ron Shipp
is someone most of us didn't believe for a number of reasons.
He appeared to be an alcoholic and I think he was a groupie. I
seriously do. I'm not going to say I don't believe the part about
the dream, but to me, his testimony was all about notoriety.
That's what I thought. I really thought he was trying to cash
in. And because of that I couldn't put any weight on the dream
part and that was even before the family members' testimony
about who Ron was and what happened the night he spoke
with O.J. Now O.J. could have told him he dreamed about
killing Nicole. But to state you followed him to the bedroom, or
something like that, and then have the family on the other side
saying, 'No, he never was near him,' that's a contradiction.
Ron Shipp had said that O.J. and he had a chat and that's
when he talked about the dream and all that. But why didn't
he say something right then? He wasn't an officer at the time,
but he was really good friends with Nicole. And then the family
says, 'Well, Shipp never did leave—he wasn't in there with O.J.
alone.' And then Shipp gets turned around and gets frustrated.
I'm watching this and thinking, *Don't blow it out of the water
because we're listening to you. You're emotional now. Come on,
what's the matter here? Are you telling us this just because
you're mad at him now? What's up?*

Juror Carrie Bess: "I know Ron Shipp used to go by O.J.'s and
he used to run people by there that he knew, but I discredit
Ron Shipp for two reasons. Number one, after he got irritated
there, he jumps and says, 'O.J. just wanted to use people.
That's all he wanted me around for. If he didn't have no use
for me, that's why he kicked me out.' It looks like he's so angry
that he'll say anything to get back at him. Like I'm saying, I
was listening to each witness and thinking, *Where are you
coming from? Are you going to discredit yourself in here?* Even
though Ron Shipp had a drinking problem, it doesn't mean he
wasn't telling the truth. Because in every bit of slander there's
a trace of truth. But the point is whether you're going to pick
the part that you need to pick out and stick to it. So I felt he
was a liar."

Cooley, Bess & Rubin–Jackson, *Madam Foreman: A Rush to Judgment?*, pp. 91–93 (Dove Books, 1995).

(h) At the conclusion of the trial, Judge Ito gave the following
special instruction to the jury:

"Witness Ron Shipp testified to a statement alleged to have been made by the defendant concerning dreams. You must first determine whether such statement was made by the defendant. If you find the statement was not made by the defendant, you shall disregard the statement. If you find that the statement referred to subconscious thoughts while asleep, you are to disregard the statement. If you find that the statement referred to an expression of a desire or expectation, you may give to such statement the weight to which you feel it is entitled. Evidence of oral statements by a defendant should be viewed with caution."

If the admission of the "dream" testimony was erroneous, would this instruction have cured the error?

(i) Only a handful of appellate courts have ruled on the question of whether a defendant's description of a "dream" is admissible to prove his state of mind. In *State v. Tyler,* 840 P.2d 413 (Kan. 1992), the Kansas Supreme Court held it was an abuse of discretion to admit evidence of a defendant's sleep-induced dream to prove his state of mind, but found the error harmless. In *State v. White,* 156 S.E.2d 721 (N.C. 1967), the North Carolina Supreme Court concluded it was error to admit a dream, but the evidence was so obviously worthless that no jury would have attached any weight to it!

"What a dream means, if anything, presents an occurrence filled with mystery. As to the meaning of a dream, we can only conjecture. The evidence as to the statement of the defendant that he dreamed he shot Bud leaves the meaning of the dream in the realm of mere conjecture, surmise, and speculation, and one surmise may be as good as another. Nobody knows.... Bacon, in his Essay of Prophecies, says in respect to prophecies and dreams, other than divine prophecies: 'My judgement is, that they ought all to be despised; and ought to serve but for winter talk by the fireside.' Even if the evidence were incompetent as contended by defendant, it is, in our opinion, so speculative and uncertain as to have had no probative force on the minds of a jury and would not justify a new trial of this case." 156 S.E.2d at 724.

In *People v. Henne,* 518 N.E.2d 1276 (Ill.App.Ct. 1988), the Illinois Court of Appeals rejected the appeal of a defendant who did not testify at his trial after a ruling that his statement to a polygraph examiner could be admitted to impeach his testimony. When asked to explain inconsistencies in the polygraph results, the defendant responded "he had terrible dreams about hurting people since childhood and it was possible he could have assaulted the victim, but if he did, he forgot about it." *Id.* at 1281. The court held that since defendant did not testify, he failed to properly preserve the question for review. If O.J. Simpson had testified at his criminal trial, could he have been asked, on cross-examination, "have you ever had dreams about killing Nicole?" See Chapter VI(C), *infra*.

C. THE BRONCO CHAIN OF CUSTODY

1. THE EVIDENCE

O.J. Simpson's white Ford Bronco was seized from the street in front of his Rockingham home on June 13, 1994, pursuant to a search warrant. It was towed to the L.A.P.D. "Print Shed" at 151 N. San Pedro St., Los Angeles, where it was searched by Criminalists Fung and Mazzola on June 14, 1994. They removed a cap, a section of the driver's side carpet, and took swatches of twelve suspected blood stains. The automobile was then removed to Viertel's Tow Yard, 1155 N. Temple St., for storage. Although it was parked in an "Evidentiary Hold" area, there was no official evidentiary hold placed on the vehicle. It was not locked or otherwise secured, and no record was maintained of who entered the vehicle or when, although numerous persons had access to it. No inventory was taken of the contents of the vehicle. On June 15, 1994, John Meraz, an employee of the tow yard, removed some credit card receipts from the vehicle as "souvenirs." They bore the signatures of O.J. Simpson and/or Nicole Brown Simpson. The theft was not reported to the Los Angeles Police Department until July 11, 1994, and the receipts were never recovered.

During its unsecured storage at Viertel's Tow Yard, five subsequent searches took place:

(1) On June 28, 1994, Criminalist Fung removed a shovel, a white towel and a plastic sheet from the rear cargo area;

(2) On August 3, 1994, thirty items were removed from the center console, glove box and rear cargo area, including various papers, business cards, notes and a pair of golf shoes;

(3) On August 10, 1994, the pads were removed from the brake and accelerator pedals;

(4) On August 11, 1994, sample fibers were removed from ten different locations on the interior carpet;

(5) On August 30, 1994, the vehicle was towed to a third location where "luminol" tests were performed to detect blood stains not visible to the naked eye.

At the time the vehicle was towed on August 30, extensive unexplained exterior damage to the car was noted by tow driver Edward

Arensdorf. John Meraz testified that the noted damage was not on the car on June 15.

2. THE TACTICAL CONTEXT

All evidence removed from the Bronco was challenged in the defendant's Motions to Suppress Evidence based on Fourth Amendment grounds. Although the motions were denied, the hearings revealed the lapse in security with respect to the vehicle's storage. The defense then filed a separate motion, challenging the evidence removed after June 15 on grounds of a failure in the "chain of custody." Another motion challenged the admissibility of "Luminol" test results under the "Kelly–Frye" standard for admissibility of scientific evidence. That motion is separately treated in Chapter V(A), *infra*. A separate motion was also filed claiming the loss of exculpatory evidence through the negligence of the Los Angeles Police Department, arguing that evidence the car contained credit card receipts signed by Nicole Brown Simpson would have corroborated her frequent use of the car and offered an explanation for why stains matching her D.N.A. might be found in the vehicle.

3. DEFENSE ARGUMENT

Any evidentiary inferences the prosecution will ask the jury to draw from evidence removed from the Bronco or laboratory analysis of such evidence will absolutely depend upon the conclusion that such evidence was present in the Bronco at the time it was seized from in front of the defendant's residence. Thus, it was critical for the police to maintain the security of the vehicle from the time of its seizure until the evidence was removed. Their failure to do so in the face of evidence of actual tampering, unrecorded access to the vehicle and unexplained damage to the vehicle renders any evidence seized inadmissible.

The California standard for the admissibility of such evidence was established by Justice Traynor in his opinion for the California Supreme Court in *People v. Riser,* 47 Cal.2d 566, 580–81 (1956):

> "Undoubtedly the party relying on an expert analysis of demonstrative evidence must show that it is in fact the evidence found at the scene of the crime, and that between receipt and analysis there has been no substitution or tampering (citations omitted), but it has never been suggested by the cases, what the practicalities of proof could not tolerate, that this burden is an absolute one requiring the party to negative all possibility of tampering (citations omitted).

> The burden on the party offering the evidence is to show to the satisfaction of the trial court that, taking all the circum-

stances into account including the ease or difficulty with which the particular evidence could have been altered, it is reasonably certain there was no alteration.

The requirement of reasonable certainty is not met when some vital link in the chain of possession is not accounted for, because then it is likely as not that the evidence analyzed was not the evidence originally received. Left to such speculation the court must exclude the evidence."

Although the *Riser* court declined to exclude fingerprints from glass articles left unguarded in a sheriff's office bookcase for four hours, the court based its conclusion on the absence of any evidence of actual tampering, any showing that fingerprints could be forged, and the lack of any suggestion "that anyone who might have been interested in tampering with the prints knew that the bottles and glasses were in Deputy Sheriff Lochry's bookcase." 47 Cal.2d at 581.

Here, of course, the Bronco was left unsecured for a period of at least six weeks, and there is undisputed evidence of actual tampering. Blood evidence is especially susceptible to tampering, and the vehicle's location was well known to numerous garage employees and police personnel in a widely publicized case.

Courts have been especially vigilant in strictly enforcing the demands of a secure "chain of custody" in cases involving analysis of blood. As a New York court put it:

"Blood specimens to be used as evidence in trials such as this should be handled with the greatest of care and all persons who handle the specimen should be ready to identify it and testify to its custody and unchanged condition."

People v. Sansalone, 146 N.Y.S.2d 359, 361 (1955). The *Sansalone* court rejected blood alcohol analysis based on a specimen which a police officer took home and kept in his refrigerator overnight, because 4–5 unidentified persons had access to the refrigerator. Other cases rejecting blood analysis evidence because of a breach in the chain of custody include: *Novak v. District of Columbia*, 160 F.2d 588 (D.C. Cir. 1947); *State v. Reenstierna*, 140 A.2d 572 (N.H. Sup. Ct. 1958); *Rodgers v. Commonwealth*, 90 S.E.2d 257 (Va. Sup. Ct. 1955); *Benton v. Pellum*, 100 S.E.2d 534 (S.C. Sup. Ct. 1957); *People v. Lyall*, 127 N.W.2d 345 (Mich. Sup. Ct. 1963); *Bruyere v. Castalacci*, 200 A.2d 226 (R.I. Sup. Ct. 1964). These cases repeatedly emphasize a point that, by now, should be common knowledge among police engaged in the investigation of a crime:

"A blood specimen is something that could be conceivably tampered with and for that reason if the analysis of a blood specimen is to be offered and admitted in evidence on the issue of intoxication, extreme caution should be used in handling the specimen."

Wooley v. Hafner's Wagon Wheel, Inc., 196 N.E.2d 119, 123 (Ill. App. 1960). If extreme caution is appropriate in a drunk driving case, the court's intolerance of sloppy handling of evidence can only increase in a homicide case where the defendant faces a potential sentence of life without possibility of parole.

The establishment that particular items such as pads from the pedals of the automobile or portions of the carpet were the same as those in the vehicle when it was seized will not overcome the breach in the chain of custody. These items are relevant only because of the potential presence of stains that the prosecution will contend were present at the moment the vehicle was seized. In this respect, the situation is analogous to *Robinson v. Commonwealth,* 183 S.E.2d 179 (Va. Sup. Ct. 1971), in which the Supreme Court of Virginia reversed a conviction for rape because there had been a breach in the chain of custody of the panties and blouse of the rape victim between the time of their delivery to police at a hospital and their analysis for stains and hairs at a police laboratory. Although there was no dispute they were the same panties and blouse, the Court concluded:

"It is not reasonably certain from the testimony presented that these exhibits were in the same condition when analyzed as they were when taken from the victim."

183 S.E.2d at 80.

4. PROSECUTION ARGUMENT

The chain of custody of the Bronco is reasonably certain; any doubt thereon is an issue of weight for the jury to decide; therefore the evidence from the Bronco should be allowed to go to the jury.

In the case of *People v. Williams,* 48 Cal.3d 1112 (1989), the defendant was sentenced to death following his convictions for the rape, robbery, kidnapping and murder of a female. The Supreme Court reversed the conviction for failure to grant the defendant's motion for change of venue under the unusual circumstances of that case.[5] The Court addressed the issue of chain of custody of fingerprint evidence for the guidance of the trial court on retrial.

In *Williams,* there was "no doubt that the evidence in question was mishandled." *Id.* at 1132. Before trial the prosecution told the

---

5. Among other factors making the case unusual was the fact that the defendant's brother had been tried in a severed trial for the same crimes prior to defendant's trial. (The two brothers aided and abetted each other in the crimes). In 1983, the Supreme Court granted a writ ordering a change of venue in the brother's trial, thereby setting precedent in the case with regard to the trial of this brother for the same murders. (48 Cal.3d at 1117–18).

defense that it had not identified the defendant's fingerprints on any item in the house in which the victim had been murdered. The prosecution introduced evidence that the defendant possessed items stolen from the house. However, the only evidence which actually placed him inside the house was the testimony of a neighbor that he thought he heard the defendant's voice inside the house. However, that testimony had been impeached.

As the Supreme Court explained, the situation changed dramatically when the prosecutor disclosed during a recess in the trial that a fingerprint of the defendant had been identified on a business card found inside the house during the initial investigation fourteen months earlier. The defense objected to its admission. After an extended evidentiary hearing, the trial court admitted the evidence.

During the evidentiary hearing, a sheriff's department fingerprint analyst testified that he had a distinct recollection of having found the card on the kitchen floor and that he had placed it in a bag with other items. After he testified, however, the prosecution found a photograph of the crime scene which showed the card lying on a bed in the house. Thereafter, the fingerprint analyst was recalled to the stand and totally changed his testimony. He now said that he had earlier assumed he found the card in the kitchen because it was in a bag with other items seized from the kitchen. His new position was that he had no independent recollection of where in the house he found the card.

Another Sheriff's lab employee testified he processed the evidence taken from the house for fingerprints. He said he took a photograph of the latent print on the card. He said it was possible he had inadvertently comingled the contents of separate bags containing evidence from the kitchen and the bedroom, but he had no independent recollection of doing so.

The photographs of all the latent prints were forwarded to another fingerprint examiner who compared them with exemplar prints taken from people who had been inside the house. For some unexplained reason, he never compared the photograph of the print on the business card with the exemplar from the defendant. He realized his mistake during the recess in the trial.

A fingerprint analyst for the Department of Justice testified during the hearing on the admissibility of the fingerprint match that, because of fading with the passage of time, it was no longer possible to compare the actual latent print on the business card with the defendant's exemplar. He further testified, however, that he compared the photograph of the print with the defendant's exemplar and they were identical. He also said it is possible to use a person's fingerprint to place a print on another surface, but it did not appear to him that such tampering had occurred.

The trial court ruled that a sufficient "prima facie" showing of relevancy and chain of custody had been made to admit the fingerprint evidence. The court gave a jury instruction requiring the jurors to find, *inter alia,* before considering the evidence of the print on the card, that the prosecution had proven beyond a reasonable doubt and to a moral certainty that the business card had not been altered. On appeal, the defense challenged the trial court's ruling that the business card was admissible. The Supreme Court made several observations regarding the evidence:

> "[T]he prosecution was unable to explain satisfactorily two anomalies in the facts and circumstances of the handling of the fingerprint evidence in question. First, the evidence concerning the card's location in the [house] was inconsistent; the photograph placed it in the bedroom, yet the evidence bag in which it was contained came from the kitchen. The inconsistent testimony made the circumstances seem even more suspicious. Nevertheless, defendant adduced no evidence that the card itself had been tampered with or that another card had been substituted in its place. As the trial court observed, whether originally seized from the bedroom or the kitchen, the evidence showed that the card was 'from the house, that's the overwhelming significance in this case.'
>
> The second anomaly surrounding the evidence was the prosecution's inexplicable failure, until midtrial, to compare the latent fingerprint on the card with defendant's exemplar. There was no evidence, however, of prosecutorial bad faith or suppression of the evidence. Moreover, there is nothing in the record to suggest that the belated disclosure resulted in the denial of a fair trial." 48 Cal.3d at 1134–35.

Despite all these problems with chain of custody of the fingerprint evidence, the Supreme Court concluded that the fingerprint evidence was properly admitted. *Id.* at 1135. The Court also laid to rest a defense argument that the trial court used an erroneous standard in ruling on the admissibility of the evidence and allowing it to go to the jury. The Court disposed of this argument as follows:

> "The contentions are without merit. '[W]hen it is the barest speculation that there was tampering, it is proper to admit the evidence and let what doubt remains go to its weight.' (*People v. Riser, supra,* 47 Cal.2d at 581). Notwithstanding the prosecution's errors in the handling of the evidence, the trial court properly concluded that the prosecution had made at least a prima facie showing that the evidence had not been tampered with. Therefore, the trial court did not err in admitting the

evidence, permitting the jury hear all of the facts and circumstances surroundings its discovery and disclosure, and requiring the jury to find beyond a reasonable doubt that the card had not been tampered with before considering it."

48 Cal.3d at 1135. The Supreme Court thereby indicated it was satisfied by the "prima facie" showing on chain of custody made by the prosecution, notwithstanding the fact that the evidence in issue unquestionably had been mishandled.

. . . It is equally well-settled that when all vital links in the chain of custody are established, any doubt that remains goes to the weight of the evidence and not its admissibility. (*E.g., People v. Riser, supra; People v. Lewis,* 191 Cal. App. 3d 1288, 1299 (1987); *People v. Lozano,* 57 Cal. App.3d 490, 495 (1976); *People v. Ham,* 7 Cal.App.3d 768, 782 (1970). Federal law is in accord. (*E.g., United States v. Robinson,* 967 F.2d 287, 292 (9th Cir. 1992) ("A defect in the chain of custody . . . goes to the weight to be afforded the evidence"); *United States v. Harrington,* 923 F.2d 1371, 1374 (9th Cir. 1991) ("Merely raising the possibility of tampering is not sufficient to render evidence inadmissible. (Citation). The possibility of a break in the chain of custody goes only to the weight of the evidence").

In this case, the People established during the evidentiary hearing that, once the Bronco was placed into the evidence hold section of Viertel's tow, it was kept secured within that section during the entire duration of its stay at Viertel's. To gain access to it, one had to show police or law enforcement identification and the locked door to the yard would have to be opened by a Viertel's employee. When the Bronco was towed to Keystone in Van Nuys, it was kept secured in a special concrete building where it remains today.

The evidence produced by the defense that the tow truck driver who towed the Bronco to Viertel's may have taken some paperwork out of the Bronco does not break the chain of custody of the Bronco evidence, nor does it constitute evidence of tampering of any attached part of its interior. In other words, there was no showing at all of any tampering to the interior structure of the passenger compartment of the vehicle. Furthermore, the showing made by the defense that tow truck driver Meraz *may* have removed papers from the vehicle for their souvenir value in this high-profile case does not support an inference that the tow truck driver or anyone else placed items into the Bronco that were not there to begin with. Moreover, since the tow truck driver was suspended from work the same day he towed the Bronco (June 15), he had no further access to the vehicle.

The defense argument that there was "extensive unexplained damage" to the vehicle was not borne out by the testimony at the hearing. To the contrary, the minor damage to the vehicle (various scratch marks on it) was likely caused by its general use, as testified to by the General Manager at Keystone Tow (who went over the vehicle with a fine tooth comb when it arrived at Keystone).

In *People v. Williams, supra,* 48 Cal.3d at 1132, our Supreme Court ruled that, even though there was "no doubt that the evidence in question was mishandled," the trial court properly ruled that the prosecution had made the requisite prima facie showing on foundation and properly admitted the evidence. Here, there is no evidence that anything inside the Bronco was mishandled in any way, save the *possible removal* of some papers. The People have established the vital links in the chain of custody of the Bronco and its contents and have produced sufficient evidence to show the Bronco was kept secure throughout its stay at both Viertel's and Keystone Tow. These showings fully satisfy the requirements of the case law. Accordingly, the evidence from the Bronco should be admitted so that the jury may give it the weight to which it finds that evidence to be entitled.

5. JUDGES' RULINGS

Judge Lance Ito issued the following order on November 14, 1994, denying the defendant's motion to exclude evidence recovered from the Bronco after June 15, 1994:

"The court has read and considered the defendant's motion to suppress evidence seized from the defendant's 1994 Ford Bronco automobile while it was in the custody of the Los Angeles Police Department on the basis of a break in the chain of custody. More specifically, the defendant argues that the prosecution cannot establish there was no alteration or tampering with the contents of the Bronco after 15 June 1994.

The evidence adduced after two days of testimony indicates that the Bronco was taken to a police department facility known as the 'print shack' upon its seizure from in front of the defendant's residence pursuant to a search warrant on 13 June 1994. A Detective Richard Haro was assigned the task of accomplishing the move of the Bronco on 15 June 1994 from the 'print shack' to the storage lot of the official police garage, Viertel's. Haro, after filling out the departmental automobile impound form, contacted John Meraz, a tow driver for Viertel's who then towed the Bronco to one of the lots within the fence of Viertel's tow yard. At this point, the evidence is in conflict as to precisely where Meraz left the Bronco; however, it is clear that the Bronco was then almost immediately moved to the interior 'police hold' area of the tow and storage operation, first against the east wall, and then twenty minutes later to the west wall to facilitate its surveillance by the manager, Robert Jones.

While at Viertel's the Bronco was searched on five occasions by personnel of the Los Angeles Police Department. The Bronco was moved on 24 August 1994 from Viertel's to Keystone Towing for Luminol testing. The tow driver from Keystone Tow, Edward Arensdorf, prepared a report indicating the condition of the Bronco was physically different than the condition reported by Haro. It also appears that on 15 June 1994, certain items, described as Visa 'vouchers' from a laundry or dry cleaners in Westwood, one in the name of Nicole and the other in the name of O.J. dated sometime in March of 1994, were removed from the driver's door side pocket by John Meraz. Meraz showed these 'vouchers' to fellow Viertel's employees and testified that he then returned these items to the Bronco. These items were never recovered by the police.

The defense contends this record indicates appallingly sloppy treatment of an important piece of prosecution evidence. Items of potentially exculpatory value were stolen from the Bronco, no special evidentiary hold was communicated to the police garage by investigators, discrepancies between the condition of the Bronco as recorded by Haro and observed by Meraz and as recorded by Arensdorf indicate an inexplicable change in condition, and subsequent searches and examinations of the Bronco and its contents were haphazardly documented.

The prosecution contends that the discrepancies between Haro and Meraz observations and those of Arensdorf are explained by Arensdorf's greater attention to detail, that the reports concerning the subsequent searches and testing of the Bronco and its contents, while slow in being produced, do not suggest any tampering, and that the apparent theft of items from the Bronco, while unfortunate, does not impact the unbroken chain of custody. The prosecution further contends there was a 'hold' placed on the Bronco by Detective Haro.

This record indicates that from the time the Bronco was seized from in front of the defendant's residence to the time frame indicated by the testimony for this motion, the Bronco was in the custody of the Los Angeles Police Department or its agents. The Bronco was moved from the 'print shack' to lot T–3 or T–5 at Viertel's, then almost immediately moved inside to the T–2, first against east wall and then against the west wall, where it stayed until 24 August when it was moved to Keystone for Luminol testing. There exists no concrete evidence of tampering. The theft of two credit card receipts or Arensdorf's detail of the condition of the Bronco when towed to Keystone do not necessarily reflect tampering. Where the indicia of tampering is speculative in nature, the evidence, if otherwise admissible, should be admitted and the jury should weigh the impact of any doubt raised by the particular facts of this case. *People v., Williams* (1989) 48 Cal.3d 1112. Accordingly, the challenge to the admissibility of the evidence seized from the Bronco is denied."

Judge Fujisaki rejected the chain of custody objection for the civil trial as well.

6. COMMENTS AND QUESTIONS

(a) The California Evidence Code, like the Federal Rules, establishes two alternatives for the resolution of foundational or other preliminary facts. If the relevance of the proffered evidence depends on the existence of the preliminary fact, the evidence is inadmissible unless the court finds "that there is evidence sufficient to sustain a finding of the existence of the preliminary fact." The jury may be instructed to disregard the proffered evidence unless they find that the preliminary fact does exist. California Evidence Code, § 403. Other preliminary factual issues are decided by the court, and the jury may not be instructed to disregard the evidence if its determination of the preliminary fact differs from the court's determination. California Evidence Code, § 405. Which provision governs the determination of chain of custody?

(b) Should the jury have been told of Judge Ito's ruling that "there exists no concrete evidence of tampering"?

(c) In the *Williams* case cited by the prosecution and relied upon by Judge Ito, the jury was told that they must find "beyond a reasonable doubt and to a moral certainty that the business card had not been altered." Should the jury in the *Simpson* case have been instructed that they could not consider the evidence removed from the Bronco unless they found it had not been altered "beyond a reasonable doubt"?

(d) At the conclusion of the evidence, the defense offered the following proposed jury instruction:

"Evidence of the analysis of blood or hairs or fibers or similar evidence recovered from a crime scene may not be considered until you first determine the evidence was preserved in an unaltered and unchanged condition from the time of its seizure at a crime scene until the time it was analyzed. This requirement, the purpose of which is to prevent contamination of or tampering with evidence, is known as the 'chain of custody requirement. Only if you determine that a reasonable chain of custody of such evidence was accounted for may you then consider the results of any analysis or testing of such evidence. If you determine that a reasonable chain of custody of such evidence was not established, however, you must disregard such evidence and not consider it for any purpose."

This proposed jury instruction was rejected. The only instruction the jury received regarding preliminary facts was the instruction reproduced in Chapter I(D), *infra*.

(e) The evidence presented at the hearing on the admissibility of items removed from the Bronco was again produced at both trials for the jury. An additional witness was also produced, a salesman who visited Viertel's tow yard and was allowed to enter the Bronco and handle the controls.

As a result of this evidence and other evidence of possible tampering, the jury apparently gave little credence to *any* of the evidence recovered from the Bronco. Jury Foreman Armanda Cooley said, "I had problems understanding how they found the blood smears on the console of the Bronco. Why were they seen after they had torn the inside of this car completely up?" *Madam Foreman: A Rush to Judgment?*, *supra* at p. 122. How might this problem have been anticipated and defused by the Prosecution?

D. JURY INSTRUCTIONS RE: BLOOD EVIDENCE

1. PROPOSED JURY INSTRUCTION

The prosecution offered evidence that blood drops found beside the bloody footprints at the Bundy crime scene were "matched" through D.N.A. analysis with O.J. Simpson's blood. They also offered evidence matching Simpson's blood with a blood stain allegedly found on the back gate of the Bundy crime scene three weeks after the murders, and matching Nicole Brown Simpson's blood with a stain located on a sock recovered from Simpson's residence. The stain was not located until two months after the murders, and defense experts claimed the configuration of the stain showed the blood was applied after the sock had been removed from the wearer's foot. The defense offered the following two special jury instructions to deal with this evidence:

SPECIAL INSTRUCTION NO. D2

"Evidence of the comparison of blood drops allegedly found on the walkways and driveways of the Bundy crime scene with a blood sample provided by Mr. Simpson has been introduced for the purpose of showing the identity of the perpetrator of the murders. Before you may even consider such evidence, you must first determine whether the blood drops allegedly found at the crime scene were deposited by the perpetrator of the murders on June 12, 1994. If you determine this fact to be true, such evidence may then be considered by you for the purpose of determining whether it tends to show the identity of the perpetrator of the murders. If you determine that the alleged blood drops may have been deposited at some other time, however, you must disregard this evidence and not consider it for any purpose."

SPECIAL INSTRUCTION NO. D3

"Evidence of the comparison of blood which was not discovered on the back gate at the Bundy crime scene until July 3, 1994, and of blood which was not discovered on a sock allegedly found in Mr. Simpson's bedroom until August 4, 1994 with a blood sample provided by Mr. Simpson and a blood sample recovered from the body of Nicole Brown Simpson has been introduced for the purpose of showing the identity of the perpetrator of the murders. Before you may even consider such evidence, you must first determine whether the blood found on the back gate and the sock was deposited by the perpetrator or victim of the murders on June 12, 1994. If you determine such fact to be true, such evidence may then be considered by you for the purpose of determining whether it tends to show the identity of the perpetrator of the murders. If you determine that blood may have been deposited on the back gate or socks at some time subsequent to June 12, 1994, however, you must disregard this evidence and not consider it for any purpose."

2. THE TACTICAL CONTEXT

The blood on the sock and the blood on the back gate were keystones in the defense argument that blood evidence had been "planted" in the case. Defense experts testified the stain on the back gate was suspicious for two reasons: (1) although it was not "discovered" until two weeks after the crime scene had been cleaned up, the samples were far less degraded that the samples recovered the morning after the murders; (2) analysis of the sample showed the presence of EDTA, a preservative used to prevent coagulation of blood specimens in test tubes, but not found in natural blood. The stain on the sock was not observed by the detectives who seized it, the criminalists who initially examined it, or the defense experts who initially examined it. The stain soaked through to the opposite surface, a phenomenon which would not have occurred if there was a foot in the sock when the blood came in contact with it.

The requested jury instructions were designed to focus the attention of the jury on the specific issues raised by the evidence of tampering *before* they considered the evidence of D.N.A. matches.

3. DEFENSE ARGUMENT

The sole authority cited by the defense in support of Special Instructions D2 and D3 was Section 4.03(c) of the California Evidence Code, which provides:

> "If the court admits the proffered evidence under this section, the court ... may, and on request shall, instruct the jury to determine whether the preliminary fact exists and to disregard the proffered evidence unless the jury finds that the preliminary fact does exist."

4. PROSECUTION ARGUMENT

The prosecution presented an "advisory brief" expressing general objections to "pinpoint" jury instructions focusing the jury's attention on particular factual issues:

> "A jury instruction cannot refer to disputed, irrelevant or misstated evidence. In *People v. Hernandez,* 18 Cal.App.3d 651, 660 (1971), the defendant was charged with rape. The defense requested a pinpoint instruction that in determining whether there was a rape, the jury should consider several pieces of evidence such as the victim's alleged failure to flee after the alleged rape. The court found that the instruction was improper since it was 'argumentative' and 'called upon the jury to consider specific evidence concerning which there was a factual dispute.' "

As an alternative, the Prosecution offered People's Special Instruction No. 1, as follows:

> "The Court has admitted physical evidence (such as blood, hair, and fiber evidence) and experts' opinions concerning analysis of such physical evidence. This physical evidence and these expert's opinions may have a tendency in reason to prove elements of the crimes charged or the identity of a perpetrator of such crimes or both. You are the sole judges of whether such evidence does in fact have a tendency in reason to prove any issue in this case. If after your review and consideration of all of the circumstances surrounding any specific item of physical evidence or expert opinion you find that such evidence does not have any tendency in reason to prove any element of the crimes charged, you are instructed to disregard such evidence as such a finding renders this evidence irrelevant."

5. JUDGES' RULINGS

Judge Ito rejected the proposed instructions offered by the defense, and instructed the jury as follows:

"The court has admitted physical evidence such as blood, hair and fiber evidence, and experts' opinions concerning the analysis of such physical evidence. You are the sole judges of whether any such evidence has a tendency (*sic.*) in reason to prove any fact at issue in this case. You should carefully review and consider of all the circumstances surrounding each item of evidence, including but not limited to its discovery, collection, storage and analysis. If you determine any item of evidence does not have a tendency in reason to prove any element of the crimes charged or the identity of the perpetrator of the crimes charged, you must disregard such evidence."

At the civil trial, no special instructions were proposed or given regarding the preliminary factual findings required for consideration of any evidence.

6. COMMENTS AND QUESTIONS

(a) Are a judges' rulings on relevancy of evidence made pursuant to California Evidence Code Section 403 or Section 405? If made pursuant to Section 405, Section 405(b)(2) provides:

"If the proffered evidence is admitted, the jury shall not be instructed to disregard the evidence if its determination of the fact differs from the court's determination of the preliminary fact."

(b) Consider the breadth of Judge Ito's instruction carefully. If it were actually literally followed by a jury, would they be required to disregard all evidence which was offered to show that evidence had been "planted"? How would such evidence prove an element of the crime or the identity of the perpetrator? Why is evidence that blood may have been "planted" relevant?

(c) If the jury concluded that blood evidence had actually been planted, could it then infer that *other* evidence produced by officers of the Los Angeles Police Department should be distrusted? If so, did the defense really want the jury to be instructed that if blood were deposited on the back gate or the sock some time subsequent to June 12, the evidence may not be considered "for any purpose"?

Chapter II

CHARACTER EVIDENCE

A. PRIOR SPOUSAL ABUSE BY SIMPSON

1. THE EVIDENCE

O.J. Simpson and Nicole Brown Simpson first met in June of 1977, when she was employed as a hostess in a Beverly Hills restaurant. After Mr. Simpson's divorce from his first wife in 1978, they began living together. They were married on February 2, 1985, with their wedding reception at the Rockingham residence. Their daughter Sydney was born on October 17, 1985, and their son Justin was born August 6, 1988.

In late 1984 or early 1985, police were summoned to the Rockingham residence. No police reports were ever filed relating to this incident, but Detective Mark Fuhrman gave the following account in a letter dated January 18, 1989:

"During the fall or winter of 1985, I responded to a 415 family dispute at 360 N. Rockingham. Upon arrival I observed a male black pacing on the driveway and a female wht. sitting on a veh. crying. I inquired if the persons I observed were the residents, at which time the male black stated, 'Yeah, I own this, I'm O.J. Simpson.' My attention turned to the female, who was sobbing, and asked her if she was alright but before she could speak the male black (Simpson) interrupted stating, 'She's my wife, she's okay!' During my conversation with the female I noticed that she was sitting in front of a shattered windshield (Mercedes–Benz, I believe) and I asked, 'Who broke the windshield?' with the female responding, 'He did (pointing to Simpson) ... He hit the windshield with a baseball bat!' Upon hearing the female's statement Simpson exclaimed, 'I broke the windshield ... it's mine ... there's no trouble here.'

I turned to the female and asked if she would like to make a report and she stated, 'No.' "

The second occasion when police were called to intervene in a dispute occurred on New Year's morning, January 1, 1989. After both had been drinking to celebrate New Year's Eve, they got into an argument in the bedroom of their Rockingham residence. Mr. Simpson allegedly hit Nicole on the forehead and slapped her several times. Photographs taken later that day showed several bruises. Police responded to a 911 call and found Nicole hiding in bushes near the house, clad in a bra and sweatpants. Although she stated she did not wish to prosecute three days later, misdemeanor charges of spousal battery were filed, and Mr. Simpson entered a plea of "no contest." He was sentenced to probation conditional on counseling. He successfully completed all the terms and conditions of probation.

The third occasion police were called to intervene occurred after O.J. Simpson and Nicole Brown Simpson were divorced in October, 1992. Nicole moved to a house on Gretna Green Way with the children. Kato Kaelin lived in a guest house on the premises. Beginning in March of 1993, the Simpsons attempted a reconciliation, and Mr. Simpson became a frequent visitor to the premises. His visit on October 25, 1993 resulted in the tape recorded 911 call considered in greater detail in Chapter III(A), *infra*. The incident was described in a police report by Sgt. R. Lerner of L.A.P.D.:

"At approx 2200 hours my partner and I responded to a 'domestic dispute' radio call at 325 S. Gretna Green. The P/R was Nicole Brown Simpson, estranged wife of the suspect, O.J. Simpson. She called the police, in fear, because the suspect had broken into her residence by kicking in the rear double doors and was still at the location.

When we arrived, I observed the white Ford Bronco (described in the contents of the call as the vehicle driven by the suspect) parked in front of the house. The P/R answered the door and directed us to the suspect's location, which was in a small guest house to the rear of P/R's residence. He was speaking with the individual residing in the guest house (M/W, name unknown). When I approached Mr. Simpson, I could see and hear that he was emotionally upset. He was pacing back and forth and talking loudly to the guest house resident. My partner and I took turns attempting to calm Mr. Simpson. We learned, from the suspect, that he and P/R had been together earlier in the day at which time he had found a picture of P/R's ex-boyfriend in their photo album. Mr. Simpson told me that he and P/R had reached a reconciliation agreement. He was no longer to date other women or keep pictures or other memorabilia of his prior dating relationships. P/R was also required, according to the arrangement, to destroy all evidence of her past relationships as well. Mr. Simpson told me that he kept his side of the bargain and felt betrayed when he found that Nicole had not kept hers. They argued for an undetermined length of time and then he left. He called several times during the evening trying to settle their disagreement but to no avail. During their last telephone conversation, Ms. Brown hung up on the suspect and took her phone off the hook. At appox. 2140 Mr. Simpson drove to the P/R's residence but was denied admittance. The suspect walked to the back of the residence, kicked in the double french doors and entered the house. The P/R said she was in fear for her safety so she called the police.

We kept the involved parties separated and calmed them. The P/R was not eager to prosecute the suspect but required our assistance in getting him to leave. Due to the sensitive nature of the call and the parties involved, we requested our supervisor, Sgt. Craig Lally, to respond to the scene. Sgt. Lally made a phone call, I believe, to a City Attorney who gave legal advice. I was instructed to complete a 'domestic violence involved' crime report entitled 'Trespass/Vandalism' listing the victim as Brown, Nicole. The victim was reluctant to make a citizen's arrest and we found no evidence of battery, so the suspect was allowed to leave the location."

Sgt. Craig Lally's report is considered in connection with the hearsay issues it raises, in Chapter III(B), *infra*.

2. THE TACTICAL CONTEXT

The admissibility of the evidence of prior spousal abuse was challenged in an *in limine* motion filed under seal while jury selection was in progress. At that point, the judge had not yet decided whether to sequester the jury. The defense was, of course, concerned that prospective jurors not learn the details of the evidence being challenged through media reports before its admissibility had been determined. Upon completion of jury selection, Judge Ito ruled that the jury would be sequestered, and set argument of the motion *in limine* after the jury had been locked up. At that point, the contents of the motion was publicly released for the first time. If Judge Ito had decided against the sequestration of the jury, the defense intended to seek an *in camera* hearing of the motion, to avoid the danger of prejudicing the jurors through exposure to media coverage of the motion.

The defense recognized that the evidence of the first incident might actually help the defense, by showing the timing and nature of the first encounter between O.J. Simpson and Detective Mark Fuhrman. The incident was contemporaneous with Fuhrman's statements to Kathleeen Bell, expressing hostility toward racially mixed couples, and could supply a motive for Fuhrman to plant evidence to incriminate Simpson. The incident was included in the motion, however, with the thought in mind that even if the motion succeeded, the defense might choose to offer evidence of this incident itself in the course of cross-examining or impeaching the testimony of Detective Fuhrman.

3. DEFENSE ARGUMENT

a. *Evidence of Prior Specific Instances of Conduct Is Not Admissible to Show Propensity.*

The prosecution cannot argue that Mr. Simpson's alleged history of abuse towards Brown demonstrates that he was disposed to commit murder, since evidence of uncharged offenses is *never* admissible to prove propensity. California Evidence Code § 1101[6]; *People v. Thompson,* 27 Cal.3d 303, 165 Cal.Rptr.289 (1980). This is not because it is irrelevant, but as Justice Jackson explained in *Michelson v. United States,* 355 U.S. 469, 496 (1948), because:

> "it is said to weigh too much with the jury and to so overpersuade them as to prejudice one with a bad general record and deny him a fair opportunity to defend against a particular charge. The overriding policy of excluding such evidence, despite its admitted probative value, is the practical experience that its disallowance tends to prevent confusion of issues, unfair surprise and undue prejudice."

Accord, *People v. Guerrero,* 16 Cal.3d 719, 724 (1976). The substantial risk that such evidence will be utilized by a jury for the forbidden purpose of showing propensity requires that any alternative purpose proffered by the prosecution—motive, opportunity, intent, preparation, plan, knowledge, identity, absence of mistake

---

6. California Evidence Code Section 1101 provides:

"(a) Except as provided in this section and in Sections 1102, 1103 and 1108 evidence of a person's character or a trait of his character (whether in the form of an opinion, evidence of reputation, or evidence of specific instances of his or her conduct) is inadmissible when offered to prove his or her conduct on a specified occasion.

(b) Nothing in this section prohibits the admission of evidence that a person committed a crime, civil wrong or other act when relevant to prove some fact (such as motive, opportunity, intent, preparation, plan, knowledge, identity, absence of mistake or accident, or whether a defendant in a prosecution for an unlawful sexual act or attempted unlawful sexual act did not reasonably and in good faith believe that the victim consented) other than his or her disposition to commit such an act.

(c) Nothing in this section affects the admissibility of evidence offered to support or attack the credibility of a witness."

or accident—be clearly identified and the inferences sought to be drawn from the evidence be precisely specified.

b. Evidence of Prior Specific Instances of Conduct Is Not Admissible to Show Identity.

Evidence of uncharged crimes or prior bad acts is admissible to prove identity, but only if it reveals a *modus operandi* unique to the defendant—the standard required by the California Supreme Court since *People v. Haston,* 69 Cal.2d 233, 70 Cal.Rptr. 419 (1969), and which the prosecution cannot possibly meet in this case. The Court has never deviated from the rigorous test announced in *Haston. People v. Banks,* 2 Cal.3d 127, 84 Cal.Rptr. 367 (1970); *People v. Alcala,* 36 Cal.3d 604, 205 Cal.Rptr. 775 (1984). In reaffirming *Haston,* the Court recently declared "the pattern and characteristics of the crimes must be so unusual and distinctive as to be like a signature." *People v. Ewoldt,* 7 Cal.4th 380, 27 Cal.Rptr.2d 646 (1994).

None of the prior incidents bear any resemblance to the brutal murders of Nicole Brown Simpson and Ronald Goldman. The murders were committed with knives, and the absence of outcries suggest stealth may have been involved. The only prior incident of physical assault involved a bedroom argument five years before which allegedly escalated to slaps and punches. The 1984–85 and 1993 incidents involved loud confrontations and damage to property.

The only way any of these incidents could support an inference that O.J. Simpson was the individual who committed these murders is by resort to a forbidden—and in this case illogical inference of propensity: that husbands who display overt anger toward their spouses are likely to kill them, and if their spouses are subsequently murdered under any circumstances, are more likely than others to have been the perpetrators. The careful requirement of "signature" facts would be abandoned in favor of a broad rule that made *any* prior incidents of abuse admissible in *any* prosecution of a husband or wife for the murder of their spouse or ex-spouse.[7]

---

7. One court, disregarding Supreme Court precedent, came close to enunciating such a rule, which has not been followed in any subsequent cases. In *People v. Zack,* 184 Cal.App.3d 409, 415 (2nd D.C.A. 1986), the court held that "where a defendant is charged with a violent crime and has or had a previous relationship with a victim, prior assaults upon the same victim, when offered on disputed issues, *e.g.,* identity, intent, motive, etc., are admissible based solely upon the consideration of identical perpetrator and victim without resort to a distinctive modus operandi analysis of other factors." The extraordinarily broad rule announced in *Zack*—which flouts controlling precedent and treats as immaterial the particular facts of a particular case—is based on the erroneous assumption that any marital discord that results in an "assault", however minor, is logically a prelude to murder. Even the *Zack* rule, of course, would not admit prior incidents which did not involve a physical assault upon the victim.

Studies estimate that as many as four million women are battered annually by husbands or boyfriends. *Developments in the Law—Domestic Violence,* 106 Harv.L.Rev.1498, 1574 n.1 (1993). Yet in 1992, according to the FBI Uniform Crime Reports, a total of 913 women were killed by their husbands, and 519 were killed by their boyfriends. Thus, the ratio of murders to batterings is .000375 to 1.

The assumption underlying the prosecution's theory of admissibility is particularly speculative since Mr. Simpson's prior allegedly abusive behavior consists of, at most, minor acts of aggression which are common to many marital relationships. A recent study shows how common mild aggression against spouses is: 31.6% of the women surveyed reported a husband pushing, grabbing or shoving; 17.6% reported slapping; and 16% reported a husband throwing something at her. L.L. Lockhart, *A Reexamination of the Effects of Race and Social Class on the Incidence of Marital Violence: A Search for More Differences,* 49 J. Marriage and Family 603, 606 (1987).

c. Evidence of Prior Specific Instances of Conduct Is Not Admissible to Show Motive or Intent.

Here, the critical issue is not intent, since Mr. Simpson has denied participating in the murders. Moreover, the prior alleged misconduct is so wildly different from the charged murders, no logical inference can be drawn that both were done with the same criminal intent.

Motive evidence is often indistinguishable from character evidence. Thus, when prior crimes or bad acts are offered to prove motive, the courts must be watchful that the evidence is not being offered as a way to circumvent the prohibition against character evidence. *People v. Gibson,* 56 Cal.App.3d 119, 129, 128 Cal.Rptr. 302 (1976). An argument that a defendant's "explosive temper" reflected a motive to kill, for example, would be so improper and prejudicial as to require reversal. *State v. Wood,* 880 P.2d 771 (Ida.Ct.App. 1994).

Evidence consisting of isolated alleged "threats" made during a marital fight, or physical mistreatment of a type that is not indicative of an intent to kill, will not support a logical inference of intent or motive, especially when the incidents precede the murder by a long lapse of time. *People v. Deeney,* 145 Cal.App.3d 647, 193 Cal.Rptr. 698 (1983).

d. Evidence of Prior Specific Instances of Conduct Is Not Admissible to Show a Common Plan or Scheme.

For evidence to be probative of a common scheme or design, "the common features must indicate the existence of a plan rather

than a series of similar spontaneous acts...." *People v. Ewoldt,* 7
Cal.4th 380, 402, 27 Cal.Rptr.2d 646, 658 (1994). Generally, other
crimes evidence is admitted for the purpose of showing a "common
plan or scheme" when the defendant has engaged in similar acts
with respect to several victims. *Ewoldt,* 7 Cal.4th at 403 (sexual
abuse of stepdaughters). Simpson is not charged with committing
the same general type of offense against different alleged victims
pursuant to some common scheme. Moreover, Simpson's alleged
assault of Brown five years earlier, and his more recent alleged
conduct towards her, reflect a "series of spontaneous acts" that
often occur in intimate relationships marked by discord, and are
not indicative of a plan to commit murder.

e. The Admission of Prior Instances of Conduct Would Violate Defendant's State and Federal Constitutional Rights.

The United States Supreme Court has not yet expressed its
opinion whether a state law would violate the Due Process Clause if
it permitted the use of "prior crimes" evidence to show propensity
to commit a charged crime. *Estelle v. McGuire,* 502 U.S. 62 (1991).
In considering a case remanded for further consideration in light of
Estelle v. McGuire, however, the U.S. Court of Appeals for the
Ninth Circuit granted a writ of habeas corpus on the grounds that a
California court's admission of other acts evidence probative only of
propensity was violative of the Due Process Clause of the United
States Constitution. In that case, the defendant had been convicted
of murdering his mother by slitting her throat on the basis of
evidence showing prior fascination with knives. *McKinney v. Rees,*
993 F.2d 1378, 1384–86 (9th Cir. 1993). The court concluded:

> "It is part of our community's sense of fair play that people are
> convicted because of what they have done, not who they are."

f. The Prejudicial Impact of Evidence of Prior Specific Instances of Conduct Outweighs Its Probative Value.

Even if the Court determines that evidence of prior specific
instances of conduct is probative of an issue in dispute and comes
within one of the exceptions outlined in California Evidence Code
§ 1101(b), the Court must then engage in the weighing process
required by California Evidence Code § 352, which provides that:

> "the court in its discretion may exclude evidence if its proba-
> tive value is substantially outweighed by the probability that
> its admission will (a) necessitate undue consumption of time or
> (b) create substantial danger of undue prejudice, of confusing
> the issues, or of misleading the jury."

In this case, the admission of evidence of prior specific instances of conduct presents grave risks of undue consumption of time by creating the need for lengthy cross-examination of witnesses, presentation of expert witnesses, and the production of evidence of good character which would not otherwise be offered. This will greatly extend the duration of a trial already projected to last as long as six months. This concern is elevated by the prospect of sequestration of the jury.

The risks of undue prejudice, confusion or misleading the jury are also of grave concern. The specific instances of domestic discord offered in this case are widely separated in time. The first, in late 1984 or early 1985, actually preceded the marriage of O.J. Simpson and Nicole Brown Simpson. The second occurred five and one-half years before the murder. While remoteness ordinarily goes to the weight to be accorded evidence, it is especially significant in exercising discretion pursuant to Section 352 where the danger of prejudice is grave. *People v. Thomas,* 20 Cal.3d 457, 466, 143 Cal.Rptr. 215 (1978).

The defense in this case is simply that Mr. Simpson did not kill the victims of this homicide. The prejudice to this defense from evidence that he struck his wife on a single prior occasion, or broke a windshield or a door, far transcends any benefit to the prosecution's proof of intent, or other issues that are not seriously disputed in this case. *People v. Gibson,* 56 Cal.App.3d 119, 128 Cal.Rptr.302 (1976).

g.   Out of Court Statements by Nicole Brown Simpson Expressing Fear of Defendant Are Inadmissible Hearsay.

[This argument is fully presented in Chapter III, Problems (A) and (B), *infra*].

4.   PROSECUTION ARGUMENT

a.   Introduction.

The defense has filed a motion seeking to exclude evidence that would correctly and fully portray the seventeen year relationship between Nicole Brown Simpson and the defendant. In cases where defendant is charged with a violent crime and has or had a relationship with the victim [hereinafter, "relationship violence cases"], evidence characterizing the relationship is admissible. Such evidence includes evidence demonstrating jealousy, quarrels, hostility, manipulation, violence, or aggression [hereinafter, "abuse and control evidence"]. It is admissible, among other things, to prove a motive for murder. Motive is relevant to establish the identity and intent of the perpetrator.

... All of the acts of abuse and control leading up to victim's murder were part of a systematic plan to control her. All of these acts were designed with a goal in mind, that being control. Nicole Brown's murder was the final manifestation of this design—the ultimate act of control. All the acts of abuse and control discussed in this brief were part of this grand design. To the extent that she was breaking away, the only choice left to defendant was to control her through her death—*i.e.,* "if I can't have her no one will." The evidence shows that the defendant was an extremely jealous and possessive man. Murdering Nicole was also the ultimate act of control and retribution. Contrary to defendant's theory that the abuse and control evidence consists of a series of unrelated acts irrelevant to the murder, victim's murder was the end of an unbroken chain constituting a continuing course of conduct. This motive for murder is well recognized in the scientific literature and by California courts. In short, this is a domestic violence case involving murder, not a murder case involving domestic violence.

> **b. *Without Resort to Traditional Evidence Code Section 1101(b) Analysis, Where a Defendant Is Charged with a Violent Crime and Has or Had a Previous Relationship With a Victim, Evidence Demonstrating Jealousy, Quarrels, Hostility, or Aggression Between Defendant and Victim Is Admissible to Prove Motive, and thus, the Perpetrator's Identity and Intent.***

An extensive body of California case authority establishes this rule. It is stated clearly in *People v. Zack,* 184 Cal.App.3d 409, 414 (1986). There, the defendant, who was charged with the first degree murder of his wife, claimed he had not killed his wife and presented an alibi defense. Along with overwhelming circumstantial evidence, the prosecutor presented evidence that defendant had previously assaulted his wife on several occasions. On one occasion victim received two black eyes. The Court of Appeal ruled that such evidence was properly admitted:

> "Without resort to a 'distinctive modus operandi,' 'signature,' 'calling card' [or] analysis of other factors ... '... the common mark of the identical perpetrator and identical victim in both the charged and uncharged offenses is so distinctive that it adds persuasive support to the inference that the defendant and not some other person was the perpetrator ...' and renders the prior evidence admissible on the issue of identity. From these precedents, as well as common sense, experience, and logic, we distill the following rule: Where a defendant is charged with a violent crime and has or had a previous relationship with a victim, prior assaults upon the same victim, when offered on disputed issues, e.g., identity, intent, motive,

et cetera, are admissible based solely upon the consideration of identical perpetrator and victim without resort to a 'distinctive modus operandi' analysis of other factors."

Id. at 414–15 (citations omitted).

The defense correctly points out that usually, under Evidence Code Section 1101(b), where evidence of prior crimes is being admitted to prove identity, there must be a distinctive modus operandi. They have misstated California law, however, in assuming this rule applies in domestic violence cases. *Zack* clearly holds that this traditional 1101(b) analysis is inapplicable in domestic violence cases. Rather, in such cases there is a per se rule favoring admissibility of evidence regarding the relationship between defendant and victim. This special rule favoring the admissibility of such evidence in domestic violence cases is similar to the special rule favoring prior crimes evidence involving the same victim in sexual assault cases. "In sex offense cases, our Supreme Court has set forth a less stringent test for the admission of evidence of uncharged offenses...." when the prior offenses involved the same victim and defendant. *People v. Salazar,* 144 Cal.App.3d 799, 810 (1983), (citing *People v. Thompson,* 27 Cal.3d 303, 315 (1980). *Zack* explains the policy reasons supporting this rule:

> "A trial is a search for the truth.... The rules of evidence are designed to further this search, and to that end the Legislature has expressly provided for the admissibility of other acts to show '... motive, opportunity, intent, preparation, plan, knowledge, identity, or absence of mistake or accident....' Appellant was not entitled to have the jury determine his guilt or innocence on a false presentation that his and the victim's relationship and their parting were peaceful and friendly."

Zack, supra, at 415. *Zack* is on all fours with our case. In both cases, the victim and defendant had a long relationship with a pronounced pattern of abuse and violence. In each case identity was the primary issue and in both cases the evidence is highly probative of the defendant's motive to kill and hence helps to identify him as the perpetrator.

The defense attempts to dispose of *Zack* simply by stating, in a footnote, that it was wrongly decided. However, ... *Zack* is a correct and controlling statement of law, based on longstanding California precedent.... The California Supreme Court approved of *People v. Zack,* in *People v. Allison,* 48 Cal.3d 879, 896 n.7 (1989). The Court approved of *Zack's* rule that evidence of prior assaults on the victim is admissible to prevent the jury from being misled. *Id.*

c. The Rule of Haston Is Inapplicable in Relationship Violence Cases.

In their brief, the defense refers to the case of *People v. Haston*, 69 Cal.2d 233 (1969), as standing for the proposition that evidence of other crimes cannot be introduced into evidence on the ultimate issue of identity unless they are "distinctive." *Haston* is not a relationship violence case and does not discuss the relationship violence line of cases. In *Haston*, the defendant was charged with robbery and identity was in issue. Evidence of other similar robberies was introduced into trial. The Court stated that a large number of similarities is insufficient to admit past acts if the acts were committed with merely a common or ordinary modus operandi.

What is significant about *Haston* is that the prior acts introduced did not involve the same defendant and victim. *Haston* does not apply in the context of relationship violence cases. As stated in *People v. Beamon*, 8 Cal.3d 625, 633 (1973), under the *Haston* test "even ignoring other similarities, the common mark of the identical perpetrator and identical victim in both the charged and uncharged offenses is so distinctive that it adds persuasive support to the inference that defendant and not some other person was the perpetrator." In a relationship violence case, the "distinctive modus operandi" test is clearly inapplicable.

> "Common sense, experience and logic compel the conclusion that the 'distinctive modus operandi'', 'signature', 'calling card' analysis in the cases relied upon by the appellant (e.g., *People v. Nottingham*, 172 Cal.App.3d 484 (1985)) is inapplicable in the present context. Here, given the brutal and unique nature of the murder, appellant's prior assaults upon the decedent, of necessity, could not survive a 'distinctive modus operandi' analysis. *One cannot kill the same person twice.* Yet appellant expressly contends that he had not previously broken the decedent's two ankles,nor had he previously inflicted twenty-one wounds to her body, nor had he previously bludgeoned her about the head."

Zack, supra at 415 (emphasis added). This analysis reveals precisely why the distinctive modus operandi test is inapplicable in relationship violence cases. Application of that test would defy logic and common sense. One indeed cannot kill the same person twice.

d. Applying Traditional Evidence Code Section 1101(b) Analysis, the Evidence Regarding the Relationship Between Victim and Defendant Is Admissible.

Evidence Code Section 1101(b) provides for the admission of prior crimes evidence for any purpose other than to prove a defendant's criminal disposition. In *People v. Sully*, 53 Cal.3d 1195

(1991), the California Supreme Court clarified that the introduction of prior crime evidence is a matter left to the sound discretion of the trial judge, and a matter will not be overturned on appeal absent an "abuse of the trial court's discretion." *Id.* at 1226. In the exercise of its sound discretion, this court should rule admissible the evidence relating to defendant's relationship with victim. The evidence is admissible to prove the motive and thus the perpetrator's identity. The evidence is admissible to prove motive and thus intent.

In *People v. Gallego,* 52 Cal.3d 115 (1990), the Court held that "when evidence of an uncharged offense is introduced to prove intent, the prosecution need not show the same quantum of 'similarity' as when uncharged conduct is used to prove identity." *Id.* at 172. The Court explained that:

> "We have long recognized that if a person acts similarly in similar situations, he probably harbors the same intent in each instance, and that such prior conduct may be relevant circumstantial evidence of the actor's most recent intent. The inference to be drawn is not that the actor is disposed to commit such acts; instead, the inference to be drawn is that, in light of the first event, the actor, at the time of the second event, must have had the intent attributed to him by the prosecution."

Id. at 171.

The evidence is also relevant to prove common plan, scheme and design. Evidence of prior offenses directed against the same victim are admissible under this theory, even if there is no issue as to identity or intent.

> "To establish the existence of a common design or plan, the common features must indicate the existence of a plan rather than a series of similar spontaneous acts, but the plan thus revealed need not be distinctive or unusual.... [E]vidence that the defendant has committed uncharged criminal acts that are similar to the charged offense may be relevant if these acts demonstrate circumstantially that the defendant committed the charged offense pursuant to the same design or plan he or she used in committing the uncharged acts. Unlike evidence of uncharged acts used to prove identity, the plan need not be unusual or distinctive; it need only exist to support the inference that the defendant employed that plan in committing the charged offense."

People v. Ewoldt, 7 Cal.4th 380, 402 (1994). *Ewoldt* demonstrates that defendant misapprehends this basis for admissibility. Defendant seems to assume that the term "plan" means that at the time defendant committed the earlier offense he contemplated committing the charged offense. Rather, cases like *Ewoldt* clarify that a continuing course of conduct, even over many years, towards the same victim (or similar victims) constitutes a common plan. Evidence of a pattern of abuse systematically directed against Nicole Brown clearly falls within this definition. While the defendant committed many different types of abusive acts against Nicole Brown Simpson they were all committed with the same intent and purpose—to control victim's life. This was his "grand design." When it appeared to him that she was escaping that control, he committed the murder as the final act of control. This legal theory of admissibility makes evidence of property destruction or stalking relevant as evidencing defendant's design to control victim. Therefore, the People should not be limited to proving acts of violence alone.

e.   The Evidence Proffered Is Highly Probative and Not Excludable Under Evidence Code Section 352.

The probative value of evidence of uncharged misconduct is enhanced if the source is independent of the evidence of the charged offense. *Ewoldt, supra* at 404. In this case, the evidence directly relating to the murder is circumstantial and forensic. By contrast, the People will prove the prior misconduct by having police officers, who did not investigate the charged offense, testify about their observations of victim after the incidents and her excited utterances describing what happened. The People will present a 911 tape to prove the 1993 incident. Additionally, the People will also call civilian witnesses who observed acts of abuse and control. Because the sources of the People's proof of the defendant's assaultive conduct is independent of the evidence of the murders, the probative value of the prior assaultive conduct is enhanced.

There is negligible danger of undue prejudice in admitting this evidence. "Danger of undue prejudice" means the likelihood "that a jury will be led astray and convict an innocent man because of his bad record...." *People v. Schader,* 71 Cal.2d 761, 774 (1969). If the evidence describing a defendant's uncharged act is no stronger and no more inflammatory that the evidence concerning the charged offense, the potential for prejudice is decreased. *Ewoldt, supra* at 405. Here, the evidence of the murder is as strong or stronger than the evidence of defendant's abuse and control. Evidence of the murder is also much more "inflammatory" than the evidence of defendant's abuse and control. Therefore, the argument that the jury will improperly convict the defendant of two heinous murders to punish him for his abuse and control of victim is meritless.

The prejudicial impact of uncharged acts is also decreased if the conduct resulted in a criminal conviction. *Balcolm,* 7 Cal.4th 761. The reason is that there is no risk the jury will convict defendant of the charged offense to punish him for prior crimes for which he went unpunished. Since defendant was convicted of the 1989 incident, the jury will learn that defendant was, in fact, punished for abusing victim.

5. DEFENSE REPLY ARGUMENT

a. *Introduction.*

The People are to be commended for the candor with which they acknowledge the revolutionary new approach they are taking to the presentation of evidence in this case. We are informed that "this is a domestic violence case involving murder, not a murder case involving domestic violence." As a consequence of attaching this label to the case, we are told that "a special rule permits abuse and control evidence," including all forms of verbal or psychological abuse, whether they involved violence or not.

There are three things wrong with this scenario. First, the "special rule" simply does not exist in the statutes or case law of California. It is simply wishful thinking by overzealous prosecutors that turns the law on its head. Second, the admissible evidence will not support the attempt to portray Nicole Brown Simpson as a "battered wife." Finally, the People are actually suggesting a trial directed to the question of who killed Nicole Brown Simpson and Ronald Goldman on June 12, 1994, should instead be transformed into a general inquiry into the character of O.J. Simpson, calling upon him to explain every aspect of a sixteen year relationship. Simply putting a special label on a case, whether that label be "organized crime," "gang activity," or "domestic violence", does not permit prosecutors to drive a truck over the rules of evidence and transform a trial into a sleazy tabloid dramatization.

b. *People v. Zack Establishes No "Special Rule" Permitting Evidence of Prior Abuse.*

Seeking to avoid the strictures of California Evidence Code § 1101, the People distort the limited holding of *People v. Zack,* 184 Cal.App. 409, 414 (1986) into a "special rule" to open the door to all evidence of prior "abuse" in cases where one accused of murder had a prior relationship with any of the victims.

Zack itself involved the presentation of evidence of prior physical beating of the victim by the defendant within a four-year period preceding her murder, in which she was literally beaten to death. Most significant, and completely overlooked in the distorted analysis by the People, is that this evidence was presented in *rebuttal* to the defendant's testimony that "his and the victim's relationship and their parting were peaceful and friendly." 184 Cal.App.3d at 415. It is especially interesting to note how the holding of *Zack* was characterized in the single California Supreme Court opinion cited by the People as giving approval to *Zack*. In *People v. Allison,* 48 Cal.3d 879, 896 n.7 (1989), the Court actually quotes *People v. Goodwin,* 202 Cal.App.3d 940 (1988), which cited *Zack* as follows:

"The weakness in [defendant's] testimony should not be ignored or given preferential treatment not granted to the testimony of any other witnesses. As it has been aptly noted in other contexts, a defendant who elects to testify in his own behalf is not entitled to a false aura of veracity. (*People v. Beagle,* 6 Cal.3d 441, 453 (1972) [impeachment with prior conviction]; *People v. Zack,* 184 Cal.App.3d 409, 415 [impeachment with evidence of prior assaults on decedent]. [Defendant] was not entitled to have the jury determine his guilt or innocence guided by jury instructions which would ignore the false or inconsistent testimony of any witness, including [himself]."

Secondly, even in its broadest, most expansive form, the *Zack* court limited the rule it propounded to evidence of "prior assaults upon the same victim." 184 Cal.App.3d at 415. To stretch this into a "special rule" that broadly admits all evidence of abuse in any form is not warranted by anything the *Zack* court said, nor for that matter, any California case has ever said.

c. *Prior Acts Are Not Relevant to Show Motive, Identity, Intent or Common Plan.*

The first step in any prosecutorial attempt to employ the limited exceptions to the general preclusion of bad character evidence contained in Evidence Code Section 1101(b) is to clearly identify the purpose of the evidence and the inferences to be drawn. The People's Response identifies a variety of purposes without ever articulating the inferences they will ask a jury to draw. Among the "motives" they ascribe to the defendant at various points are "control," rage and jealousy. The apparent inference process proceeds something like this:

O.J. Simpson struck his wife with his fists during an argument after a New Year's Eve party at which both had too much to drink five years ago;

Therefore, the defendant wanted to "control" his wife;

Nicole Simpson was slashed and stabbed on June 12, 1994 by someone who wanted to "control" her;

Therefore, it is more likely that O.J. Simpson was the person who slashed and stabbed her.

The logical fallacies in this chain of inferences are readily apparent. A much more persuasive chain of inferences would simply be:

O.J. Simpson struck his wife with his fists during an argument after a New Year's Eve party at which both had too much to drink five years ago;

Therefore, O.J. Simpson is a bad person;

Therefore, it is more likely that O.J. Simpson was the person who slashed and stabbed Nicole Simpson.

This use of evidence of prior acts as "propensity" evidence is precisely what is forbidden. Yet the prosecution cannot articulate a chain of inferences which is not a thinly disguised attempt to suggest propensity.

The suggestion the evidence is admissible to prove the motive *and thus the perpetrator's identity* suggests that identity can be inferred from motive, thus short-circuiting the requirement that prior acts bear "signature fact" similarities to support an inference of identity. The cases relied upon are inevitably cases where identity was not in issue; the defendant conceded he did the act, and the issue being litigated was the state of mind with which it was done. Here, the key issue in the case is simply one of identity. The prosecution's case will stand or fall on their ability to prove beyond a reasonable doubt that O.J. Simpson was the person who killed Nicole Brown Simpson and Ronald Goldman. Noticeably absent among the theories of admissibility articulated by the prosecution is a direct inference of identity. The reason should be abundantly clear—that the alleged acts bear no resemblance to the act of murder perpetrated here. The requirement of similarity cannot be avoided by the simple expedient of canting talismanic words like "motive" or "intent."

The suggestion of a "common scheme or plan" also lacks any articulated inference. As the California Supreme Court noted in *People v. Ewoldt,* 7 Cal.4th 380, 402 (1994), there must be "such a concurrence of common features that the various acts are naturally to be explained as caused by the general plan of which they are the individual manifestation." The prosecution makes no effort to identify *any* common features other than that Nicole Brown Simpson was the victim of each incident. In this respect, the argument is indistinguishable from the argument that there is some "special rule" that permits all evidence of abusive behavior by a spouse whenever he or she is accused of the murder of the other spouse.

Finally, it should be noted that the People suggest a highly misleading standard for analysis of the admissibility of evidence under Section 1101. They suggest the admission or exclusion of such evidence is a matter of "sound discretion of the trial judge." A trial court does not have "discretion" to admit irrelevant evidence. California Evidence Code § 350. Only *after* the court has determined that evidence is admissible under § 1101 is an exercise of discretion called for, to weigh probative value against the risk of undue consumption of time and danger of undue prejudice or confusion. California Evidence Code § 352.

d. Probative Value of the Evidence of Prior Acts is Outweighed by the Risks of Undue Consumption of Time and Undue Prejudice.

In responding to the Defendant's objection pursuant to California Evidence Code § 352, the People do not even address the issue of undue consumption of time. The prospect of doubling the length of this trial to litigate the ups and downs of a sixteen-year relationship should give the court great pause. Each of the incidents enumerated in the Defendant's Motion and the People's Response would itself occupy a mini-trial, with numerous issues of credibility and circumstances of extenuation. Ultimately, their value in resolving the central issue of who killed Nicole Brown Simpson and Ronald Goldman is highly questionable. The potential to distract the jury from that central issue is enormous.

6. JUDGES' RULING

On January 18, 1995, Judge Ito issued the following ruling:

The prosecution bases its argument for the admissibility of prior acts of violence committed by this defendant upon Nicole Brown Simpson upon *People v.Zack,* 184 Cal.App.3d 409 (1986). In that case, also involving a charge of homicide within a male/female relationship and the defense of alibi, the trial court admitted evidence of Zack's prior assaults upon the decedent. The *Zack* court cited to *People v. Daniels,* 16 Cal.App.3d 36, 46 (1971), which held: 'Evidence showing jealousy, quarrels, antagonism or enmity between an accused and the victim of a violent offense is proof of a motive to commit the offense.... Evidence relevant as proof of motive or behavior pattern is not inadmissible because it also is proof of prior crimes....' This argument, however, must be measured against our Supreme Court's latest holdings concerning Evidence Code Section 1101(b). In *People v. Ewoldt,* 7 Cal.4th 380, 403 (1994), the high court observed, 'The greatest degree of similarity is required for evidence of uncharged misconduct to be relevant to prove identity. For identity to be established, the uncharged misconduct and the charged offense must share common features that are sufficiently distinctive to support the inference that the same person committed both acts. [cite] The pattern and characteristics of the crimes must be so unusual and distinctive as to be like a signature. [cite]." The *Ewoldt* court cites its earlier opinion in *People v. Miller,* 50 Cal.3d 954, 987 (1990), noting, "... The inference of identity, moreover, need not depend on one or more unique or nearly unique common features; features of substantial but lesser distinctiveness may yield a distinctive combination when considered together." This language is particularly instructive as it is virtually identical to that which precedes the following comment from our high court in *People v. Beamon,* 8 Cal.3d 625, 633: "... We have no difficulty in concluding that, even ignoring other similarities, the common mark of identical perpetrator and identical victim in both the charged and uncharged offenses is so distinctive that it adds persuasive support to the inference that defendant and not some other person was the perpetrator of both offenses involving [the victim]." In clear and unmistakable language, the *Zack* court goes on to provide guidance to the trial courts: "... From these precedents, as well as common sense, experience, and logic, we distill the following rule: Where a defendant is charged with a violent crime and had or had a previous relationship with a victim, prior assaults upon the same victim, when offered on disputed issues, e.g., identity, intent, motive, et cetera, are admissible based solely upon the consideration of identical perpetrator and victim without resort to a 'distinctive modus operandi' analysis of other factors." *Zack* at 415. It is the relationship between the alleged perpetrator and the victim that provides the necessary uniqueness required under Evidence Code Section 1101(b). It is therefore the *in limine* holding of this court that evidence of defendant's prior assaults upon Nicole Brown Simpson may be admitted at trial as to the issues of motive, intent, plan and identity. Those incidents [include] ... the 1985 incident in which Simpson beat her car with a baseball bat. This evidence is relevant as to the nature and quality of the relationship, it is part of a pattern of conduct by the defendant towards Brown Simpson and an incident of physical violence against her; and the 1989 incident resulting in defendant's conviction for spousal abuse where Nicole Brown Simpson was the victim, including various letters containing admissions of the defendant and police photos of Brown Simpson's injuries. This evidence is relevant as to the nature and quality of the relationship, it is part of a pattern of conduct by the defendant towards Brown Simpson and an incident of physical violence against her.

[These incidents] involve either a direct observation of defendant engaged in assaultive conduct against Brown Simpson or an admission of such conduct by the defendant. The probative value is strong and outweighs any danger of undue prejudice, confusion of the issues or misleading the jury. The 352 objection is therefore denied.

[Judge Ito also overruled the defense objection to the 1993 incident on the 911 tape, although not on the basis that it was an instance of physical violence or assaultive behavior toward the same victim.

This ruling is reproduced in Chapter III(A) *infra,* treating the hearsay objections. Objections were sustained with respect to some incidents deemed "remote" or having "slight" probative value.]

All of the incidents of prior spousal abuse admitted at the criminal trial were also admitted at the civil trial. Many were utilized in the cross examination of defendant O.J. Simpson.

7. COMMENTS AND QUESTIONS

(a) The ruling excluding some evidence of spousal abuse in the criminal trial applied only to the prosecution's case in chief. The prospect of the excluded evidence being utilized to cross-examine and impeach the defendant's testimony was a weighty consideration in determining whether the defendant should testify:

"Simpson would be the last witness called by the defense. From a tactical standpoint, there was a real risk to ending the trial with a rehash of all of the domestic discord evidence with which the trial had begun. Not only would all of that evidence be replayed, but a good deal of additional evidence of discord that had been excluded by our pretrial motion was excluded only from the prosecutor's opening case and could still be used to rebut the defense case. Cross-examination would open new doors and bring much of that evidence before the jury for the first time."

Uelmen, *Lessons From the Trial: The People v. O.J. Simpson* (Andrews & McMeel, 1996), at 157–58. At the civil trial, the door was opened wide to the use of prior incidents of abuse when O.J. Simpson flatly denied that he *ever* struck Nicole Brown Simpson:

"Q. And how many times, Mr. Simpson, in the course of these physical altercations, did you hit Nicole?

A. Never.

Q. How many times did you strike Nicole?

A. Never.

Q. How many times did you slap Nicole?

A. Never.

Q. How many times did you kick her?

A. Never.

Q. How many times did you beat her, sir?

A. Never."

(b) The prosecution did not even offer all of the evidence of prior spousal abuse that Judge Ito ruled admissible. What considerations might lead a lawyer to decline to offer evidence that a judge has already ruled admissible? Can a prosecutor "save" evidence for rebuttal, because it will have a more dramatic impact at the end of a trial, to refute the defendant's anticipated testimony? What if the defendant never testifies? Consider these post-trial comments of Marcia Clark:

> "... I knew from experience, both personal and professional, that the very mention of the words 'domestic violence' aroused volative emotions in people. There was no telling what kind of response they might elicit from our jury. The fact that most of our jurors were women was not comfort to me: female jurors often view the victims of domestic violence with uncompre- hending disdain. On top of this, we had the complications of race and celebrity. This did not mean that our female jurors couldn't be brought around, but we would have to proceed cautiously.
>
> If it appeared that the domestic violence evidence was alienating our jury, someone would have to make the strategic call to stand down. It would not be a popular move, certainly not within our office. But somewhere down the line a tough decision might have to be made. And even as I lifted a glass to victory, I realized the person to make it would have to be me."

Marcia Clark, *Without A Doubt,* pp. 257–58 (Viking Penguin, 1997).

(c) How would a lawyer assess whether domestic violence evidence was "alienating" the jury? Jury Foreman Armanda Cooley suggests the prosecution may have "stood down" too soon:

> "The prosecution was trying to build up a case based on the rage that Mr. Simpson had built up through the time periods between 1985 and 1994, and the information that they gave us about that period of spousal abuse was really just not enough information to indicate that this man had built up all this rage over all this time. We only had one incident with three little episodes, and it wasn't until we got out that we heard about all these other incidents. I hear about these other episodes and I'm thinking, *Well, damn, I can truly see spousal abuse or some type of rage will build up within a person if I would have heard all this stuff.*"

Armanda Cooley, Carrie Bess and Marsha Rubin–Jackson, *Madam Foreman: A Rush to Judgement?,* p. 198 (Dove Books, 1995).

(d) The instructions to the jury included the standard CALJIC instructions utilized when past criminal acts are admitted for the limited purposes included in California Evidence Code Section 1101(b). The instruction informed the jury:

> "Evidence has been introduced for the purpose of showing that the defendant committed crimes other than that for which he

is on trial. Such evidence, if believed, was not received and may not be considered by you to prove that the defendant is a person of bad character or that he has a disposition to commit crimes.

Such evidence was received and may be considered by you only for the limited purpose of determining if it tends to show:

(1) a characteristic method, plan or scheme in the commission of criminal acts similar to the method, plan or scheme used in the commission of the offense in this case which would further tend to show the existence of the intent which is a necessary element of the crime charged, the identity of the person who committed the crime, if any, of which the defendant is accused or a clear connection between the other offense and the one of which the defendant is accused, so that it may be inferred that if the defendant committed the other offenses, the defendant also committed the crimes charged in this case;

(2) the existence of the intent which is a necessary element of the crime charged;

(3) the identity of the person who committed the crime, if any, of which the defendant is accused;

(4) a motive for the commission of the crime charged.

For the limited purpose for which you may consider such evidence, you must weigh it in the same manner as you do all the other evidence in this case. You are not permitted to consider such evidence for any other purpose.

Within the meaning of the preceding instruction, such other crime or crimes purportedly committed by a defendant must be proved by a preponderance of the evidence. You must not consider such evidence for any purpose unless you are satisfied that the defendant committed such other crime or crimes."

What level of education do you think is necessary for a juror to understand this instruction? Do you understand it?

(e) After the criminal trial of O.J. Simpson, the California legislature amended the California Evidence Code to facilitate the admission of evidence of prior spousal abuse. California Evidence Code Section 1109 now provides:

"(a) Except as provided in subdivision (e), in a criminal action in which the defendant is accused of an offense involving domestic violence, evidence of the defendant's commission of other domestic violence is not made inadmissible by Section 1101, if the evidence is not inadmissible pursuant to Section 352.

(b) In an action in which evidence is to be offered under this section, the people shall disclose the evidence to the defendant, including statements of witnesses or a summary of the substance of any testimony that is expected to be offered, at least 30 days before the scheduled date of trial or at a later time as the court may allow for good cause.

(c) This section shall not be construed to limit or preclude the admission or consideration of evidence under any other statute or case law;

(d) As used in this section, 'domestic violence' has the meaning set forth in Section 13700 of the Penal Code.

(e) Evidence of acts occurring more than 10 years before the charged offense is inadmissible under this section, unless the court determines that the admission of this evidence is in the interest of justice."

California Penal Code Section 13700 provides the following definitions:

"(a) 'Abuse' means intentionally or recklessly causing or attempting to cause bodily injury, or placing another person in reasonable apprehension of imminent serious bodily injury to himself or herself, or another.

(b) 'Domestic violence' means abuse committed against an adult or a fully emancipated minor who is a spouse, former spouse, cohabitant, former cohabitant, or a person with whom the suspect has had a child or is having or has had a dating or engagement relationship. For purposes of this subdivision, 'cohabitant' means two unrelated adult persons living together for a substantial period of time, resulting in some permanency of relationship. Factors that may determine whether persons are cohabiting include, but are not limited to, (1) sexual relations between the parties while sharing the same living quarters; (2) sharing of income or expenses; (3) joint use or ownership of property; (4) whether the parties hold themselves out as husband and wife; (5) the continuity of the relationship; and (6) the length of the relationship."

To what extent is the new code section broader than Judge Ito's ruling? To what extent is it narrower? Note that incidents which may not be admissible under Section 1109 may still be offered for the limited purposes specified under Section 1101(b).

Why is the new code section limited to criminal cases? Isn't the risk of prejudice *greater* in criminal cases than civil cases?

The new code section apparently permits the evidence to be considered to show *propensity*. Can an argument be made, based on cases cited by the defense, that this new code section is unconstitutional?

(f) The defense *in limine* motion addressing the admissibility of evidence of prior spousal abuse requested the court to admonish prosecutors against using the terms "battering," "stalking," or "spousal abuse." The motion itself was labeled a motion to exclude evidence of "domestic discord." While Judge Ito denied this request, can you envision situations where it might be appropriate to limit the use of inflammatory labels in court?

(g) Professor Roger Park concludes that Judge Ito's decision admitting evidence of prior spousal abuse "is consistent with authority throughout the country. [Citing Annotation, 24 ALR5th 465 (1994)]. While the issue was under consideration by Judge Ito, it was covered with 'this is a horse race' commentary, but in retrospect the case presents an instance in which the evidence law was relatively clear." Park, *Character Evidence Issues in the O.J. Simpson Case—Or, Rationales of the Character Evidence Ban, With Illustrations From the Simpson Case*, 67 U.Colo.L.Rev. 747, 753 (1996).

B. PRIOR POLICE MISCONDUCT BY FUHRMAN

1. THE EVIDENCE

Laura Hart McKinny first met Officer Mark Fuhrman in Westwood in February, 1985. Over the course of the next ten years, she met with Fuhrman to conduct tape recorded interviews while he served as a "technical advisor" for her development of a screenplay about the experiences of women police officers in L.A.P.D. The transcripts of the interviews contained eighteen examples of Detective Fuhrman admitting participation in police misconduct, or offering approving comments with respect to misconduct. This misconduct included illegal use of deadly force, beating suspects to extract confessions, planting evidence, framing innocent persons, and lying or covering up misconduct by other police officers. Five of the extracts from the transcripts included in a defense "offer of proof" are reproduced here:

3. (Transcript of April 2, 1985, p. 25, describing arrest of a narcotics user).

> "So if that's considered falsifying a report, and if some hype, you know, says Ah, you know, whatever, I shot two days ago, and you find a mark that looks like three days ago, pick the scab, squeeze it, looks like serum's coming out, as if it were hours old. It's a hard find. You just can't find the mark, cause

he's down. His eyes don't lie. That's not falsifying a report.
That's putting a criminal in jail. That's being a policeman.''

7. (Transcript of April 2, 1985, p. 33–34, describing the manufacturing of probable cause for arrest of a suspect in Westwood).

"He was a nigger. He didn't belong. Two questions. And
you're going: Where do you live? 22nd and Western. Where
were you going? Well, I'm going to Fatburger. Where's Fatburger. He didn't know where Fatburger was? Get in the car.

Q. So under what did you arrest him?

A. I didn't arrest him under anything, just took him to the
station, ran him for prints, gave them to the detectives to
compare with what they've got in the area. I'll probably arrest
a criminal that way.

Q. So you're allowed to just pick somebody up that you think
doesn't belong in an area and arrest him?

A. I don't know.

Q. Well, I mean, you did, so—

A. I don't know. I don't know that the Supreme Court or the
Superior Court says, and I don't really give a shit. . . . If I was
pushed into saying why I did it, I'd say suspicion of burglary.
I'd be able to correlate exactly what I said into a reasonable
probable cause for arrest.''

9. (Transcript of April [day unknown], 1985, pp. 32–33, describing how police officers cover up the unlawful use of force):

"But that gives a lot of credibility, when you've got a real
heavy investigation. We had one. I had sixty-six allegations of
brutality: ADW, under color of authority, assault and battery
under color authority. Torture, all kinds of stuff. Two guys,
well, there was four guys. Two of my buddies were shot and
ambushed, policemen. Both alive and I was first unit on the
scene. Four suspects ran into a second story in a apartment . . .
projects apartment. We kicked the door down. We grabbed a
girl that lived there, one of their girlfriends. Grabbed her by
the hair and stuck a gun to her head, and used her as a
barricade. Walked up and told 'em: 'I've got this girl, I'll blow
her fucking brains out, if you come out with a gun. Held her
like this, threw the bitch down the stairs—deadbolted the door,
''let's play, boys.' ''

Q. Can we use that in the story?

A. It hasn't been seven years. Statute of limitations. I have
300 and something pages Internal Affairs investigation just on
that one incident. I got several other ones. I must have about
three thousand or four thousand pages of Internal Affairs

Investigations out there. Anyway, we basically tortured them.
There was four policemen, four guys. We broke 'em. Numerous
bones in each one of them. Their faces were just mush. They
had pictures on the walls, there was blood all the way to the
ceiling with finger marks like they were trying to crawl out of
the room. They showed us pictures of the room. It was unbe-
lievable. There was blood everywhere. All the walls. All the
furniture. All the floor. It was just everywhere. These guys,
they have to shave so much hair off, one guy they shaved it all
off. Like seventy stitches in his head. You know, knees cracked,
oh, it was just ... We had 'em begging that they'd never be
gang members again, begging us. So with 66 allegations, I had
a demonstration in front of Hollenbeck Station chanting my
name. Captain had to take them all into roll call, and that's
where the Internal Affairs investigation started. It lasted eighteen months. I was on a photo lineup, suspect lineup. I was
picked out by twelve people. So I was pretty proud of that. I
was the last one interviewed. The prime suspect is always the
last one interviewed. They didn't get any of our unit—38
guys—they didn't get one day. I didn't get one day. The
custodian, the jailer of the Sheriff's Department got five days
since he beat one of the guys at the very end. . . . Boy, you
know, and started. . . . Immediately after we beat those guys,
we went downstairs to the garden hose in the back of the place.
We washed our hands. We had blood all over our legs, everything. With a dark blue uniform, you know, and in the dark
you can't see it. But when you get in the light and it looks like
somebody took red paint and painted all over you. We had to
clean our badges off with water, there was blood all over 'em.
Our faces had blood on them. We had to clean all that. We
checked each other. Then we went out, and we were directing
traffic. And the chiefs and everything were coming down because the two officers were shot. 'Where are the suspects?' 'I
think some of these officers over here got them, and they took
them to the station. So now, nobody really knows who arrested
them. We handcuffed them and threw them down two flights of
stairs, you know. That's how they came. That's where a lot of
people saw, you know. 'Look out! Here comes one. Oh my God.
Look out, he's falling.' I mean, you don't shoot a policeman.
That's all there is to it. But anyway, the point is—well, they
know I did it. They know damn well I did it. There's nothing
they could do but I could—most of those guys work the 77th
together. We came in as a gang unit. We were tight. I mean, we
could have murdered people and got away with it. We were
tight. We all knew what to say. We didn't have to call each
other at home, and say, 'okay.' We all knew what to say. Most
real good policemen understand that they would just love to

take certain people and just take them to the alley, and blow their brains out.

Q.   Certain people.

A.   All gang members for one. All dope dealers for two. Pimps, three. There's probably your three most worthless type of people in a large city."

10.   (Transcript of April 15, 1985, pp. 3–5, describing necessity for police officers to be willing to lie):

"Well I really love being a policeman when I can be a policeman. It's like my partner now. He's so hung up with the rules and stuff. I get pissed sometimes and go: 'you just don't fucking even understand. This job is not rules. This is a feeling. Fuck the rules, we'll make them up later. He's a college graduate, a Catholic college. He was going to be a fucking priest. He's got more morals than he's got hair on his head. He doesn't know what to do about it.

Q.   What do you mean he's got more morals?

A.   He doesn't know how to be a policeman. 'I can't lie.' Oh, you make me fucking sick to my guts. You know, you do what you have to do to put these fucking assholes in jail. If you don't, you fucking get out of the fucking game. He just wants to be one of the boys. Doesn't want to play—pay the dues.

Q.   So how does he deal with it?

A.   He doesn't lie. Well, I know for a fact in this Internal Affairs investigation, he has a ten days suspension. He'll roll.

Q.   I'm sorry, I don't understand.

A.   He'll drop the dime on me, squeal, tell the truth ... He won't take any time.

Q.   You serious?

A.   Not a policeman at heart. He's considered one of the good guys.

Q.   He won't take any suspension at all?

A.   He'll say ... he didn't realize. He goes: 'I got a wife and kid to think of.' I says, 'Fuck you. Don't tell me because you've got a wife and kid.... You're either my partner all the way or get the fuck out of this car. We die for each other. We live for each other, that's how it is in the car. You lie for me, up to six months suspension. Don't ever get fired for me. Don't get indicted for me. But, you'll take six months for me, 'cause I'll take it for you. If you don't, get the fuck out of here. It shouldn't have to be said."

15. (Transcript of April 23, 1985, p. 44, describing providing testimony for events he did not witness):

"I've been on several calls in West L.A., and I'm the third or fourth car, and I end up handling the whole situation. You got a bunch of munchkins out in front with their guns. 'What are you doing? The call is on the other side of the house.' You know, the guy broke in here, and everybody is waiting where he broke in, like he'll go out the door. I mean, it's ridiculous, you know, they're just sitting there. So, I just go in, kick the door in, the guy's going out the garage. We beat the shit out of him. He's just a bloody mess. Handcuff him, there, I'm leaving. [mimics high female voice] 'Thank you.' This is embarrassing. Then you go to court, and I'm the only one knows how to testify. You have five officers on the case and I'm the only one who knows how to testify. The D.A. goes, 'yah, but you were the fourth car, but would you testify?' 'Yah,' I say, 'I saw him do that, yeah, yeah, okay, bye.' Why do I have to do everything? That's what it's coming down to. I have to fight the guy. I have to catch the guy. I have to keep the guys mouth shut at the station because they're not going to do it for a female. I can just walk by and say: 'shut up or I'm going to kick your face in.' "

2. TACTICAL CONTEXT

The Fuhrman tapes were discovered after Detective Mark Fuhrman had testified. He was excused subject to recall for further cross-examination. The defense wanted to utilize the tapes to conduct further cross examination on his denial that he had moved or planted any evidence in the Simpson case. Thus, the offer of proof was made to define the parameters of further cross-examination. The tapes would be used to impeach Fuhrman only if he denied making the statements which had been recorded. The prosecution sought to prevent the admission of the tapes for any purpose.

The tapes also contained forty-two instances of Detective Fuhrman using the word "nigger," an epithet he had denied every uttering in the previous ten years. The admissibility of this portion of the tapes is considered in Chapter IV(B), *infra*, dealing with the impeachment of witnesses.

3. DEFENSE ARGUMENT

a. Introduction.

Detective Mark Fuhrman is subject to recall for further cross-examination. He previously offered testimony in which he denied moving or planting evidence in this case, ... and denied that a conversation ever took place in 1985 or 1986 with Kathleen Bell in which he suggested he would find a reason to stop a "nigger" driving a car with a white woman. He also described an incident in which he intervened in a dispute between O.J. Simpson and Nicole Brown Simpson in 1985 or 1986 at their Rockingham residence.

The defense will contend that the excerpts are highly relevant and probative evidence for further cross-examination of Detective Fuhrman, ... and as evidence of his conduct in the investigation of this case.

b.   The Evidence of Prior Misconduct is Admissible Under California Evidence Code Section 1101(b).

California Evidence Code Section 1101(b) provides that:

"Nothing in this section prohibits the admission of evidence that a person committed a crime, civil wrong, or other act when relevant to prove some fact (such as motive, opportunity, intent, preparation, plan, knowledge, identity, absence of mistake or accident ...) other than his or her disposition to commit such an act."

This, of course, was the provision relied upon by the Court to rule that prior instances of abusive behavior by the defendant were admissible to prove intent, motive and identity in this case. By the same principle, prior instances of planting or manufacturing evidence, covering up police misconduct, ignoring police department policies and regulations in order to make arrests or harass suspects in criminal cases are relevant to show Detective Fuhrman's motive, opportunity, intent, preparation and plan to engage in such activity in this case.

The admission by Detective Fuhrman of numerous incidents of police misconduct which he engaged in or assisted in covering up are relevant *both* to assess his credibility *and* to prove his conduct on June 13, 1994. California Evidence Code Section 787 creates no obstacle to such admissibility. It provides:

"Subject to Section 788, evidence of specific instances of his conduct relevant only as tending to prove a trait of his character is inadmissible to attack or support the credibility of a witness."

In *People v. Mascarenas,* 21 Cal.App.3d 660, 668–69 (1971), the Court ruled it was error to exclude evidence that in previous cases a police informant had stolen wine to ingratiate himself with a suspect, and falsely accused an innocent person. The Court concluded that the evidence in both instances was *not* precluded by Section 787. With respect to the prior theft, the Court held:

"Evidence Code Section 1101 provides in subsection (b) that evidence of commission of a crime is admissible to prove a relevant fact 'such as [a] plan.' Here the evidence of Eric's theft of the wine was relevant to an issue other than proof of a trait of character to attack his credibility. It tended to prove a plan on his part to steal to accomplish his objective. A principle issue at trial concerned the manner in which Eric acquired possession of the prescription bottle labeled with appellant's name and containing 30 codeine tablets. Eric testified that appellant sold him the bottle of pills while appellant produced testimony that Eric stole the codeine. Evidence that Eric stole on another occasion to accomplish his mission of making a case for Officer Legerski was relevant as tending to corroborate the testimony offered by appellant that Eric had stolen for that same purpose in the case at bench. The evidence being relevant to a purpose other than that stated in Evidence Code Section 787 is not barred by that section. The evidence being relevant to a purpose stated in Evidence Code Section 1101, subdivision (b) is admissible pursuant to that section."

The parallels to this case are readily apparent. For example, Incident No. 3 in the offer of proof presents Detective Fuhrman's description of how to manufacture evidence of fresh blood to justify a false arrest of a drug addict by picking a scab and squeezing it. He concludes, "That's not falsifying a report. That's putting a criminal in jail. That's being a policeman."

In this case, a speck of blood on the Bronco door was the chief justification offered by Detective Fuhrman to lead fellow officers "over the wall" into Mr. Simpson's home in the early morning hours of June 13, 1994. If he regards the manufacturing of false blood evidence as "good police work" when it puts someone he has decided is a "criminal" in jail, the credibility of his discovery of blood on the Bronco is greatly impacted by the existence of a "plan" under Evidence Code Section 1101(b). The *Mascarenas* court also addressed the admissibility of false accusations of others:

"Although generally the *character* of a witness may not be attacked by evidence of specific wrongful acts . . ., this rule is not controlling where the inquiry goes beyond character and involves a basic fact in issue. *People v. Clark*, 63 Cal.2d 503, 505. The proposition has been applied to authorize the introduction by the defense in charges of sexual violations upon minors of evidence of prior false charges by the minor or his siblings, *People v. Clark, supra* at 506, or by his parent. *People v. Scholl*, 225 Cal. App.2d 558, 564. The admissibility of evidence of prior false charges is rationalized by the strong possibility that the charge against the defendant may be the result of youthful fantasy or be motivated by malice and by the fact that the only available witnesses are likely to be the alleged victim and the defendant. A similar situation exists in the case at bench.''

While the risk of a false accusation in this case arises from racial animus rather than youthful fantasy, the principle is the same. The fact that Detective Fuhrman will make up facts to justify an arrest, or will testify to events he did not observe, speaks volumes about the credibility of his denial that he moved or planted evidence in this case.

The admissibility of prior false accusations has been reaffirmed in recent rulings that note that Proposition Eight's ''truth in evidence'' provision has the effect of repealing Section 787, so evidence of specific instances of conduct are admissible even if their *only* relevance is to show a trait of character of a witness. As the Court concluded in *People v. Adams,* 198 Cal.App.3d 10, 18 (1988):

''Section 28(d) was not designed to liberalize the rules of admissibility only for evidence favorable to the prosecution while retaining restrictions on the admissibility of evidence tending to prove a defendant's innocence, but to ensure that those who are actually guilty do not escape conviction through restrictions on the admissibility of relevant evidence.''

Accord, People v. Franklin, 25 Cal. App.4th 328, 334–37 (1994) (evidence of witness' prior false accusation of another person of sexual misconduct admissible.)

c. Evidence of Prior Instances of Police Misconduct is Relevant to Show Habit and Custom.

California Evidence Code Section 1105 provides:

''Any otherwise admissible evidence of habit or custom is admissible to prove conduct on a specified occasion in conformity with the habit or custom.''

Detective Fuhrman in the tapes describes a custom under which police officers are expected to lie and cover up for each other. He boasts of an arrest in which he participated in brutally beating the suspects but getting away with it because all of the 38 police officers in his unit ''were tight ... we all knew what to say. We didn't have to call each other at home.'' He complains of having a partner who had too many morals to lie, who was ''not a policeman at heart,'' because he wouldn't ''play the game'' of lying to cover up his partner's misconduct. In the context of the prosecution contention that Detective Fuhrman could not have moved or tampered with evidence in this case because there were too many other police officers at the scene, this evidence is highly relevant, coming from his own lips.

The admissibility of prior instances of police misconduct to establish habit or custom was confirmed by the California Supreme Court in *People v. Memro,* 38 Cal.3d 658, 681 (1985). The issue arose in the context of a *Pitchess* motion to discover prior instances in which the arresting officers or other officers of the South Gate Police Department used coercive techniques to extract confessions. The People argued that discovery was properly denied because the prior incidents would not be admissible evidence that coercive techniques were used to extract the defendant's confession. The Court responded:

> "The Evidence Code clearly supported appellant's theory of discovery. Discovery might lead to evidence of habit or custom admissible to show that a person acted in conformity with that habit or custom on a given occasion. Evid. Code § 1105. 'Habit' or 'custom' is often established by evidence of repeated instances of similar conduct. *See, e.g., Dincau v. Tamayose,* 131 Cal.App.3d 780, 793–96 (1982). Plainly, evidence that the interrogating officers had a custom or habit of obtaining confessions by violence, force, threat or unlawful aggressive behavior would have been admissible on the issue of whether the confession had been coerced."

Likewise, evidence that the investigating officers in this case had a custom or habit of lying and covering up each other's misconduct would be admissible on the issue of a coverup of the planting or moving of evidence in this case.

The *Memro* court offered yet another rationale for the admissibility of the evidence of previous misconduct, however:

> "Furthermore, evidence of reputation, opinion, and specific instances of conduct is admissible to show, inter alia, motive, intent or plan. Evid. Code § 1101(b). Evidence that the interrogating officers had acted according to a plan or with a motive to coerce appellant's confession, or had intended to do so, would have been relevant to appellant's claim of involuntariness. Reputation or opinion evidence would also have been relevant on this issue."

Repeated examples are available to demonstrate the use of different practices depending on the race of the suspect, or the presence of witnesses. Thus, motive, intent and plan to ignore the rules when the suspect is an African American are clearly evident from the pattern of incidents described on the "Fuhrman Tapes."

d. The Probative Value of the Evidence Substantially Outweighs Any Prejudicial Impact or Risk of Undue Consumption of Time.

The probative value of interviews of Detective Fuhrman in 1985 and 1986 lies in the fact that they are precisely coterminous with his visit to the Rockingham residence and first encounter with O.J. Simpson and Nicole Brown Simpson, and are also coterminous with his meetings with Kathleen Bell. The remarkable similarity of the tenor or his taped interview comments and his remarks to Kathleen Bell will provide solid corroboration of Kathleen Bell's testimony. All of the interviews are within the ten year period encompassed by Detective Fuhrman's flat and unqualified assertion that anyone who quotes him as using the word "nigger" in the past ten years would be a liar.

It must be noted, of course, that the argument of "remoteness" was rejected in the context of prior incidents involving Mr. Simpson and his wife with respect to events occurring in 1985. It would indeed be ironic and inconsistent for the Court to find that relevant inferences can be drawn against Mr. Simpson from incidents that allegedly occurred in 1985, but interviews of Detective Fuhrman conducted in 1985 are "too remote" to have relevance in this case.

The defendant has proffered a very selective and tightly edited array of excerpts from the "Fuhrman Tapes." Although the tapes contain something to offend nearly everyone, only the portions that directly contradict the testimony offered, prove bias or prejudice directly relevant to this case, directly corroborate other witnesses, or demonstrate an attitude toward those directly involved in this case have been selected.

Any risk of undue consumption of time has been minimized, by reducing over sixteen hours of tapes to less than one hour. Any danger of undue prejudice has been minimized by judicious editing. Detective Fuhrman's central role in the investigation and prosecution of this case requires that the defendant be given wide latitude in challenging his credibility, showing his bias, and demonstrating his motive, intent, plan, custom and habit.

e. The Jury Must Assess the Credibility of Detective Fuhrman's Statements.

The public reaction of prosecutors to the revelation of the "Fuhrman Tapes" suggests they will attempt to characterize Detective Fuhrman's statements as fictional "role-playing," or exaggerated braggadocio. These are arguments that go to the weight of the evidence, rather than its admissibility. It will be for the jury to assess whether such characterizations of the evidence are appropriate, based on any testimony of the participants and the context involved.

Even if such characterizations were found to be accurate, it would not affect the relevance of the tapes. Detective Fuhrman's flat denial of the use of racial epithets included no "exception" for role-playing. And, of course, any propensity for braggadocio is highly relevant to the credibility of his testimony in this case. It will indeed be ironic for the prosecution, which presented Detective Fuhrman as the astute police officer whose remarkable investigative skills led to finding the principle evidence linking the defendant to the murder of his ex-wife, to then dismiss his admissions of lying, manufacturing evidence and covering up police misconduct in other cases as the exaggerated ranting of a megalomaniac. You can't have it both ways.

4. PROSECUTION ARGUMENT

a. The Proffered Allegations of Misconduct Are Temporally Remote.

With the exception of one statement made April 7, 1987, all of the proffered statements were made in the course of meetings during the months of April and August in 1985. Assuming the incidents recounted in the statements in those interviews are true, they reflect a course of conduct that preceded Detective Fuhrman's involvement in this case by at least ten years.

As this court is well aware, in evaluating the use of prior felony convictions, or for that matter, since the advent of Proposition Eight, other past acts of misconduct, the factor of temporal remoteness is given strong consideration. This factor is deemed to be highly relevant to the issue of admissibility for the simple fact that a defendant or witness' conduct at a previous time must be relevant to inform the jury of the state of mind of the defendant or witness in the case at hand. The more remote the conduct, the less probative such evidence is to the time frame relevant to the case under consideration.

As our Supreme Court pointed out in *People v. Clair,* 2 Cal.4th 629 (1992) regarding a trial court's exercise of discretion in deciding whether to admit prior convictions for impeachment:

> "We made plain [in *People v. Castro,* 38 Cal.3d 301 (1985)] that in exercising their discretion, trial courts should continue to be guided ... by the factors set forth in *People v. Beagle,* 6 Cal.3d 441 (1972). [citations]. *When the witness subject to impeachment is not the defendant, those factors prominently include whether the conviction (1) reflects on honesty, and (2) is near in time.*"

2 Cal.4th at 653–655.

b. The Defense Has Proffered No Evidence to Demonstrate the Statements Made by Mark Fuhrman Describing Acts of Misconduct Have Any Basis in Fact.

The proffered evidence has no relevance unless the statements are, in fact, true. As a simple matter of foundation, in order to demonstrate the admissibility of these statements, it must be shown that the events and statements of personal philosophy are true. If not true they are inadmissible.

This aspect of the proffer presents the most problematic issue of admissibility due to the fact that the statements were made in the context of the creation of a screenplay in which the author's avowed intent was to create scenes of the most graphic violence in order to underscore her theme for dramatic effect. The characters in that screenplay were drawn in the most polarized, indeed caricaturized, light possible in order to highlight the conflict which formed the premise of the story. Mark Fuhrman was aware of the dramatic intent and theme of this movie and offered his contribution with the above stated goals in mind. There is no dispute that this was not meant to be an accurate factual account of any vignette included in the story. For this reason, Ms. McKinney made no effort to verify any of the stories told to her by Mark Fuhrman.

. . . In this regard, due at least in part to the fact that the recounted incidents occurred so long ago, it will likely never be known to what extent the incidents are the product of Mark Fuhrman's imagination, overheard conversations in a bar frequented by police officers, incidents recounted by others embellished by Mark Fuhrman in the telling, or a truthful account of an incident that actually occurred. If the incidents are fictional they have no bearing on Detective Fuhrman's credibility whatsoever. Yet the effort to prove or disprove each incident will certainly require the prodigious consumption of time as this court convenes the mini-trial of Mark Fuhrman's past acts.

Nor is this an issue which the jury can legitimately resolve. In the absence of any factual foundation, the jury will essentially be asked to speculate with no factual basis to believe that any of the alleged acts ever occurred. Without some evidence external to the statements alone, there is no other evidence against which to weigh them to determine what is fact and what is fiction. Yet the temptation will be strong to believe all statements to be true despite the obvious countervailing fact that they were made in the context of preparing a work of fiction.

c. The Proffered Evidence Does Not Qualify for Admission Under California Evidence Code Section 1101(b).

The rationale of Evidence Code Section 1101(b) was applied to witnesses (as distinguished from defendants) in *People v. Mascarenas,* 21 Cal.App.3d 660, 668 (1971). The defense has cited this case in support of the admissibility of the proffered prior acts. However, in reality, when the holding is reviewed in light of the facts and circumstances of that case, it becomes clear that the reverse is true.

In *Mascarenas,* unlike the instant case, the People's case was solely dependent on the uncorroborated testimony of a 16 year old minor, an aspiring narcotics officer, who had volunteered for undercover police work. As was emphasized by the Court of Appeal, the minor's testimony constituted the only evidence which in any way tended to establish the defendant's guilt:

> "Eric's testimony is the only evidence in any way tending to establish appellant's guilt. That testimony is totally uncorroborated, there apparently having been no effort made to supply Eric with marked funds for a transaction or to conduct a surveillance of his meetings with appellant."

21 Cal.App.3d at 664–65.

> "The prosecution's case was by no means overwhelming. There was not a scintilla of corroboration of Eric's testimony."

21 Cal.App.3d at 669. This language makes it clear that the focal point of the analysis for the Court of Appeal was the uncorroborated nature of the minor's testimony. Furthermore, the Court of Appeal was also careful to point out the substantial similarity of the prior conduct to the alleged conduct in that case. The obviously close factual nexus between the prior conduct and the alleged recent conduct of the uncorroborated minor highlights the distinction between *Mascarenas* and the instant case.

In the case at hand, not only is the testimony of Mark Fuhrman concerning his discovery of the Rockingham glove corroborated in several ways, it has been established that he had no opportunity to move or plant evidence as alleged. Even more importantly, unlike *Mascarenas,* this case does not hinge on the testimony of Mark Fuhrman or the Rockingham glove at all. If his testimony and the glove were completely disregarded there would still be overwhelming evidence of the defendant's guilt.

When one examines the proffered acts for the similarity described in *Mascarenas* the dramatic differences between the proffer and the alleged conduct become manifest. Acts of excessive force and the willingness to cover for a partner, after the fact, who has committed violations that would justify temporary suspension, although not indictment or incarceration, bear no reasonable similarity to the conduct the defense seeks to prove in the instant case. In no passage did Mark Fuhrman discuss the movement of evidence to implicate a party in a serious felony. Nor is there any indication that, as a detective, he would commit such felonious conduct. Nor is there any passage in which Mark Fuhrman indicates that he ever engaged in the pre-planned conspiracy to move evidence. Rather, the few references in the proffer to a willingness to cover for a partner involves the suppression of information after the fact concerning acts of misconduct that involved the use of force in the apprehension of suspects.

d.   The Proffered Evidence Does Not Constitute Admissible Evidence of Habit or Custom.

"Habit" has been defined as "a person's regular or consistent response to a repeated situation" and "custom" has been defined as "the routine practice or behavior on the part of a group or organization that is equivalent to the habit of an individual." *People v. Memro,* 38 Cal.3d 658, 681 n.22 (1985).

The question whether habit evidence is admissible is essentially one of threshold relevancy and is addressed to the sound discretion of the trial court. *People v. Green,* 27 Cal.3d 1, 19 (1980). As stated in the very case cited by defendant, *People v. Memro, supra* at 681, central to this threshold issue of relevancy is that the court must find "evidence of repeated instances of similar conduct" sufficient for the trial court to conclude a habit was present.

In the case at hand, the material proffered by the defense fails to meet this test of threshold relevancy in that it is neither similar to any conduct speculatively attributed to Detective Fuhrman nor is it even "conduct" as described in the several cases interpreting Evidence Code Section 1105.

The individual events or apparent statements of belief described by Detective Fuhrman in the McKinney audiotapes and their corresponding transcripts are wholly dissimilar to the conduct the defense wishes to attribute to Detective Fuhrman in the instant case. Even assuming, arguendo, the 18 proffered matters have some basis in reality and are not fictionally created in some manner, an analysis of the material—discrete incident or belief by discrete incident or belief—reveals no repeated instances of similar conduct sufficient to form a habit or custom.

e.   The Court Should Exercise Its Discretion Under Evidence Code Section 352 to Exclude the Proffered Materials.

Whether the defendant seeks to introduce the proffered McKinney material for purposes as yet unspecified by the defendant under Evidence Code Section 1101(b) or for purposes of establishing conduct in conformity with habit or custom under Section 1105, the restrictions of Evidence Code Section 352 still apply. The People submit that the introduction of such proffered evidence for either of these purposes will unfairly prejudice the jury, confuse the issues before the jury, and unduly consume time.

The defendant does not have a constitutional right to collaterally impeach a witness where the relevancy or probative value of the proffered evidence is slight. In *People v. Jennings,* 53 Cal.3d

334 (1991), the California Supreme Court affirmed the exclusion of collateral impeachment evidence by application of Evidence Code Section 352:

> "Because the evidence in question would impeach the witness on collateral matters and was only slightly probative of their veracity, application of Evidence Code Section 352 to exclude the evidence did not infringe defendant's constitutional right to confront the witnesses against him."

53 Cal.3d at 372. The evidence proffered by the defense is clearly collateral impeachment and its probative value, if any, is so underwhelmingly slight as to compel its exclusion under Evidence Code Section 352.

The prejudicial effect of this collateral impeachment has been the subject of rare consensus among commentators that have addressed the issue. As one law professor stated:

> "This is such incendiary stuff it could exert a powerful effect on the jury.... If what Cochran says is on the tapes is true, the case is over. It will raise enough of a cloud that enough of the evidence will be tainted to result in an acquittal. When juries get indignant and their sense of justice is tapped, cases are won or lost."

Paul Rothstein, Georgetown Law School professor, as reported in the Los Angeles Times, Aug. 8, 1995, Part A., p. 15. As another observer noted:

> "It's going to be devastating.... It does more than eliminate Fuhrman as a witness. It really tars the whole prosecution. He's part of their team, and if they didn't know about this, how can [jurors] believe anything?"

Defense lawyer Harland Braun, as reported in the San Diego Union–Tribune, Aug. 8, 1995, p.29.

Evidence Code Section 352 was enacted for precisely the situation at issue here. The prejudicial effect on the prosecution is so manifest that the defense is gleefully calling the admissibility of the tapes the single biggest ruling the court will make. The fact that this ruling is so critical, when it goes, not to the direct proof of any key point in the case, but only to impeach collateral testimony, demonstrates just how prejudicial it is to the People. If the defense can make or break the case on mere collateral impeachment, that fact alone shows that the tapes, *ipso facto,* are overwhelmingly prejudicial. In other words, collateral impeachment, by definition, simply cannot be that important to a case without being more prejudicial than probative. The critical importance of the tapes to the outcome of this trial demonstrates their prejudicial effect.

The simple and basic truth of the background against which these tape recordings must be viewed is that Mark Fuhrman had no opportunity to do what the defense seeks to prove through their admission. There is now no question of this fact, it has been established through the sworn testimony of numerous witnesses.

Nor is there any legitimate argument that there are other aspects of his testimony that would justify this highly prejudicial, yet wholly collateral impeachment. The balance of Mark Fuhrman's testimony was largely cumulative to the testimony of other witnesses.... Rather, what is patently obvious is that this is the last ditch effort of the defense to distract this jury from the evidence by the flagrant manipulation of issues of great social importance but which have no relevance to the legitimate issues in this case. The admission of this evidence would serve only to demean the integrity of these proceedings and tax the ability of the jury to fairly and impartially decide this case on the evidence and the law.

5. JUDGES' RULINGS

On August 31, 1995, Judge Lance Ito issued the following order, rejecting all eighteen incidents included in the defense proffer:

"The defense seeks to offer 18 incidents of alleged misconduct to attack Fuhrman's credibility, to support the argument that Furhman planted evidence and to support the testimony of Bell. The defense cites Evidence Code Sections 780 (Credibility of Witnesses), 1101(b) (Prior Bad Acts) and 1105 (Habit and Custom to Prove Specific Behavior). As noted in the ruling of 20 January 1995, there must be some evidence in the record from which counsel might argue, however reasonably or unreasonably, that Fuhrman moved a glove from the Bundy crime scene to the defendant's Rockingham residence for the purpose of placing blame for two brutal and savage murders upon the defendant. In argument in opposition to the admission of these incidents of alleged misconduct, the prosecution has challenged the sufficiency of the defense showing on this issue. The defense proffers and argument did not add to the defense proffer filed 23 January 1995 despite the challenge from the prosecution and inquiry by the court. That proffer essentially argues that because Fuhrman allegedly suppressed information given to him by Rosa Lopez that was arguably favorable to the defendant, it can be assumed that he would plant the glove. This assertion is not supported by the record. The underlying assumption requires a leap in both law and logic that is too broad to be made based upon the evidence before the jury. It is a theory without factual support. It fails to support the admissibility of these incidents of alleged misconduct as prior bad acts or evidence of custom and habit.

While the current state of the record does not indicate evidence that would reach the minimal threshold necessary to find inquiry into the planting of evidence theory relevant, and the court so finds, the defense has not yet rested its case. The court will therefore analyze each incident, assuming *arguendo*, the minimal threshold of relevance is later met.

. . .

3. Hype arrest:

This case does not involve an arrest by Fuhrman. Because the proffer goes to a collateral matter, the probative value is therefore non-existent. The Evidence Code Section 350 objection is sustained. No factual basis has been offered in support. Admission would require diversion into what would essentially be a trial of a violation of Health and Safety Code 11550, being under the influence of a controlled substance, which would necessitate undue consumption of time. The Evidence Code Section 352 objection is sustained.

. . .

7. Manufacturing probable cause for arrest:

This case does not involve an arrest made by Fuhrman. The incident does not speak to racial animosity. It is not relevant. The Evidence Code Section 350 objection is sustained. Presentation of this incident would require undue expenditure of the court's time given its negligible probative value. The Evidence Code Section 352 objection is sustained.

. . .

9. Cover up of unlawful use of force.

This case does not involve any police officers as victims, any pursuit of a suspect where there is any allegation of unnecessary force used in the arrest, or any cover up of unnecessary force used upon an arrestee. The proffer lacks relevance to this case. The proffer does not include any mention of a basis in fact. The argument of the parties indicates there is substantial factual dispute as to whether any actual incident matches the scenario painted by Fuhrman. There is a substantial danger that the proof of the underlying incident, if such be available, would necessitate the undue consumption of the court's time. [The court notes that the jury has been sequestered since mid-January. The undue consumption of time is a critical factor to be considered by the trial court under these unique circumstances.] The court also finds that having balanced the indirect nature of the probative value of the proffered evidence with the danger of undue prejudice, the court finds that defense counsel's characterization of this incident as a 'blockbuster' most eloquently speaks to the inflammatory nature of this incident, creating the substantial danger of undue prejudice. The Evidence Code Section 352 objection is sustained.

    10.   Necessity for police officers to be willing to lie.

No argument or allegation has been made that Fuhrman has been lying to cover for his partner, Det. Phillips, nor has there been any argument or allegation that Phillips has been lying to cover for Fuhrman. There is no direct relevance to this case. The Evidence Code Section 350 objection is sustained. Presentation of this incident would require the undue and unwarranted expenditure of the court's time. The Evidence Code Section 352 objection is sustained.

   . . .

    15.   Testimony for events not witnessed.

The proffer does not suggest any actual basis in fact. Given the collateral nature of the issue at hand, the lack of any apparent factual basis, the conglomerative character of the statement and the inferential nature of the statement, the court finds its probative value to be severely limited such that its presentation would require an undue consumption of time. The Evidence Code Section 352 objection is sustained."

At the civil trial, Detective Mark Fuhrman was never called as a witness by either side, so the issue of the scope of cross-examination on prior bad acts was not presented.

6. COMMENTS AND QUESTIONS

(a) Judge Ito imposes a threshold requirement of proof that Fuhrman actually planted evidence in this case before evidence can be offered of prior acts. Was such a requirement imposed on the prosecution before they could offer evidence of prior spousal abuse? The evidence of prior spousal abuse was the first evidence offered by the prosecution at commencement of the criminal trial.

(b) Consider the analysis of Professor Roger Park:

"Judge Ito's assertion that the evidence of other acts by Fuhrman is not even *relevant* unless a minimum threshold is met showing the glove was planted relies upon a conditional relevancy theory that is at least technically fallacious. Evidence that Fuhrman was a racist and an evidence tamperer on other occasions is not *irrelevant* in the absence of evidence *aliunde* sufficient to support a finding that the glove was moved. Evidence of racism and fabrication proclivity met the minimal requirement of relevance by making a fact of consequence somewhat more likely than it would have been without the evidence.

As an illustration, suppose that the defense had evidence that Fuhrman, LAPD Detectives Vanatter and Ron Phillips, and the other police investigators belonged to a chapter of the Aryan Brotherhood pledged to uphold white supremacy by lying, murdering, and fabricating evidence. Clearly, *that* evidence would increase the likelihood that Fuhrman planted the glove, even without any predicate incident-specific evidence of planting."

Park, *Character Evidence Issues in the O.J. Simpson Case—Or, Rationales of the Character Evidence Ban, With Illustrations From the Simpson Case,* 67 U.Colo.L.Rev. 747, 763–64 (1996).

(c) The assertion that Fuhrman suppressed information given by Rosa Lopez was a relatively minor aspect of the offer of proof regarding Fuhrman's manipulation of evidence. Primary reliance was placed on inconsistencies between Fuhrman's testimony and the testimony of fellow officers, and the physical condition and location of the Rockingham glove being inconsistent with having been dropped the night before. Evidence offered after the proffer of the Fuhrman tapes also suggested that evidence offered by the prosecution that Fuhrman had no access to the crime scene evidence before he went to Rockingham was inconsistent with crime scene photos, and that the prosecution misrepresented the sequence of the crime scene photos to cover up the fact that he did have complete access.

(d) With respect to each of the proffered incidents, Judge Ito notes that there is no proffer of independent factual proof of the incidents. Before cross-examining a witness with respect to his own prior statements describing an incident, must counsel proffer independent evidence to prove the incidents actually occurred as the statements describe them? What if the witness admits, on cross examination, that his prior statements are accurate? What if the witness explains the statements as lies or exaggeration or imaginary role-playing?

(e) Compare the degree of similarity between the prior incidents and this case with the degree of similarity required for the evidence of spousal abuse. In the context of spousal abuse, the identity of the alleged perpetrator and the victim was held to be sufficient:

"Judge Ito rejected the specific incidents where Fuhrman made up probable cause for an arrest by finding there was not sufficient similarity between those incidents and the Simpson case, because Fuhrman did not make the arrest of O.J. Simpson! In other words, the fact that an officer planted blood on another suspect he arrested is irrelevant to show he planted blood on this suspect, because this suspect was subsequently arrested by some other officer. This reasoning was patently specious."

Uelmen, *Lessons From the Trial: The People v. O.J. Simpson*, p. 153 (Andrews & McMeel, 1996).

(f) The argument that Fuhrman's statements were a charade for Laura McKinney's benefit, and did not express his actual opinions and beliefs was apparently given little credence by Judge Ito. Laura McKinney testified Fuhrman was not "role playing," but was providing, at her request, his own perceptions and experiences.

(g) The arguments on this issue are a good example of the intrusiveness of media coverage of a high profile trial, to the extent it affects the behavior of participants in the trial. Note the prosecution's use of the commentary of pundits to support their arguments against admission of the evidence. Could a judge call up a prominent law professor and ask how the professor thinks he should rule in a pending matter? Is it ever appropriate for a judge to consider the comments of prominent law professors that he heard on television while the matter was under submission? If not, should such comments be quoted in briefs and pleadings?

Chapter III

HEARSAY AND EXCEPTIONS

A. THE "911" TAPES

1. THE EVIDENCE

The prosecution offered evidence of two audiotapes of 911 emergency calls placed by Nicole Brown Simpson. The first tape, from the January 1, 1989 incident, included no description of the incident itself. The second tape, from the October 25, 1993 incident, was much more graphic, and Simpson's voice could actually be heard, yelling at Nicole Brown Simpson while she was holding the telephone. A full transcript of the 1993 tape follows:

"O   911 Emergency.

N   Yeah, can you send someone to my house?

O   What's the problem there?

N   Well, my ex-husband or my husband just broke into my house and he's ranting and raving. Now he's just walked out in the front yard.

O   Has he been drinking or anything?

N   No, but he's crazy.

O   He is black, white or Hispanic?

N   Black.

O   What's he wearing right now?

N   Black pants and a golf shirt.

O   What color shirt?

N   I think it's black and white.

O   And you said he hasn't been drinking?

N   No.

O   Did he hit you?

N   No.

O   Do you have a restraining order against him?

N   No.

O   What's your name?

N   Nicole Simpson.

O   And the address?

N   325 Gretna Green Way.

O   Is that a house or an apartment?

N   It's a house.

O   Okay, we'll send the police out.

N   Thank you.

O   Uh-huh.

O   Any West L.A. unit, domestic violence, 325 South Gretna Green Way, Code 4221...25."

     . . .

"O   911 Emergency.

N   Could you get someone over here now to 325 Gretna Green, he's back? Please.

O   Okay. What does he look like?

N   He's O.J. Simpson, I think you know his record. Could you just send somebody over here?

O   Okay, what is he doing there?

N   He just drove up again. Could you just send somebody over?

O   He just drove up? Okay, wait a minute. What kind of car is he in?

N   He's in a white Bronco. But first of all, he broke the back door down to get in.

O   Okay, wait a minute. What's your name?

N   Nicole Simpson.

O   Okay. Is he the sportscaster or whatever?

N   Yeah.

O   Okay. And what does he—

N   Thank you.

O   Wait a minute, we're sending the police. What is he doing, is he threatening you?

N   He's fucking going nuts.

O   Okay, has he threatened you in any way, or—or is he just harassing you?

N   You're going to hear him in a minute, he's about to come in again.

O   Okay, just stay on the line.

N   I don't want to stay on the line, he's gonna beat the shit out of me.

O   Wait a minute. Wait, just stay on the line so we can know what's going on until the police get there, okay? Okay, Nicole?

N   Uh-huh.

O   Just a moment. Does he have any weapons?

N   I don't know.

O   Okay.

N   He went home and now he's back.

O   Okay.

N   The kids are up there sleeping and I don't want anything to happen.

O   Okay, just a moment. Is he on drugs or anything?

N   No.

O   Okay. Just stay on the line just in case he comes in, I need to hear what's going on, all right?

N   Can you can hear him outside?

O   Is he yelling?

N   Yep.

O   Okay. Is he—has he been drinking?

N   No.

O   Okay. West L.A., all units, addition on a domestic violence, 325 South Gretna Green Way. The suspect has returned in a white Bronco, monitor comment. Incident 4221. Okay, Nicole?

N   Mmh-mmnh.

O   Is he still outdoors or—

N   Uh-huh, he's in the back yard.

O   He's in the back yard?

N   He's screaming at my roommate about me and at me here.

O   Okay. Okay, what is he saying?

N Oh, something about some guy I know and hookers and . . . and I started this shit before and ____

O Mmnh-mmnh.

N And it's all my fault, and now what am I going to do, get the police in on this and the whole thing.

O Okay.

N It's all my fault, I started this before. Brother. I just don't want my kids exposed to this.

O Okay. Now, has he hit you today or no?

N No.

O Okay. You don't need any paramedics or anything?

N Uhn-uhn.

O Okay. You just want him to leave?

N He broke my door. He broke the whole back door in.

O And then he left and he came back?

N Then he came and he practically knocked my upstairs door down, but he pounded it and then he screamed and hollered and I tried to get him out of the bedroom 'cause the kids were sleeping in there.

O Mmnh-mmnh. Okay.

N And then he wanted somebody's phone number and I gave him my phone book and was dow—or I gave—put my phone book down to write—write down the phone number that he wanted and then he took my phone book with all my stuff in it.

O Okay. So basically you guys have just been arguing?

[Voice of O.J. Simpson, hereafter "S"]:

  . . . O.J., worked his ass off for . . . but she's a drug addict and her fucking girlfriend . . .

O Is he inside right now?

N Yes. Yeah.

O Okay, just a moment.

S . . . call the police . . .

O Is he talking to you?

N Yeah.

O Are you locked in a room or something?

N No, he can come right in. I'm not going where the kids are 'cause . . .

O Do you think he's going to hit you?

N I don't know.

O Okay. Stay on the line, don't hang it up, okay?

N Okay.

O What is he saying?

N What?

O What is he saying?

N What else?

S ... goddam ... who goddam ...

O All units, there's a domestic violence at 30——correction——South Gretna Green Way. The suspect has now entered ...

N O.J., the kids are sleeping.

S You didn't give a shit about the kids ... fucking ... in the living room, they were here. You didn't care about the kids then. Oh, it's different now. I'm talking ... if you're gonna shake your head ...

O Is he still yelling at you? Just stay on the line, okay? Is he upset with something that you did?

N A long time ago, it always comes back.

O Is—is your roommate talking to him?

N No one can talk, listen to him.

O I know. Does he have any weapons or anything with him—

N No.

O —right now?

N Uhn-uhn.

O Okay. Where is he standing?

N In the back doorway, in the house.

O Okay.

S ... I don't give a shit anymore ... mother fucker ...

N Could you just please—O.J.? O.J.? O.J.? O.J., could you please leave. Please. Please leave.

S I'm not leaving ... fucking ... when I'm leaving ...

N Please leave.

S ... fucking ...

N O.J., please, the kids ... the kids are asleep ... please.

O Is he leaving?

N No.

O Does he know you're on the phone with the police?

N No

O Okay. Where are the kids at right now?

N Up in my room.

O Can they hear him yelling?

N I don't know.

S ... fucking ...

N ... the only one that's quiet.

O Is there someone up there with the kids?

N No.

O What is he saying now? Nicole, are you still on the line?

N Yeah.

O Do you think he's still going to hit you?

N I don't know. He's not gonna leave, he just said that. He just said he ain't leaving.

S ... Hey, I ... I had to read this bullshit all week in the National Enquirer, the words exactly ...

O Are you the only one in there with him?

N Right now, yeah.

O And he's talking to you?

N Yeah. And he's also talking to me—the guy that lives out back is just standing there.

O Oh, okay.

N He just came home.

O Oh, okay. Is he arguing with him too?

N Oh, absolutely not, he hasn't said a word.

O Oh, okay. Okay.

N Nobody is arguing.

O Yeah. Has this happened before or no?

N Many times.

O Okay. The police should be on their way, it just seems like a long time 'cause it's kind of busy in that division—right now.

S ... goddam ...

O ... regarding Gretna Green Way, the suspect is still there and yelling very loudly. Is he still arguing?

N Mmnh-mmnh.

O   Oh. Was someone knocking on your door?

N   No, that was him.

O   Oh, he was knocking on the door?

N   There's a—there's a locked bedroom and he's wondering why.

O   Oh, okay, he's knocking on the locked door?

N   Yeah.

You know what, O.J., that window above you is also open. Could you just go, please. Can I get off the phone, now?

O   You want to hang—you—you feel safe hanging up?

N   Well, all right.

O   You want to wait 'til the police get there?

N   Yes.

O   Nicole?

N   Mmnh-mmnh.

O   Is he still arguing with you?

N   Mmnh-mmnh. He's moved a little bit, . . .

O   Okay. But he doesn't know you're—Okay. Are the kids still asleep?

N   Yeah . . . like a rock.

O   What part of the house is he in right now?

N   Downstairs.

O   Downstairs?

N   Mmnh-mmnh.

O   And you're upstairs?

N   No, I'm downstairs in the kitchen. . . . Now he's walking around. Around the kitchen.

S   . . . and I try my goddam best. I ain't putting up with no . . . fucking . . .

O   Do you see the police, Nicole?

N   No, but I will go out there right now.

O   Okay, you want to go out there?

N   Yeah.

O   Okay.

N   I'm gonna hang up.

O   Okay.''

2. THE TACTICAL CONTEXT

The "911" tapes were released to the media by the Los Angeles Police Department within a week after O.J. Simpson's arrest, and were widely broadcast in television news reports. The defense immediately moved to conduct *voir dire* of the grand jury, to ascertain whether they had been exposed to prejudicial news reports of the tapes although they had not been submitted as evidence in the grand jury hearing. After determining that grand jurors had heard the tapes, the court dismissed the grand jury. The defense also questioned prospective trial jurors about their exposure to the tapes, and learned that most of the potential jurors had been exposed to the news reports about the tapes. If the tapes were inadmissible as evidence, of course, the defense would have a strong claim that the defendant had been prejudiced by their improper pretrial release. If the tapes were deemed admissible, however, the error in their pretrial release would, in all likelihood, be deemed harmless. In this context, the prosecution had a powerful unspoken advantage in litigating the admissibility of the tapes. By deeming them admissible, the trial judge could "clean up" the record and eliminate a potentially reversible error.

The defense challenged the admissibility of the tapes in the pretrial *in limine* motion seeking to exclude evidence of spousal abuse, arguing that even if the October 25, 1993 incident was deemed admissible, it could not be proven by means of the "911" tapes, because they were inadmissible hearsay.

3. DEFENSE ARGUMENT

a. *The "911" Tapes Are Not Admissible as "Spontaneous Statements."*

Presumably, the prosecution will argue that the 911 calls constitute 'spontaneous statements,' admissible pursuant to Section 1240 of the California Evidence Code.[8] For a statement to be admissible under this section (1) it must 'purport to describe or explain and act or condition perceived by the declarant', and (2) the 'statement must be made spontaneously, while the declarant is under the stress of excitement caused by the perception.' *People v. Farmer,* 47 Cal.3d 888, 901, 254 Cal.Rptr. 508 (1989). As the California Su-

---

8. California Evidence Code § 1240 provides:

"Evidence of a statement is not made inadmissible by the hearsay rule if the statement:

(a) Purports to narrate, describe, or explain an act, condition, or event perceived by the declarant; and

(b) Was made spontaneously while the declarant was under the stress of excitement caused by such perception."

preme Court has explained, 'the basis for the circumstantial trustworthiness of spontaneous utterances is that in the stress of previous excitement, the reflective faculties may be stilled and the utterance may become the instinctive and uninhibited expression of the speaker's actual impressions and belief.' *Id.* at 903.

The two 911 calls placed by Brown on October 25, 1993 do not qualify as 'spontaneous statements.' Obviously, the 911 operator's statements are not admissible as 'spontaneous' utterances and they clearly do not fall within any other recognized exception to the hearsay rule. They would have to be redacted, which would render the remaining statements, to a large degree, incomprehensible.

Moreover, Brown's statements also fail to meet the rigorous requirements of this hearsay exception. In the first 911 call, Brown sounds annoyed, but otherwise calm and collected. There is no indication that the 'stress' of the event was such that her powers of reflection were stilled.

The second 911 call lasted almost fourteen minutes. Listening to the tape, it is apparent that in the first few seconds Brown was excited, but she quickly composed herself and was able to reflect and respond to the questions asked by the 911 operator in a deliberate fashion. Brown showed concern for her children, and she tried to calm down Simpson and convince him to leave. Brown informed the operator that her housemate was present, talking to Simpson, and at one point she even stated that she did not think she was in any danger. She was obviously in control of her responses.

While some 911 calls may constitute 'spontaneous' statements, they must bear all the earmarks of such statements. Not every 911 call is alike. Statements made by a victim of a violent crime, who is suffering from trauma, even if in response to a 911 operator's questions, constitute 'spontaneous' statements because it is assumed that a person who is 'distraught and in severe shock' is unlikely to lie. *Farmer,* 47Cal.3d at 904. But, as the California Supreme Court has recognized, that is a far cry from the situation presented here: 'an uninjured witness whose excitement might wane—and would thus be in a position to fabricate answers—through the sobering interrogation of an investigator.' *Id.* at 904. Under those circumstances, answers to extensive questioning are likely to be 'self-serving.' *Id.*

The fact that a 911 call has been placed is not by itself indicative of an 'emergency' situation what would render everything said by the party making the call inherently reliable. The police themselves recognize that 911 reports can be false, or reflect only a partial truth, and they evaluate their responses to such calls accordingly. *See, e.g.,* Dolan, Hendricks & Meagher, *Police Practices and Attitudes Toward Domestic Violence,* 14 J. Police Sci. and Admin. 187 (1986) (indicating that the frequency of calls from a particular household is an important factor in an officer's determination both to arrest and *not* to arrest when confronted with a domestic violence call); Hickman, *Note, It's Time to Call 911 for Government Immunity,* 43 Case W.Res.L.Rev. 1067, n.118 (1993) (citing inappropriate use of 911 services). *See also, Leonzal v. Grogan,* 516 N.W.2d 210, 214 (Minn. 1994) ('The weighing of ... the odds the 911 report was false is a matter of discretion appropriately reserved to the officers'); *Keller v. Georgia,* 431 S.E.2d 411 (Ga.App. 1993) (arrest for making false 911 call). Especially in incidents involving domestic disputes, there is a risk that the true motivation for a 911 call is anger and a desire to 'get even,' or gain an advantage in pending or contemplated divorce or custody battles.

b. Many Statements Contained on the 911 Tape Are Inadmissible Opinions.

California Evidence Code Section 1240 limits the exception for "spontaneous statements" to statements that purport to "narrate, describe or explain" the event the declarant is observing. Even if Brown's placing of the 911 call is treated as a "spontaneous statement," each of her out-of-court statements during the phone call must be examined to ensure its admissibility. But many of the statements made by Brown in response to the 911 operator's questions—indeed, the most prejudicial statements—cannot possibly be introduced for any legitimate purpose. At one point, Brown opined, "I don't want to stay on the line, he's gonna beat the shit out of me," and at another, "He's going fucking nuts." Certainly, Brown's view about Simpson's likely actions cannot be introduced for the truth—as proof that Simpson was indeed "going nuts" or was going to "beat the shit out of [her]"—since nothing of the sort occurred.

Moreover, these are statements of Brown's opinion. They would be excludable under the opinion rule if offered as direct testimony, and cannot be transformed into admissible evidence by invoking the spontaneous statement exception to the hearsay rule. *People v. Miron,* 210 Cal.App.3d 580, 258 Cal.Rptr. 494 (1980) (excluding, as opinion evidence, hearsay statement that a "man was trying to kill us").

Finally, the prosecution cannot avoid the hearsay bar by contending that these statements are not being introduced for the truth but as evidence of Brown's state of mind, since Brown's state of mind, particularly her state of mind a full eight months before the murder, is irrelevant to any issue in this case.

c. The Admission of the 911 Tapes Would Violate the Defendant's Constitutional Rights to Confront and Cross Examine the Witnesses Against Him.

Although the prosecutors understandably relish a dramatic opportunity to present the anguished voice of the victim of this homicide as a witness against the defendant, the fact remains that the defendant will never have the opportunity to confront and cross-examine this testimony. Statements by an angry spouse are notoriously unreliable. The use of hearsay exceptions to permit snippets of domestic discord to be admitted without the opportunity to confront and cross-examine the declarant would present an egregious denial of the right of confrontation guaranteed by the Due Process Clause of the federal constitution and specifically guaranteed by Article I, Section 15 of the California constitution. Hearsay must bear "indicia of reliability" and "circumstantial guarantees of trustworthiness" if it is to meet constitutional requirements. *Ohio v. Roberts,* 448 U.S. 56 (1980); *Idaho v. Wright,* 497 U.S. 805 (1990).

4. PROSECUTION ARGUMENT

1. 911 Tapes are Business Records Under Evidence Code Section 1271.

In *People v. De La Plane,* 88 Cal.App.3d 223 (1979), the Court of Appeal held that tape recordings of 911 phone calls fall within the business records exception to the hearsay rule. There the trial court permitted the jury to hear tape recordings of incoming and outgoing telephone calls to the police station on the morning of the murder in question. In the first of those calls a woman reported that shots had been fired. The second call contained double hearsay. An officer reported that the father of the victim had named defendant as a suspect. At trial the court admitted the entire tape on the basis that the prosecution did not offer it for the truth of the matter asserted but instead offered it to establish the time the calls were made.

The court held that the tapes themselves constituted a business record and the time stampings on those tapes were a business entry on that record. However, based on the failure of the prosecution to present either any factual basis for a hearsay exception or even to assert any theory for an applicable exception, the court found that the statements contained within the tape were hearsay.

The teaching of *De Le Plane* is that tape recordings of 911 phone calls do satisfy all of Evidence Code Section 1271 requirements for admission as a business record. However, hearsay statements contained therein must independently qualify under other exceptions to the hearsay rule.

2.   Statements Contained Within the Tape Constitute the "Res Gestae" of an Act of Domestic Violence in Progress.

Evidence Code Section 1241 provides that 'Evidence of a statement is not made inadmissible by the hearsay rule if the statement: (a) Is offered to explain, qualify, or make understandable conduct of the declarant; and (b) Was made while the declarant was engaged in such conduct.' This section codifies the so called 'res gestae' or 'verbal acts' rule which allows the admission of statements made during the actual transaction at issue. *People v. Marchialette,* 45 Cal.App.3d 974 (1975). Thus, if a witness had seen the events of October 25, 1993, they would be permitted to testify to hearing the sounds of defendant banging on the door, the statements he made, the tone of his voice, the victim's responses to him, and so forth. That this evidence is captured on a recording rather than being presented by an eyewitness does not make the statement any less admissible. It simply makes the evidence more accurate, less subject to dispute and more persuasive.

3.   Defendant's Statements on the Tape are Admissions Under Evidence Code Section 1220.

As the Court of Appeal explained in *People v. Zack,* 184 Cal.App.3d 409, 417 (1986), regarding admissions of a criminal defendant under Evidence Code Section 1220:

'Statements to be admissions need not be incriminating. [citations]. As aptly stated by Witkin, "... any prior statement of a party may be offered against him, even though it may not have been against his interest or even may have been self-serving when made."

Thus, all of the statements of the defendant on the 911 tapes are admissible under section 1220.

4.   The Statements of Victim Nicole Brown Simpson Constitute Excited Utterances Under Evidence Code Section 1240.

In determining the admissibility of an excited utterance:

'[t]he foundation, or preliminary fact, require[s] only proof by a preponderance of the evidence. [citations]. In making its factual determination the trial court exercises discretion. [citation]. If substantial evidence supports the exercise of that discretion we must uphold it.'

People v. Anthony O., 5 Cal.App.4th 428, 433–34 (1992).

The California Supreme Court has previously found 911 phone call statements to have been made spontaneously. *People v. Farmer*, 47 Cal.3d at 904. While the defense correctly cites to *Farmer* as binding authority, they quote only selected portions of that opinion and largely ignore both its facts and its holding.

In *Farmer*, the defendant was found guilty of felony murder stemming from the commission of a burglary. On the night in question, a police dispatcher received a phone call from a woman claiming that her brother had been shot. The dispatcher then called the victim and recorded the ensuing conversation in which the victim stated that he had been shot in the stomach three times and described his assailant who was known to him. During the trial, the court admitted this tape in its entirety. Included on it was extensive questioning of the victim by the dispatcher.

Based upon this record, the California Supreme Court held that the trial court did not err in admitting the entire tape recording as a spontaneous statement. In so holding, the court rejected the defendant's argument that the victim's statements lacked spontaneity because they had been obtained as the result of direct police questioning. Rather, the court reasoned that 'the crucial element in determining whether a declaration is sufficiently reliable to be admissible under this exception to the hearsay rule is thus not the nature of the statement but the mental state of the speaker.' *Id.* at 903. Since it was clear that the victim was excited when the statements were made the entire conversation was admissible. See also, *People v. Forgason*, 99 Cal.App.3d 356, 365 (1979) (battery victim indicated that '[defendant] had always hit her, but this is the first time she got kicked'); *Gonzalez*, 193 A.D.2d at 361 (attempted murder victim made a 911 phone call while hiding under his desk); *Slaton*, 135 Mich.App. at 354 (felony murder victim told 911 operator that individuals had broken into his basement and were attempting to enter his house by breaking his door down); *United States v. Campbell*, 782 F.Supp. 1258, 1259–61 (N.D.Ill.) (911 call giving description of shooting); *Bowling v. Commonwealth*, 12 Va.App. 166, 176 (1991) (robbery victim's conversation with 911 operator describing robbery).

Farmer is directly on point. In fact, a comparison of the 911 calls in these cases reveals that the calls Nicole Simpson made are even more spontaneous than in *Farmer*. First, Nicole Brown Simpson made both of her emergency calls of her own volition. In *Farmer*, it was the police dispatcher who called the victim. Second, in this case the 911 calls and the statements therein were made contemporaneously with the event itself. In *Farmer* the call did not take place until the actual commission of the crime had been completed. Third, the questioning by the dispatcher in the instant case is less suggestive than in *Farmer*.

In *Farmer* it was the dispatcher who initially mentioned the shooting. The officer also suggested both the gender and the possible ethnicity of the assailant. The officer even forced the victim to give a description of his attacker and led him through that description. In the instant case it was Nicole Simpson who informed the officer of the situation. She was also the one who volunteered the name of her assailant. Finally, she detailed the events as they were transpiring without coaxing from the dispatcher. All of the aforementioned factors are clear indications of the spontaneity of the statements made under the stress of excitement.

In fact, the defense even concedes that during at least a portion of these calls she was under the stress of the event. Implicit in this concession is that the event must have been startling enough to cause this excited state. However, the defense argument that this excitement dissipated during the course of the incident is factually incorrect. The content of the 911 calls indicates that she remained entrenched in the midst of this assault during the entire time.

These tapes clearly illustrate that the stress of the situation continued through the entire duration of the calls. The fact that Nicole Simpson attempted to calm her outraged assailant is not evidence that she was not under the stress of the situation. Rather, it is an indication that the defendant's conduct that evening was extreme and outrageous, that she recognized that fact, and attempted to quiet the situation before she incurred any physical harm.

The element of spontaneity is clearly established in our case because the statement was made contemporaneously with the stressful event. In *People v. Garcia,* 178 Cal.App.3d 814, 821 (1986), shortly before the victim was shot, he called his fiancé and said that the defendant 'went crazy and he's going to shoot me.' This is almost identical to victim Brown's stating that defendant 'went nuts' and was going to 'beat the shit' out of her. In *Garcia,* as in our case, angry yelling could be heard over the telephone. The *Garcia* court found the statement 'clearly admissible' because it was made contemporaneously with defendant's yelling at the victim and just before victim was shot. The Court of Appeal explained:

'It is rare, but not unknown, for there to be available spontaneous declarations made during the very transaction at issue. Because of this rarity, most of the cases have been concerned with declarations made shortly after the event. Excited statements made close in time to the event are generally regarded as admissible. [citations]. A statement made contemporaneously with one criminal event has been regarded as "clearly admissible" in a prosecution for a subsequent crime. *People v. Worthington,* 38 Cal.App.3d 359, 366–67 (1974). In *Worthington,* the defendant was charged with murdering a mother and child. Two days before the killings a witness had heard the mother angrily order the defendant out of the daughter's bedroom, saying, "He's trying to go down on my daughter." The statement was admitted to prove the defendant had been trying to molest the daughter and thus to establish his motive at the time of the killing.

Id. at 821. The second requirement of Evidence Code Section 1240 is that the proffered statement must narrate, describe or explain the event perceived. Again, *Farmer* is factually squarely on point with the instant case. First, in both cases the victim identifies the assailant who was known to them. Second, both victims describe the circumstances surrounding the incidents. In fact, the account of the incident in this case is an even more detailed narration of the events as they transpired than the description provided to the police in *Farmer*. Nicole Simpson's narration describes how the defendant arrived, how he broke into her house by breaking her door down, and his extreme and outrageous conduct while he was present at the location. Finally, both victims provide explanations of the cause of the events. In *Farmer,* the victim suggests the reason for the break-in was drug related. Nicole Simpson suggests that the cause of the defendant's actions is something which occurred 'a long time ago, it always comes back.' The factual similarity of these two cases leads to the inescapable conclusion that *Farmer* is binding authority in this case.

5.   Victim Brown's Statements Do Not Constitute Inadmissible Opinion Evidence.

The defense argues that Nicole Simpson's statements that 'He's fucking going nuts,' and 'I don't want to stay on the line, he's gonna beat the shit out of me,' must be excluded because they constitute impermissible opinion. This proposition fails because it is contrary to the holding in *Farmer*. There the court upheld the admission of the victim's speculation that his assailant had entered the apartment hoping to steal drugs. *Id.* at 905.

Similarly, the two statements in our case both describe and explain the events which transpired on that night. Since 'He's going fucking nuts' is a description, and not an opinion, it is admissible as a spontaneous statement. The statement, 'I don't want to stay on the line, he's gonna beat the shit out of me' explains the event as a domestic violence situation.

Moreover, victim Brown's statements are both relevant for a non-hearsay purpose. The statements both demonstrate victim's mental state—her fear of defendant. Her mental state is relevant to show that the statements were made under the stress of excitement. It must be remembered that the trial court merely makes a preliminary determination that the foundation for the excited utterance exception is met. *Anthony O., supra* at 433–34. However, the final determination regarding the weight to be given the evidence is for the jury. Thus, both sides are at liberty to argue to the jury the extent to which the statement was made under the stress of excitement, and hence whether it is trustworthy. The victim's statements regarding her fear are admissible because they effectively eliminate any argument that the statements were not made under the stress of excitement and therefore should be given little weight.

5. JUDGES' RULINGS

In his January 18, 1995 ruling on the admissibility of evidence of prior acts of spousal abuse, Judge Ito held the 911 tapes could be admitted:

> The prosecution seeks to present the tapes as evidence of defendant's continuing violent conduct towards Brown Simpson, the comments of the defendant as admissions of jealousy as it pertains to motive, intent, plan and identity, and the comments of Brown Simpson as excited utterances as an exception to the hearsay rule under Evidence Code Section 1240, describing an event in progress. *People v. Farmer,* 47 Cal.3d 888, 901–907 (1989) provides guidance for the trial court. Although Brown Simpson responds to a series of questions posed by the 911 operator, it is clear she is still under the stress and pressure of defendant's presence and his loud, boisterous and angry behavior. The court has examined this recording and found it to have significant probative value as it relates to the nature and quality of the relationship in late 1993 and expressions of anger and jealousy by defendant. The statement by Brown–Simpson, 'He's going to beat the shit out of me' causes the court to take pause, especially in this situation where there is no allegation that defendant actually struck Brown Simpson on this particular occasion. With that particular statement excised, the probative value clearly outweighs the prejudicial impact. The 352 objection is therefore denied.

The tapes were also admitted at the civil trial.

6.   COMMENTS AND QUESTIONS

(a) The defense asserts that Nicole Brown Simpson's state of mind at the time of the 911 call is "irrelevant." If a predicate fact for admissibility of a spontaneous statement is that the declarant was "under the stress of excitement," doesn't that make her state of mind relevant? Is it relevant for the jury in evaluating the statement, or only for the judge in deciding its admissibility? Consider the following comment to Section 405 of the California Evidence Code:

> "When hearsay evidence is offered, two preliminary fact questions may be raised. The first question relates to the authenticity of the proffered declaration—was the statement actually made by the person alleged to have made it? The second question relates to the existence of those circumstances that make the hearsay sufficiently trustworthy to be received in evidence—e.g., was the declaration spontaneous, the confession voluntary, the business record trustworthy? Under this code, questions relating to the authenticity of the proffered declaration are decided under Section 403. See the Comment to Section 403. But other preliminary fact questions are decided under Section 405."

Does the determination of spontaneity as a 405 issue remove the issue from the jury's consideration, in determining the weight they should give to the statement? Should the jury be instructed to consider some of the statements on the 911 tape only for the purpose of ascertaining the declarant's "state of mind"? Could the judge redact the statements, even if they are relevant to demonstrate "state of mind", on the grounds their probative value is outweighed by their prejudicial impact?

B.   NICOLE'S STATEMENTS IN POLICE REPORTS

1.   THE EVIDENCE

Sgt. Craig Lally was summoned to Nicole Brown Simpson's Gretna Green home on October 25, 1993, to advise the officers investigating her "911" call. He interviewed Nicole Brown Simpson, and wrote the following report:

> "I responded to a supervisor request on 10–25–93. While at the scene I spoke privately with Nicole Brown Simpson. During my conversation with Brown I asked her if she was in fear of her life or in fear of great bodily injury because of this incident. Brown stated that on this particular night she was not afraid of Mr. Simpson because he did not have 'that look in his eyes.' I

asked Brown to explain what she meant. Brown stated that on prior incidents when she was beaten by Mr. Simpson he had this look in his eyes as if possessed by the devil. She further stated that this rage is what helped to make him such a great football player. Brown stated that Mr. Simpson became very upset because he observed a photo of an ex-boyfriend in the family photo album. Brown further stated that Mr. Simpson would become very jealous over the most stupid things, while showing me a photo of the ex-boyfriend."

2. THE TACTICAL CONTEXT

Sgt. Lally's report was produced during pre-trial discovery. In challenging the admissibility of evidence of prior spousal abuse in their pretrial motion *in limine,* the defense included their objection to Sgt. Lally's report on the grounds it was inadmissible hearsay. Sgt. Lally's report raised greater concerns for the defense than statements allegedly made by Nicole Brown Simpson to friends and family that were recalled by them after her murder. The Lally report was a contemporaneously recorded statement by a witness with no apparent interest in the case. Thus, if admitted, it might be given greater weight by a jury. The statement also offered dramatic potential for prosecutorial argument to the jury.

3. DEFENSE ARGUMENT

a. The Statement to Sgt. Lally Is Not Admissible to Show "State of Mind."

Brown's out-of-court comments to others concerning her feelings about Simpson might be probative of her state of mind. But Brown's state of mind is not an issue in this case, and evidence of a declarant's state of mind is admissible only when the declarant's state of mind is "itself an issue in the action" or is "offered to prove or explain acts or conduct of the declarant." California Evidence Code, § 1250(a)(1) and (2).[9] Consequently, since neither

---

9. Section 1250 of the California Evidence Code provides:

"(a) Subject to Section 1252, evidence of a statement of the declarant's then existing state of mind, emotion, or physical sensation (including a statement of intent, plan, motive, design, mental feeling, pain or bodily health) is not made inadmissible by the hearsay rule when:

(1) The evidence is offered to prove the declarant's state of mind, emotion, or physical sensation at that time or at any other time when it is itself an issue in the action; or

(2) The evidence is offered to prove or explain acts or conduct of the declarant.

(b) This section does not make admissible evidence of a statement of memory or belief to prove the fact remembered or believed."

Brown's state of mind, nor her conduct preceding the murder, is of any relevance, her out of court statements cannot be introduced pursuant to the "state of mind" exception to the hearsay rule.

The California Supreme Court has made it crystal clear that hearsay statements by a victim expressing fear of the defendant or relating threats of physical harm are not admissible to prove that the defendant in fact threatened the victim, and cannot be rendered admissible under the guise of "state of mind" evidence unless the victim's state of mind or his conduct preceding the crime is an actual issue in dispute. *See, e.g., People v. Arcega,* 32 Cal.3rd 504, 186 Cal.Rptr. 94 (1982) (error to admit testimony by victim's mother that victim told her shortly before her murder that defendant was following her around and treating her "weird", and was going to "hurt her" or "beat her up."); *People v. Ireland,* 70 Cal.2d 522, 75 Cal.Rptr. 188 (1969) (error to admit statement by victim on the morning she was killed that her husband was going to kill her).

In *People v. Armendariz,* 37 Cal.3d 573, 209 Cal.Rptr. 644 (1984), the trial court allowed the victim's son, Alfred, to testify that his father told him some seventeen months before his murder that he was frightened that the defendant would assault him if he did not lend him money. The trial court ruled that this evidence was admissible for the limited non-hearsay purpose of explaining why Alfred then went to his father's home. The Supreme Court rejected this reasoning because "a hearsay objection to an out-of-court statement may not be overruled simply by identifying a non-hearsay purpose for admitting the statement. The trial court must also find that the non-hearsay purpose is relevant to an issue in dispute." 37 Cal.3d at 584. Since the reason the son went to his father's house seventeen months before the murder was not in issue, the evidence offered to explain his conduct was irrelevant. Accord, *People v. Ruiz,* 44 Cal.3d 589, 244 Cal.Rptr.200 (1988); *People v. Noguera,* 4 Cal.4th 599, 15 Cal.Rptr.2d 400 (1992).

Evidence that Brown told people that she was fearful of Simpson, or that he had beaten her, is classic hearsay if introduced to prove that Simpson in fact committed these acts or in fact threatened Brown with physical harm. It presents all the "traditional hearsay dangers," since Brown's memory, perception and sincerity cannot be tested by cross examination. Moreover, since Brown's state of mind is not an issue in this case, and since the defense has not raised any issue concerning her conduct preceding the murder, testimony purporting to explain her conduct or show her state of mind is irrelevant.

> **b.** **The Statement to Sgt. Lally Is Not Admissible Under the Hearsay Exception for Official Records or Business Records.**

Police reports may qualify as an exception to the hearsay rule pursuant to Section 1280 of the California Evidence Code,[10] provided certain foundational requirements are met. But statements made by others to a police officer included within a police report constitute "hearsay within hearsay" [11] and are not covered by the "official records" exception. Police officers reporting their own observations pursuant to an official duty to make accurate statements are presumed to be reliable. But, as the California courts have repeatedly recognized, statements made by others to police officers are often made with ulterior motives and lack any guarantee of trustworthiness. *People v. Baeske,* 58 Cal.App.3d 775, 130 Cal.Rptr. 35 (1976); *Jackson v. Dept. Of Motor Vehicles,* 22 Cal. App.4th 730, 736, 27 Cal.Rptr.2d 712 (1994). For the same reason, police reports are not admissible under the "business records" exception to the hearsay rule, California Evidence Code § 1271, to the extent they include narrations by persons under no business duty to report to the police.

Statements made by Brown to Sgt. Lally are not admissible pursuant to Section 1280 simply because they may be contained in a document that could be introduced into evidence were it to contain observations made by Lally during the course of his official duties. Consequently, those statements can only be admitted if they fall within another recognized exception to the hearsay rule. Clearly, they do not.

c.   The Statement to Sgt. Lally Is Not Admissible as a "Spontaneous Statement."

The statement made by Nicole Brown Simpson to Sgt. Lally was made in response to direct questions, and was not "spontaneous." Brown was not injured or in shock. By the time police responded to Brown's "911" call and took her statement, she had ample time to reflect on which she wanted to say. Her statements to Sgt. Lally were not made impulsively while under the stress of a highly traumatic event and bear no indicia of trustworthiness.

10. California Evidence Code § 1280 provides as follows:

"Evidence of a writing made as a record of an act, condition, or event is not made inadmissible by the hearsay rule when offered to prove the act, condition or event if:

(a) The writing was made by and within the scope of duty of a public employee;

(b) The writing was made at or near the time of the act, condition or event;

(c) The sources of information and method and time of preparation

were such as to indicate its trustworthiness."

11. California Evidence Code § 1201 ("Multiple Hearsay") provides as follows:

"A statement within the scope of an exception to the hearsay rule is not inadmissible on the ground that the evidence of such statement is hearsay evidence if such hearsay evidence consists of one or more statements each of which meets the requirement of an exception to the hearsay rule."

An out-of-court statement is "spontaneous" if it is made "without deliberation or reflection." *People v. Farmer,* 47 Cal.3d 888, 900, 254 Cal.Rptr. 508 (1989). It is presumed to be trustworthy because it is made while the declarant is under the stress of nervous excitement and before she has had time to reflect or contrive.

While there is no set time limit within which a so-called "spontaneous statement" must be made, the courts have allowed in statements made after the triggering event only when the declarant had suffered serious trauma and is plainly in substantial pain or shock. Under such circumstances, the victim is not likely to have had the wherewithal to manufacture a false statement. *See, e.g., People v. Raley,* 2 Cal.4th 870, 8 Cal.Rptr.2d 678 (1992) (victim had been left bleeding, suffered traumatic head injury, had been unconscious, and was close to death); *People v. Poggi,* 45 Cal.3d 306, 246 Cal.Rptr. 886 (1988) (statement by stabbing victim bleeding profusely from ultimately fatal wounds thirty minutes after attack).

4. PROSECUTION ARGUMENT

A victim's statements of fear of an accused are admissible under Evidence Code Section 1250 if the victim's conduct in conformity with that fear is relevant.

In *People v. Finch,* 213 Cal.App.2d 752 (1963), the defendant was charged with murdering his wife. Five witnesses testified to statements of the deceased relating threats, beatings and other abuse at the hands of her husband, to show that she was in mortal fear of him and would never have gone home on the fatal night had she suspected that defendant would be there. Specifically, this evidence included victim's statement that defendant "tried to kill [her] last night", and affidavits filed in her divorce action relating a number of specific acts of violence by defendant against her. This evidence was clearly relevant to refute any theory of an accidental killing. *Id.* at 765. The evidence in our case is being introduced for the same purpose.

In *Finch,* the evidence was admissible to show victim would not have gone home had she known defendant was present there. In our case, the victim's statements prove that she would not have gone outside had she known defendant was there. This corroborates our theory that she was attacked by surprise. Likewise, it helps refute the defense claim that a lone assailant could not have killed both victims. The reason is that since victim was frightened of defendant by the time of the murder, she would not have exited her house at night to knowingly confront defendant. This is particularly true if she knew a young man would be present who defendant would mistake as a lover. Therefore, she did not know defendant was present, and was taken by surprise. Thus, *Finch* compels the conclusion that they are admissible. *See also, People v. Garcia,* 178 Cal.App.3d 814 ("come over, defendant went crazy, he is going to shoot me," comes in to show victim's mental state to explain he was not aggressor); *People v. Rowland,* 4 Cal.4th 238 (1992) (in kidnapping case, victim's statement that she was going home because she had splitting headache, comes in to show victim's state of mind, to infer victim's subsequent conduct).

In *People v. Pinn,* 17 Cal.App.3d 99 (1971), a murder case, victim told a witness that defendant "was going to kill her, and she wanted to get into the house to get some clothes and find her grandmother's gun." Later, defendant was seen forcing victim to take numerous barbiturates.

> "Evidence that [victim] was afraid of [defendant] and fearful that he might kill her tended to explain her conduct in taking an overdose of barbiturate pills at [defendant's] insistence and against her will and in accompanying him to the isolated place where the fatal episode occurred. [I]t also provided a basis for the reasonable inference that [victim] probably repelled his sexual advances and that it was this action on her part which caused [defendant] to attack and inflict upon her the wounds which caused her death." *Id.* at 105–06.

Similarly, in our case, evidence of victim's fear of defendant, proves that she probably did not repel defendant's attack. This is explained as part of a psychological phenomena known as "learned helplessness." It is one of the characteristics of abused women. Victim Nicole Brown's probable lack of resistance provides another explanation as to how a lone assailant easily dispatched two victims quickly and without detection. Viewed collectively, the statements in our case show an evolution in victim's attitude towards defendant leading up to her murder from one of fear to abject terror. As in *Pinn,* the statements in our case are coming in to prove victim's fear, and her conduct in conformity therewith.

5. JUDGES' RULINGS

In his ruling of January 18, 1995 on the admissibility of evidence of spousal abuse, Judge Lance Ito ruled that statements of Nicole Brown Simpson expressing fear of the defendant would not be admissible:

> To the man or woman on the street, the relevance and probative value of such evidence is both obvious and compelling, especially those statements made just days before the homicide. It seems only just and right that a crime victim's own words be heard, especially in the court where the facts and circum-

stances of her demise are to be presented. However, the laws and appellate court decisions that must be applied by the trial court hold otherwise. In factual situations distressingly similar to the assumed facts of this case, the California Supreme Court has given clear guidance to the trial court. The courts in *People v. Arcega,* 32 Cal.3d 503 (1982), and *People v. Ireland,* 70 Cal.2d 522 (1969), have clearly held that it is reversible error to admit the hearsay statements by a homicide victim expressing fear of the defendant, even when made on the very day of the homicide. (See also *People v. Ruiz,* 44 Cal.3d 589, 607–610 (1988)). The Evidence Code Section 1250 exception argued by the prosecution on the theory of 'learned helplessness' is not supported by the offer of proof and the defense has not raised any issue concerning Brown Simpson's acts or conduct preceding the homicide.

The statements of Nicole Brown Simpson relating threats by the defendant were admitted at the civil trial, partially in reliance upon a new hearsay exception enacted by the California legislature in direct response to the criminal verdict in the criminal case, and partially based on Judge Hiroshi Fujisaki's conclusion that Nicole Brown Simpson's state of mind was relevant. California Evidence Code Section 1370 now provides:

"(a) Evidence of a statement by a declarant is not made inadmissible by the hearsay rule if all of the following conditions are met:

(1) The statement purports to narrate, describe, or explain the infliction or threat of physical injury upon the declarant.

(2) The declarant is unavailable as a witness pursuant to Section 240.

(3) The statement was made at or near the time of the infliction or threat of physical injury. Evidence of statements made more that five years before the filing of the current action or proceeding shall be inadmissible under this section.

(4) The statement was made under circumstances that would indicate its trustworthiness.

(5) The statement was made in writing, was electronically recorded, or made to a law enforcement official.

(b) For purposes of paragraph (4) of subdivision (a), circumstances relevant to the issue of trustworthiness include, but are not limited to, the following:

(1) Whether the statement was made in contemplation of pending or anticipated litigation in which the declarant was interested.

(2) Whether the declarant has a bias or motive for fabricating the statement, and the extent of any bias or motive.

(3) Whether the statement is corroborated by evidence other than statements that are admissible only pursuant to this section.

(c) A statement is admissible pursuant to this section only if the proponent of the statement makes known to the adverse party the intention to offer the statement and the particulars of the statement sufficiently in advance of the proceedings in order to provide the adverse party with a fair opportunity to prepare to meet the statement."

6. COMMENTS AND QUESTIONS

(a) Based on essentially the same arguments, Judge Ito excluded a "diary" prepared by Nicole Brown Simpson at the time of her divorce from O.J. Simpson, describing various injuries allegedly inflicted upon her by the defendant. At the civil trial, Judge Hiroshi Fujisaki ruled broadly that any statements in Nicole Brown Simpson's diaries showing threats to her by the defendant would be admissible to show "her state of mind with regards to the relationship."

Why would Nicole Brown Simpson's state of mind with regards to the relationship be relevant in the civil case, if it wasn't relevant in the criminal case?

(b) Reconsider the arguments on admissibility of the "911" tapes. Would Evidence Code Section 1370 provide an alternative basis for the admission of such tapes, even when the requisite spontaneity for Section 1240 is absent?

(c) Did the apparent reluctance in Judge Ito's ruling suggest corresponding eagerness to admit the evidence if an alternative theory became available?

"Judge Ito ruled that any statements made by Nicole Brown Simpson, expressing fear of O.J. Simpson, were inadmissible hearsay. Her state of mind was not relevant to any issue in the case. The law and precedents were so clearly on our side of that issue that Judge Ito couldn't find any way around them. Not that he did not want to. As he put it in a very revealing passage in his ruling, 'It seems only just and right that a crime victim's own words be heard, especially in the court where the facts and circumstances of her demise are to be presented. However, the laws and appellate decisions that must be applied by the trial court hold otherwise.' I felt a cold chill when I read those sentences. It was obvious Judge Ito would be looking for any opportunity the evidence might present to let in the hearsay that emanated from Nicole Brown Simpson herself. The one opportunity that might have been presented for him to do so was if O.J. Simpson took the witness stand. On cross-examination, he could be questioned about statements Nicole Brown Simpson made in his presence."

Uelmen, *Lessons From the Trial: The People v. O.J. Simpson,* p. 110 (Andrews & McMeel, 1996).

C. O.J.'s STATEMENT TO POLICE DETECTIVES

1. THE EVIDENCE

O.J. Simpson was called at a Chicago hotel early on the morning of June 13, and told by detectives of Nicole Brown Simpson's murder. He was asked to return to Los Angeles as soon as possible. He flew back that morning, and upon his arrival at his Rockingham residence, he was placed in handcuffs. The handcuffs were removed, and accompanied by Attorney Howard Weitzman, he was asked to come to Police Headquarters at Parker Center. Detectives Phil Vanatter and Tom Lange then questioned him for thirty-two minutes. Simpson agreed to be interviewed in the absence of his attorney, and the entire interview was tape-recorded. The following transcript was prepared from the audio tape. The voice of Vanatter is designated "VA," Simpson is designated "OJ," and Lange is designated "TL."

LAPD INTERVIEW OF O.J. SIMPSON, June 13, 1994

VA: .... my partner, Detective Lange, and we're in an interview room in Parker Center. The date is June 13th, 1994, and the time is 13:35 hours. And we're here with OJ Simpson. Is that Orenthal James Simpson?

OJ: Orenthal James Simpson.

VA: And what is your birthdate, Mr. Simpson?

OJ: July 9th, 1947.

VA: OK. Prior to us talking to you, as we agreed with your attorney, I'm going to give you your constitutional rights. And I would like you to listen carefully. If you don't understanding anything, tell me, OK?

OJ: Alright.

VA: OK, Mr. Simpson, you have the right to remain silent. If you give up the right to remain silent, anything you say can and will be used against you in a court of law. You have the right to speak with an attorney and to have an attorney present during questioning. If you so desire and cannot afford one, an attorney will be appointed for you without charge before questioning. Do you understand your rights?

OJ: Yes, I do.

VA: Are there any questions about that?

OJ: [unintelligible]

VA: OK, you've got to speak up louder than that . . .

OJ: OK, no.

VA: OK, do you wish to give up your right to remain silent and talk to us?

OJ: Ah, yes.

VA: OK, and you give up your right to have an attorney present while we talk?

OJ: Mmm. hmm. Yes.

VA: OK. Alright, what we're gonna do is, we want to . . . We're investigating, obviously, the death of your ex-wife and another man.

TL: Someone told us that.

VA: Yeah, and we're going to need to talk to you about that. Are you divorced from her now?

OJ: Yes.

VA: How long have you been divorced?

OJ: Officially? Probably close to two years, but we've been apart for a little over two years.

VA: Have you?

OJ: Yeah.

VA: What was your relationship with her? What was the . . .

OJ: Well, we tried to get back together, and it just didn't work. It wasn't working, and so we were going our separate ways.

VA: Recently you tried to get back together?

OJ: We tried to get back together for about a year, you know, where we started dating each other and seeing each other. She came back and wanted us to get back together, and . . .

VA: Within the last year, you're talking about?

OJ: She came back about a year and four months ago about us trying to get back together, and we gave it a shot. We gave it a shot the better part of a year. And I think we both knew it wasn't working, and probably three weeks ago or so, we said it just wasn't working, and we went our separate ways.

VA: OK, the two children are yours?

OJ: Yes.

TL: She have custody?

OJ: We have joint custody.

TL: Through the courts?

OJ: We went through the courts and everything. Everything is done. We have no problems with the kids, we do things together, you know, with the kids.

VA: How was your separation? Was that a . . . ?

OJ: The first separation?

VA: Yeah, was there problems with that?

OJ: For me, it was, big problems. I loved her, I didn't want us to separate.

VA: Uh huh. I understand that she had made a couple of crime, crime reports or something?

OJ: Ah, we have a big fight about six years ago on New Years, you know, she made a report. I didn't make a report. And then we had an altercation about a year ago maybe. It wasn't a physical argument. I kicked her door or something.

VA: And she made a police report on those two occasions?

OJ: Mmm hmm. And I stayed right there until the police came, talked to them.

TL: Were you arrested at one time for something?

OJ: No. I mean, five years ago we had a big fight, six years ago, I don't know. I know I ended up doing community service.

VA: So you weren't arrested?

OJ: No, I was never really arrested.

TL: They never booked you, or ... ?

OJ: No.

VA: Can I ask you, when's the last time you've slept?

OJ: I got a couple hours sleep last night. I mean, you know, I slept a little on the plane, not much, and when I got to the hotel I was asleep a few hours when the phone call came.

TL: Did Nicole have a housemaid that lived there?

OJ: I believe so, yes.

TL: Do you know her name at all?

OJ: Avia, Alvia, something like that.

VA: We didn't see her there. Did she have the day off perhaps?

OJ: I don't know. I don't know what schedule she's on.

TL: Phil, what do you think? We can maybe just recount last night ...

VA: Yeah. When was the last time you saw Nicole?

OJ: We were leaving a dance recital. She took off and I was talking to her parents.

VA: Where was the dance recital?

OJ: Paul Revere High School.

VA: And was that for one of your children?

OJ: Yeah, for my daughter Sydney.

VA: And what time was that yesterday?

OJ: It ended about 6:30, quarter to seven, something like that, you know, in the ball park, right in that area. And they took off.

VA: They?

OJ: Her and her family—her mother and father, sisters, my kids, you know.

VA: And then you went your own separate way?

OJ: Yeah, actually she left, and then they came back and her mother got in a car with her, and the kids all piled into her sister's car, and they ...

VA: Was Nicole driving?

OJ: Yeah.

VA: What kind of car was she driving?

OJ: Her black car, a Cherokee, Jeep Cherokee.

VA: What were you driving?

OJ: My Rolls Royce, my Bentley.

VA: Do you own that Ford Bronco that sits outside?

OJ: Hertz owns it, and Hertz lets me use it.

VA: So that's your vehicle, the one that was parked there on the street?

OJ: Mmm hmm.

VA: And it's actually owned by Hertz?

OJ: Hertz, yeah.

VA: Who's the primary driver on that? You?

OJ: I drive it, the housekeeper drives it, you know, it's kind of a....

VA: All-purpose type vehicle?

OJ: All-purpose, yeah. It's the only one that my insurance will allow me to let anybody else drive.

VA: OK.

TL: When you drive it, where do you park it at home? Where it is now, it was in the street or something.

OJ: I always park it on the street.

TL: You never take it in the ...

OJ: Oh, rarely. I mean, I'll bring it in and switch the stuff, you know, and stuff like that. I did that yesterday, you know.

TL: When did you last drive it?

OJ: Yesterday.

VA: What time yesterday?

OJ: In the morning, in the afternoon.

VA: OK, you left her, you're saying, about 6:30 or 7:00, or she left the recital?

OJ: Yeah.

VA: And you spoke with her parents.

OJ: Yeah, we were just sitting there talking.

VA: OK, what time did you leave the recital?

OJ: Right about that time. We were all leaving. We were all leaving them. Her mother said something about me joining them for dinner, and I said no thanks.

VA: Where did you go from there, OJ?

OJ: Ah, home, home for awhile, got my car for awhile, tried to find my girlfriend for awhile, came back to the house.

VA: Who was home when you got home?

OJ: Kato.

VA: Kato? Anybody else? Was your daughter there, Arnelle?

OJ: No.

VA: Isn't that her name, Arnelle?

OJ: Arnelle, yeah.

VA: So what time do you think you got back home, actually physically got home?

OJ: Seven-something.

VA: Seven-something? And then you left, and ...

OJ: Yeah, I'm trying to think did I leave? You know, I'm always ... I had to run and get my daughter some flowers. I was actually doing the recital, so I rushed and got her some flowers, and I came home, and then I called Paula as I was going to her house, and Paula wasn't home.

VA: Paula is your girlfriend?

OJ: Girlfriend, yeah.
VA: Paula who?
OJ: Barbieri.
VA: Could you spell that for me?
OJ: B–A–R–B–I–E–R–I.
VA: Do you know an address on her?
OJ: No, she lives on Wilshire, but I think she's out of town.
VA: You got a phone number?
OJ: Yeah, 470–3468.
VA: So you didn't see her last night?
OJ: No, we'd been to a big affair the night before, and then I came back home. I was basically at home. I mean, any time I was … Whatever time it took me to get to the recital and back, to get to the flower shop and back, I mean, that's the time I was out of the house.
VA: Were you scheduled to play golf this morning someplace?
OJ: In Chicago.
VA: What kind of a tournament was it?
OJ: Ah, it was Hertz, with special clients.
VA: Oh, OK. What time did you leave last night, leave the house?
OJ: To go to the airport?
VA: Mmm hmm.
OJ: About … The limo was supposed to be there at 10:45. Normally they get there a little earlier. I was rushing around—somewhere between there and 11:00.
VA: So approximately 10:45 to eleven?
OJ: Eleven o'clock, yeah, somewhere in that area.
VA: And you went by limo?
OJ: Yeah.
VA: Who's the limo service?
OJ: Ah, you have to ask my office.
TL: Did you converse with the driver at all? Did you talk to him?
OJ: No, he was a new driver. Normally I have a regular driver I drive with and converse. No, just about rushing to the airport, about how I live my life on airplanes and hotels, that type of thing.
TL: What time did your plane leave?
OJ: Ah, 11:45 the flight took off.
VA: What airlines was it?
OJ: American.
VA: American? And it was 11:45 to Chicago?
OJ: Chicago.
TL: So yesterday you did drive the white Bronco?
OJ: Mmm hmm.
TL: And where did you park it when you brought it home?
OJ: Ah, the first time probably by the mailbox. I'm trying to think, or did I bring it in the driveway? Normally, I will park it by the mailbox, sometimes …
TL: On Ashford, or Ashland?
OJ: On Ashford, yeah.

TL: Where did you park it yesterday for the last time, do you remember?

OJ: Right where it is.

TL: Where it is now?

OJ: Yeah.

TL: Where, on ... ?

OJ: Right on the street there.

TL: On Ashford?

OJ: No, on Rockingham.

TL: You parked it there?

OJ: Yes.

TL: About what time was that?

OJ: Eight-something, seven.... eight, nine o'clock, I don't know, right in that area.

TL: Did you take it to the recital?

OJ: No.

TL: What time was the recital?

OJ: Over at about 6:30. Like I said, I came home, I got my car, I was going to see my girlfriend. I was calling her, and she wasn't around.

TL: So you drove the ... You came home in the Rolls, and then you got in the Bronco ...

OJ: In the Bronco, 'cause my phone was in the Bronco. And because it's a Bronco, it's a Bronco, it's what I drive, you know. I'd rather drive it than any other car. And, you know, and as I was going over there I called her a couple of times, and she wasn't there, and I left a message, and then I checked my messages, and there were no messages. She wasn't there, and she may have to leave town. Then I came back and ended up sitting with Kato.

TL: OK, what time was this again that you parked the Bronco?

OJ: Eight-something maybe. He hadn't done a jacuzzi, we had went and got a burger, and I'd come home and kind of leisurely got ready to go. I mean, we'd done a few things ...

TL: You weren't in a hurry when you came back with the white Bronco?

OJ: No.

TL: The reason I ask you, the cars were parked kind of at a funny angle, stuck out in the street.

OJ: Well, it's parked because ... I don't know if it's a funny angle or what. It's parked because when I was hustling at the end of the day to get all my stuff, and I was getting my phone and everything off it, when I just pulled it out of the gate there, it's like it's a tight turn.

TL: So you had it inside the compound, then?

OJ: Yeah.

TL: Oh, OK.

OJ: I brought it inside the compound to get my stuff out of it, and then I put it out, and I'd run back inside the gate before the gate closes.

VA: OJ, what's your office phone number?

OJ: 820–5702.

VA: And is that Area Code 310?

OJ: Yes.

VA: How did you get the injury on your hand?

OJ: I don't know. The first time, when I was in Chicago and all, but at the house I was just running around.

VA: How did you do it in Chicago?

OJ: I broke a glass. One of you guys had just called me, and I was in the bathroom, and I just kind of went bonkers for a little bit.

TL: Is that how you cut it?

OJ: Mmm, it was cut before, but I think I just opened it again, I'm not sure.

TL: Do you recall bleeding at all in your truck, in the Bronco?

OJ: I recall bleeding at my house, and then I went to the Bronco. The last thing I did before I left, when I was rushing, was went and got my phone out of the Bronco.

TL: Mmm hmm. Where's the phone now?

OJ: In my bag.

TL: You have it ... ?

OJ: In that black bag.

TL: You brought a bag with you here?

VA: Yeah, it's

TL: So do you recall bleeding at all?

OJ: Yeah, I mean, I knew I was bleeding, but it was no big deal. I bleed all the time. I play golf and stuff, so there's always something, nicks and stuff here and there.

TL: So did you do anything? When did you put the Bandaid on it?

OJ: Actually, I asked the girl this morning for it.

TL: And she got it?

OJ: Yeah, 'cause last night with Kato, when I was leaving he was saying something to me, and I was rushing to get my phone, and I put a little thing on it, and it stopped.

VA: Do you have the keys to that Bronco?

OJ: Yeah.

VA: OK. We've impounded the Bronco. I don't know if you know that or not.

OJ: No.

VA: ... take a look at it ... Other than you, who's the last person to drive it?

OJ: Probably Gigi. When I'm out of town I don't know who drives the car, maybe my daughter, maybe Kato.

VA: The keys are available.

OJ: I leave the keys there, you know, when Gigi's there because sometimes she needs it, or Gigi was off and wasn't coming back until today, and I was coming back tonight.

VA: So you don't mind if Gigi uses it, or ...

OJ: This is the only one I can let her use. When she doesn't have her car, 'cause sometimes her husband takes her car, I let her use the car.

TL: When was the last time you were at Nicole's house?

OJ: I don't go in, I won't go in her house. I haven't been in her house in a week, maybe five days. I go to her house a lot. I mean, I'm always dropping the kids off, picking the kids up, fooling around with the dog, you know.

VA: How does that usually work? Do you drop them at the porch, or do you go in with them?

OJ: No, I don't go in the house.

VA: Is there a kind of gate out front?

OJ: Yeah.

VA: But you never go inside the house?

OJ: Up until about five days, six days ago, I haven't been in the house. Once I started seeing Paula again, I kind of avoid Nicole.

VA: Is Nicole seeing anybody else that you . . .

OJ: I have no idea. I really have absolutely no idea. I don't ask her, I don't know. Her and her girlfriends, they go out, you know, they've got some things going on right now with her girlfriends, so I'm assuming something's happening because one of the girlfriends is having a big problem with her husband because she's always saying she's with Nicole until three or four in the morning. She's not. You know, Nicole tells me she leaves her at 1:30 or two or 2:30, and the girl doesn't get home until five, and she only lives a few blocks away.

VA: Something's going on, huh?

TL: Do you know where they went, the family, for dinner last night?

OJ: No. Well, no. I didn't ask.

TL: I just thought maybe there's a regular place that they go.

OJ: No. If I was with them, we'd go to Toscano. I mean, not Toscano, Poponi's.

VA: You haven't had any problems with her lately, have you, OJ?

OJ: I always have problems with her, you know? Our relationship has been a problem relationship. Probably lately for me, and I say this only because I said it to Ron yesterday at the— Ron Fishman, whose wife is Cora—at the dance recital when he came up to me and went, "Oooh, boy, what's going on?" and everybody was beefing with everybody. And I said, "Well, I'm just glad I'm out of the mix." You know, because I was like dealing with him and his problems with his wife and Nicole and evidently some new problems that a guy named Christian was having with his girl, and he was staying at Nicole's house, and something was going on, but I don't think it's pertinent to this.

VA: Did Nicole have words with you last night?

OJ: Pardon me?

VA: Did Nicole have words with you last night?

OJ: No, not at all.

VA: Did you talk to her last night?

OJ: To ask to speak to my daughter, to congratulate my daughter, and everything.

VA: But you didn't have a conversation with her?

OJ: No, no.

VA: What were you wearing last night, OJ?

OJ: What did I wear on the golf course yesterday? Some of these kind of pants, some of these kind of pants, I mean I changed different for the whatever it was. I just had on some

VA: Just these black pants.

OJ: Just these . . . They're called Bugle Boy.

VA: Bugle Boy? Is that what you wore to the recital?

OJ: No, no, to the recital I wore . . . What did I wear to the recital? I wore a white T-shirt and some slacks.

VA: These aren't the pants?

OJ: No.

VA: Where are the pants that you wore?

OJ: They're hanging in my closet.

VA: These are washable, right? You just throw them in the laundry?

OJ: Yeah, I got 100 pair. They give them to me free, Bugle Boys, so I've got a bunch of them.

VA: Do you recall coming home and hanging them up, or . . . ?

OJ: I always hang up my clothes. I mean, it's rare that I don't hang up my clothes unless I'm laying them in my bathroom for her to do something with them, but those are the only things I don't hang up. But when you play golf, you don't necessarily dirty pants.

TL: What kind of shoes were you wearing?

OJ: Tennis shoes.

TL: Tennis shoes? Do you know what kind?

OJ: Probably Reebok, that's all I wear.

TL: Are they at home, too?

OJ: Yeah.

TL: Was this supposed to be a short trip to Chicago, so you didn't take a whole lot?

OJ: Yeah, I was coming back today.

TL: Just overnight?

OJ: Yeah.

VA: That's a hectic schedule, drive back here to play golf and come back.

OJ: Yeah, but I do it all the time.

VA: Do you?

OJ: Yeah. That's what I was complaining with the driver about, you know, about my whole life is on and off airplanes.

VA: OJ, we've got sort of a problem.

OJ: Mmm hmm.

VA: We've got some blood on and in your car, we've got some blood at your house, and sort of a problem.

OJ: Well, take my blood test.

TL: Well, we'd like to do that. We've got, of course, the cut on your finger that you aren't real clear on. Do you recall having that cut on your finger the last time you were at Nicole's house?

OJ: A week ago?

TL: Yeah.

OJ: No. It was last night.

TL: OK, so last night you cut it.

VA: Somewhere after the recital?

OJ: Somewhere when I was rushing to get out of my house.

VA: OK, after the recital.

OJ: Yeah.

VA: What do you think happened? Do you have any ideas?

OJ: I have no idea, man. You guys haven't told me anything. I have no idea. When you said to my daughter, who said something to me today, that somebody else might have been involved, I have absolutely no idea what happened. I don't know how, why or what. But you guys haven't told me anything. Every time I ask you guys, you say you're going to tell me in a bit.

VA: Well, we don't know a lot of the answers to these questions yet ourselves, OJ, OK?

OJ: I've got a bunch of guns, guns all over the place. You can take them, they're all there, I mean, you can see them. I keep them in my car for an incident that happened a month ago that my in-laws, my wife and everybody knows about.

VA: What was that?

OJ: Going down to ... And cops down there know about it because I've told two marshals about it. At a mall, I was going down for a christening, and I had just left, and it was like 3:30 in the morning, and I'm in a lane, and also the car in front of me is going real slow, and I'm slowing down 'cause I figure he sees a cop, 'cause we were all going pretty fast. And I'm going to change lanes, but there's a car next to me, and I can't change lanes. Then that goes for a while, and I'm going to slow down and go around him, but the car butts up to me, and I'm like caught between three cars. They were Oriental guys, and they were not letting me go anywhere. And finally I went on the shoulder, and I sped up, and then I held my phone up so they could see the light part of it, you know, 'cause I have tinted windows, and they kind of scattered, and I chased one of them for awhile to make him think I was chasing him before I took off.

TL: Were you in the Bronco?

OJ: No.

TL: What were you driving?

OJ: My Bentley. It has tinted windows and all, so I figured they thought they had a nice little touch ...

TL: Did you think they were trying to rip you off maybe?

OJ: Definitely, they were. And then the next thing, you know, Nicole and I went home. At four in the morning I got down there to Laguna, and when we woke up, I told her about it, and told her parents about it, told everybody about it, you know? And when I saw two marshals at a mall, I walked up and told them about it.

VA: What did they do, make a report on it?

OJ: They didn't know nothing. I mean, they'll remember me and remember I told them.

VA: Did Nicole mention that she'd been getting any threats lately to you? Anything she was concerned about or the kids' safety?

OJ: To her?

VA: Yes.

OJ: From?

VA: From anybody.

OJ: No, not at all.

VA: Was she very security conscious? Did she keep that house locked up?

OJ: Very.

VA: The intercom didn't work apparently, right?

OJ: I thought it worked.

VA: Oh, OK. Does the electronic buzzer work?

OJ: The electronic buzzer works to let people in.

VA: Do you ever park in the rear when you go over there?

OJ: Most of the time.

VA: You do park in the rear.

OJ: Most times when I'm taking the kids there, I come right into the driveway, blow the horn, and she, or a lot of times the housekeeper, either the housekeeper opens or they'll keep a garage door open up on the top of the thing, you know, but that's when I'm dropping the kids off, and I'm not going in. _____times I go to the front because the kids have to hit the buzzer and stuff.

VA: Did you say before that up until about three weeks ago you guys were going out again and trying to . . .

OJ: No, we'd been going out for about a year, and then the last six months we've had . . . it ain't been working, so we tried various things to see if we can make it work. We started trying to date, and that wasn't working, and so, you know, we just said the hell with it, you know.

VA: And that was about three weeks ago?

OJ: Yeah, about three weeks ago.

VA: So you were seeing her up to that point?

OJ: It's, it's . . . Seeing her, yeah, I mean, yeah. It was a done deal. It just wasn't happening. I mean, I was gone. I was in San Juan doing a film, and I don't think we had sex since I've been back from San Juan, and that was like two months ago. So it's been like . . . for the kids we tried to do things together. We didn't go out together, you know, we didn't really date each other. Then we decided let's try to date each other. We went out one night, and it just didn't work.

VA: When you say it didn't work, what do you mean?

OJ: Ah, the night we went out it was fun. Then the next night we went out it was actually when I was down in Laguna, and she didn't want to go out. And I said, "Well, let's go out 'cause I came all the way down here to go out," and we kind of had a beef and it just didn't work after that, you know? We were only trying to date to see if we could bring some romance back into our relationship. We just said, let's treat each other like boyfriend and girlfriend instead of, you know, like 17-year-old married people. I mean, 17 years together, whatever that is.

VA: How long were you together?

OJ: Seventeen years.

VA: Seventeen years. Did you ever hit her, OJ?

OJ: Ah, one night we had a fight. We had a fight, and she hit me. And they never took my statement, they never wanted to hear my side, and they never wanted to hear the housekeeper's side. Nicole was drunk. She did her thing, she started tearing up my house, you know? And I didn't punch her or anything, but I . . .

VA: . . . slapped her a couple of times.

OJ: No, no, I wrestled her, is what I did. I didn't slap her at all. I mean, Nicole's a strong girl. She's a . . . one of the most conditioned women. Since that period of time, she's hit me a few times, but I've never touched her after that, and I'm telling you, it's five-six years ago.

VA: What's her birthdate?

OJ: May 19th.

VA: Did you get together with her on her birthday?

OJ: Yeah, her and I and the kids, I believe.

VA: Did you give her a gift?

OJ: I gave her a gift.

VA: What'd you give her?

OJ: I gave her either a bracelet or the earrings.

VA: Did she keep them, or . . .

OJ: Oh, no, when we split she gave me both the earrings and the bracelet back. I bought her a very nice bracelet—I don't know if it was Mothers' Day or her birthday—and I bought her the earrings for the other thing, and when we split—and it's a credit to her—she felt that it wasn't right that she had it, and I said good because I want them back.

VA: Was that the very day of her birthday, May 19, or was it a few days later?

OJ: What do you mean?

VA: You gave it to her on the 19th of May, her birthday, right, this bracelet?

OJ: I may have given her the earrings. No, the bracelet. May 19th. When was Mothers' Day?

VA: Mothers' Day was around that . . .

OJ: No, it was probably her birthday, yes.

VA: And did she return it the same day?

OJ: Oh, no, she . . . I'm in a funny place here on this, alright? She returned it—both of them—three weeks ago or so, because when I say I'm in a funny place on this it was because I gave it to my girlfriend and told her it was for her, and that was three weeks ago. I told her I bought it for her. You know? What am I going to do with it?

TL: Did Mr. Weitzman, your attorney, talk to you anything about this polygraph we brought up before? What are your thoughts on that?

OJ: Should I talk about my thoughts on that? I'm sure eventually I'll do it, but it's like I've got some weird thoughts now. I've had weird thoughts.... you know, when you've been with a person for seventeen years, you think everything. I've got to understand what this thing is. If it's true blue, I don't mind doing it.

TL: Well, you're not compelled at all to take this thing, number one, and number two—I don't know if Mr. Weitzman explained it to you—this goes to the exclusion of someone as much as to the inclusion so we can eliminate people. And just to get things straight . . .

OJ: But does it work for elimination?

TL: Oh, yes. We use it for elimination more than anything.

OJ: Well, I'll talk to him about it.

TL: Understand, the reason we're talking to you is because you're the ex-husband . . .

OJ: I know I'm the number one target, and now you tell me I've got blood all over the place.

TL: Well, there's blood at your house in the driveway, and we've got a search warrant, and we're going to go get the blood. We found some in your house. Is that your blood that's there?

OJ: If it's dripped, it's what I dripped running around trying to leave.

TL: Last night?

OJ: Yeah, and I wasn't aware that it was . . . I was aware that I . . . You know, I was trying to get out of the house, I didn't even pay any attention to it. I saw it when I was in the kitchen, and I grabbed a napkin or something, and that was it. I didn't think about it after that.

VA: That was last night after you got home from the recital, when you were rushing?

OJ: That was last night when I was . . . I don't know what I was . . . I was in the car getting my junk out of the car. I was in the house throwing hangers and stuff in my suitcase. I was doing my little crazy what I do . . . I mean, I do it everywhere. Anybody who has ever picked me up says that OJ's a whirlwind, he's running, he's grabbing things, and that's what I was doing.

VA: Well, I'm going to step out, and I'm going to get a photographer to come down and photograph your hand there. And then here pretty soon we're going to take you downstairs and get some blood from you. OK? I'll be right back.

TL: So it was about five days ago you last saw Nicole? Was it at the house?

OJ: OK, the last time I saw Nicole, physically saw Nicole . . . I saw her obviously last night. The time before, I'm trying to think ... I went to Washington, DC, so I didn't see her, so I'm trying to think ... I haven't seen her since I went to Washington. I went to Washington—what's the date today?

TL: Today's Monday, the 13th of June.

OJ: OK, I went to Washington on maybe Wednesday. Thursday I think I was in ... Thursday I was in Connecticut, then Long Island Thursday afternoon and all of Friday. I got home Friday night, Friday afternoon. I played, you know ... Paula picked me up at the airport. I played golf Saturday, and when I came home I think my son was there. So I did something with my son. I don't think I saw Nicole at all then. And then I went to a big affair with Paula Saturday night, and I got up and played golf Sunday, which pissed Paula off, and I saw Nicole at ... It was about a week before, I saw her at the ...

TL: Ok, the last time you saw Nicole, was that at her house?

OJ: I don't remember. I wasn't in her house, so it couldn't have been at her house, so it was, you know, I don't physically remember the last time I saw her. I may have seen her even jogging one day.

TL: Let me get this straight. You've never physically been inside the house?

OJ: Not in the last week.

TL: Ever. I mean, how long has she lived there? About six months?

OJ: Oh, Christ, I've slept at the house many, many, many times, you know? I've done everything at the house, you know? I'm just saying ... You're talking in the last week or so.

TL: Well, whatever. Six months she's lived there?

OJ: I don't know. Roughly. I was at her house maybe two weeks ago, ten days ago. One night her and I had a long talk, you know, about how can we make it better for the kids, and I told her we'd do things better. And, OK, I can almost say when that was. That was when I ... I don't know, it was about ten days ago. And then we ... The next day I had her have her dog do a flea bath or something with me. Oh, I'll tell you, I did see her one day. One day I went ... I don't know if this was the early part of last week, I went 'cause my son had to go and get something, and he ran in, and she came to the gate, and the dog ran out, and her friend Fay and I went looking for the dog. That may have been a week ago, I don't know.

TL: [to Vanatter]: Got a photographer coming?

VA: No, we're going to take him up there.

TL: We're ready to terminate this at 14:07.

2. THE TACTICAL CONTEXT

Although the statement was largely exculpatory, the prosecution could have offered it in evidence as an admission. The defense, of course, could not offer it, since an admission can only be offered "against the declarant." California Evidence Code Section 1220. The prosecutors decided not to offer the statement, since it would allow Simpson's exculpatory account of his activities on the night of the murder to be heard by the jury without cross examination. The defense, on the other hand, was anxious to capitalize upon any opportunity which might present itself to get the statement admitted. An opportunity did present itself during the direct examination of Collin Yamauchi, a criminalist who prepared some of the blood evidence for testing. During his examination by Deputy District Attorney Rockne Harmon, the following exchange occurred:

"Q. By Mr. Harmon: Mr. Yamauchi, you've been watching television, the televised proceedings in this case occasionally?

A. Yes.

Q. Have you heard the term examiner bias?

A. Yes.

Q. Are you familiar with it?

A. Well, I'd like to hear an explanation, but I have an idea what it means.

Mr. Scheck: Objection, Your Honor.

The Court: Overruled.

Q. By Mr. Harmon: Based on what you heard in the media at the time, or, you know, before you did the test in this case, did you have an expectation of what the outcome of these tests would be?

Mr. Scheck: Objection.

The Court: Overruled.

The Witness: Well, on the 13th, the last thing I heard in the evening . . .

Mr. Scheck: Your Honor . . .

The Court: Nonresponsive. Did you have an expectation, yes or no?

The Witness: Yes.

Q. By Mr. Harmon: And what was that based on?

Mr. Scheck: Objection.

The Court: Overruled.

Mr. Scheck: Calls for hearsay.

The Court: Overruled.

The Witness: Like I was saying, I heard on the news, well, yeah, he's got an air-tight alibi. He's in Chicago and, you know, that and it's his ex-wife and this and that. And I go, oh, well, he's probably not related to the scene.

The Court: All right. Let me see counsel over at sidebar.

At sidebar:

The Court: We've got a huge problem. We just brought in a statement. I'm going to strike the answer.

Mr. Scheck: No, Your Honor. Your Honor, I'm not against it. It opens the door to his entire statement.

The Court: It does.

Ms. Clark: Wait, wait, wait."

3. DEFENSE ARGUMENT

The defense contends that the presentation of the detached declaration, "he's got an air-tight alibi", permits the admission of those portions of the defendant's statement to police on the same subject of his alibi which are necessary to make the detached declaration understood, pursuant to California Evidence Code Section 356, which provides:

> "Where part of an act, declaration, conversation, or writing is given in evidence by one party, the whole on the same subject may be inquired into by an adverse party; when a letter is read, the answer may be given; *and when a detached act, declaration, conversation, or writing is given in evidence, any other act, declaration, conversation or writing which is necessary to make it understood may also be given in evidence.*"

(Emphasis supplied). Two things become immediately apparent from the statutory language. First, the testimony that "opens the door" need *not* be an actual part of the act, declaration, conversation or writing that is offered to make it understood. Second, the "writing" that is offered to make it understood can include a tape-recorded statement. California Evidence Code Section 250.[12]

Thus, it makes no difference whether Collin Yamauchi was referring to news reports or to the actual statement of the defendant. The fact remains that an "airtight alibi" is attributed *to the defendant:*

> *"He's got* an airtight alibi."

---

12. California Evidence Code Section 250 defines "writing" to mean "handwriting, typewriting, printing, photostating, photographing, and every other means of recording upon any tangible thing any form of communication or representation, including letters, words, pictures, sounds, or symbols, or combinations thereof."

The impact upon the jury of leaving this testimony unexplained is readily apparent. They are left to speculate why this alleged "airtight alibi" has not been explained. Is it because it was false? Is it because the defense got it suppressed? The correct answer, of course, is it's because the prosecution made a tactical decision to keep it from the jury. The whole purpose of Section 356 is to say to the prosecution, "you can't have it both ways. You can't keep the defendant's exculpatory statement from the jury, and still offer to the jury a detached and misleading summary of the statement in the form, 'he's got an air-tight alibi.' "

In any event, the source of media speculation that Mr. Yamauchi would have heard was clearly the defendant's statement. It was widely reported that Attorney Howard Weitzman accompanied Mr. Simpson to Parker Center after his return from Chicago, and Mr. Weitzman issued a statement that Mr. Simpson was fully cooperating in the investigation. The operative impact of Section 356 is not dependent upon the identification of the source to which the witness attributes the detached act, declaration, conversation, or writing. It was presented as a claim by the defendant, so any other writing necessary to make that claim understood may now be given in evidence.

The purpose of Section 356 is to preserve fair play when misleading impressions are created. The misleading impression created by "He's got an airtight alibi," without any further explanation, will be extremely damaging to the defendant, because the jury will not know that the defendant never claimed he was in Chicago at the time the murders were committed, and that his denial is completely consistent with the testimony already elicited from numerous prosecution witnesses regarding his activities on the evening in question.

A helpful illustration of the rule's application appears in *Rosenberg v. Wittenborn,* 178 Cal.App.2d 846 (1960). A police officer testified that the defendant told him he had the red light at the time an accident occurred. The defendant was then permitted to elicit the full explanation on cross-examination, which gave "a very different complexion."

> "Plaintiff's attorney was trying to leave the jury with the impression that defendant by way of admission had told the officer ... that he entered the intersection against the red light,—that he said this and no more. These statements were in fact so qualified when made to the officer that they carried no implication (such as plaintiff would have the jury draw) that defendant ran the red light because he was going too fast to stop within the distance he had available.... Considerations of fair play demanded that the portion of the conversation placed

in evidence by plaintiffs be supplemented by the qualifying and enlightening portions of the conversation which gave a very different complexion than that which plaintiff's segregated passages bore."

178 Cal.App.2d at 851–52. Here, to paraphrase *Rosenberg v. Wittenborn,* the defendant's statements to the police were so qualified that they carried no implication of an "airtight alibi" that the prosecution wants the jury to believe was contrived. Considerations of fair play demand that the relevant portions of the statement be admitted which will qualify and enlighten the true nature of defendant's explanation, which will present "a very different complexion" than that conveyed by the testimony, "He's got an airtight alibi."

The damage in the unexplained attribution of an "airtight alibi" to the defendant by Collin Yamauchi is heightened by the jury's awareness through Mr. Yamauchi's previous testimony that he had been "briefed" by Dennis Fung with information from the homicide detective's investigation. Some of this information, such as the fact the defendant had a cut on the middle finger of his left hand, could only have come from the examination of Mr. Simpson by Detectives at Parker Center. Thus, his prior information about the case was *not* limited to news accounts.

Obviously, only the portions of the defendant's taped statement relating to an alibi may be relevant, but in applying the limitation of relevance, two things are made clear by the opinion of the court in *People v. Hamilton,* 48 Cal.3d 1142, 1174 (1989): relevance must be placed in the context of all of the testimony leading up to the statement "he's got an airtight alibi," and the court should not draw narrow lines around the exact subject of inquiry.

In *Hamilton,* a prosecution witness gave a tape recorded statement claiming the defendant told her he wanted his wife killed. On cross-examination, the defense showed inconsistencies between the tape and a transcript of the tape regarding the planning of the crime. Without objection, the prosecution then had the entire tape played, revealing additional statements about the defendant's motive. The Court upheld the admission of the entire tape under Evidence Code Section 356:

> "In applying Evidence Code Section 356, the courts do not draw narrow lines around the exact subject of inquiry. 'In the event a statement admitted in evidence constitutes a part of a conversation or correspondence, the opponent is entitled to have placed in evidence all that was said or written by or to the declarant in the course of such conversation or correspondence, provided the other statements have some bearing upon, or connection with, the admission or declaration in evidence.'"

48 Cal.3d at 1174.

The test of relevancy presents more complexity in the context of two different statements, if the first statement that "opens the door" is *independently comprehensible.* That was the rationale offered in *People v. Barrick,* 33 Cal.3d 115, 131–32 (1982) for excluding a distinct and separate post-arrest interrogation after the prosecution elicited a pre-arrest statement:

> "The post-arrest statement would also be admissible if necessary to understand the earlier prearrest statement, but in the present case the earlier statement is independently comprehensible."

33 Cal.3d at 131 n.4. Here, of course, the statement "He's got an airtight alibi" is hardly independently comprehensible. It raises a host of questions that can only be answered in the full context of the defendant's statement explaining his movements on the night of the homicide.

As a leading commentator on California Evidence noted in explaining the operation of Section 356, "Whenever matters are taken out of context, misleading impressions can be created." Mendez, *California Evidence,* Section 13.10, p. 244 (1993). Section 356 exists to "diminish this risk." That is all the defendant seeks to do. Considerations of fair play fully justify the admission of the relevant portions of the defendant's recorded statement which are necessary to make Mr. Yamauchi's report of the detached declaration, "He's got an airtight alibi," understood by the jury.

4. PROSECUTION ARGUMENT

By its terms, Section 356 requires that before the remainder of a conversation or writing is admissible, a portion of that conversation or writing must first have been testified to by one party.[13] For example, in *People v. Sandoval,* 4 Cal.4th 155 (1992), the prosecution offered into evidence slips of paper which had been attached to an appointment book and weekly planner. The California Supreme Court held that "contrary to defendant's contention, Evidence Code Section 356 did not require admission of the appointment book and weekly planner. *Those books simply were not part of a writing given in evidence by the prosecution."* (*Id.* at 177; emphasis added; see generally, Cal. Criminal Law, Procedure and Practice (CEB 2nd Ed., 1994), Section 30.24, pp. 732–733). Here, there was no testimony regarding any statement by the defendant. Mr. Yamauchi testi-

13. Even when a portion of a conversation or writing has been admitted, only that portion which is necessary to place the admitted portion in context is admissible under Section 356.

E.g. People v. Pride, 3 Cal.4th 195, 235 (1992) ("where one party has introduced part of a conversation, the opposing party may admit any other part necessary to place the original excerpts in context.").

fied he formed *his own conclusion* that the defendant had an "airtight alibi" because he heard *on the news* late on the evening of June 13 that the defendant was in Chicago.[14] He did not hear, nor testify to, any statement of the defendant. Consequently, Evidence Code Section 356 has no application.

The news report that the defendant was in Chicago was offered, not for the truth of the matter asserted (*i.e.*, that the defendant was in Chicago), but, rather for the nonhearsay purpose of showing the impact of that statement on the state of mind of the listener. During the cross-examination of Department of Justice Criminalist Rene Montgomery, Mr. Blasier tried to establish that the witness had an expectation that her test results would be consistent with the defendant being guilty. Consequently, during direct examination of Mr. Yamauchi, the prosecutor sought to lay to rest any notion that there had been any such expectation on Mr. Yamauchi's part by showing that, if anything, Mr. Yamauchi had a bias which would cause him to expect that his testing results would exclude the defendant as a possible suspect. The mention of news reports was properly admitted for that purpose. (See, generally, Jefferson, Evidence Benchbook, Vol. 1, Sec. 1.4, p. 57 (2d Ed. 1982)).

5. JUDGES' RULINGS

After hearing argument, Judge Ito ruled that the testimony of Collin Yamauchi had not "opened the door" to permit the defense to offer the defendant's statement to the police. The statement was never admitted into evidence at the criminal trial.

At the civil trial, O.J. Simpson was called as a hostile witness by the plaintiff, pursuant to California Evidence Code Section 776.[15] His statement to the police was frequently used during cross-examination to impeach him with prior inconsistencies. The following excerpts from the examination of O.J. Simpson by Mr. Petrocelli illustrate the use of the statement to police as a prior inconsistent statement, pursuant to California Evidence Code Sections 769, 770

---

14. Even if the *news* report had used the phrase "airtight alibi", that report could not have been based on the defendant's statement to the police. The media did not yet know at that time the content of the defendant's statement to the police. Nor does the defendant, in his statement to the police, claim that he was in Chicago at the time the murders occurred. Nor was his statement an alibi statement. Consequently, the phrase could not have been based in any

manner on the defendant's statement to the police.

15. California Evidence Code Section 776(a) provides:

"A party to the record of any civil action, or a person identified with such a party, may be called and examined as if under cross-examination by any adverse party at any time during the presentation of evidence by the party calling the witness."

and 1235.[16] In the course of his examination, Mr. Petrocelli also offered the entire statement, and the tape recording was played for the jury.

(1) "Q. By Mr. Petrocelli: And you were together, then, with Nicole about 17 years, is that right?

A.   Most of 17 years, yes.

Q.   And there were bad times, right?

A.   A few, yes.

Q.   More than a few, right?

A.   Well, like any long relationship, there was a few bad times, yes.

Q.   We're only talking about your relationship, sir, not other relationships, Okay?

A.   Yes.

Q.   And this was a passionate relationship at times, correct?

[Relevance objection overruled].

A.   Yes.

Q.   And it was a problem relationship for you throughout much of the time, true?

A.   Not true.

Q.   Did you not tell the Los Angeles police detectives who interviewed you on June 13, 1994, hours after Nicole's death, that you had always had problems with your relationship with Nicole; it was a problem relationship?

A.   Yes, we had problems in our relationship, but I don't think it was mostly a problem.

16.   California Evidence Code Section 769 provides:

"In examining a witness concerning a statement or other conduct by him that is inconsistent with any part of his testimony at the hearing, it is not necessary to disclose to him any information concerning the statement or other conduct."

California Evidence Code Section 770 provides:

"Unless the interests of justice otherwise require, extrinsic evidence of a statement made by a witness that is inconsistent with any part of his testimony at the hearing shall be excluded unless:

(a) The witness was so examined while testifying as to give him an opportunity to explain or deny the statement; or

(b) The witness has not been excused from giving further testimony in the action."

California Evidence Code Section 1235 provides:

"Evidence of a statement made by a witness is not made inadmissible by the hearsay rule if it is inconsistent with his testimony at the hearing and is offered in compliance with Section 770."

Q. Did you not say that to the police detectives on June 13, 1994? Yes or No?

A. Yes." [Transcript Nov. 22, 1996, Vol. 21, pp.8–9].

(2) "Q. By Mr. Petrocelli: And during this period of time, May 19, is when she had her birthday and you bought her an emerald bracelet and gave it to her, together with a cigarette lighter, correct?

A. I gave it to her. I didn't buy it for her, but I gave it to her, yes.

Q. Well, you bought this bracelet for her?

A. No.

Q. You did not?

A. No.

Q. You told the L.A. Police detectives who interviewed you on June 13, that you bought it for her, didn't you?

A. That's correct.

Q. Okay, and certainly on June 13, only three weeks after May 19, that is a lot closer than today, true?

A. Yes.

Q. And in fact, you told the detectives who interviewed you, Detectives Thomas Lange and Phil Vanatter, on June 13, that you were in a bad spot because you had bought the bracelet for Nicole, given it to her, she returned it to you, and you gave it to Paula and told Paula you bought it for her, true?

A. That's true.

Q. Okay. And now you're telling us that all that's false, right? Yes or no?

A. It is false.

Q. Okay.

A. It's partially true. But if you want me to explain it's a very simple explanation and I think you will understand if you give me the opportunity to explain.

Q. I think I understand, sir." [Transcript Nov. 22, 1996, Vol. 21, pp. 111–12].

(3) "Q. By Mr. Petrocelli: Answer this question: When you spoke to the police on June 13, hours after Nicole's death, you told the police that you, after the recital, made a phone call while driving over to Paula's looking for her, from your Bronco, the car you'd rather drive than any other car, using your cell phone, true?

A. I don't think I said from my Bronco, but I did imply that I was driving to Paula's right after the recital and I made a call to Paula.

Q. You implied it or you said it?

A. I don't recall but I know it was implied.

Q. Let me read it to you.

(Reading from p. 9 of transcript of police interview):

'... and as I was going over there I called her a couple times, and she wasn't there, and I left a message, and then I checked my messages, and there were no messages. She wasn't there, and she may have to leave town. Then I came back and ended up sitting with Kato.' You told the police you drove to Paula's after the recital, in your Bronco, and made a call to her from your cell phone, true or untrue?

A. True.

Q. The only time after the recital that you have any cell phone calls to Paula is at what time, looking at your cell phone records?

A. 10:03.

Q. So sir, you were in your Bronco calling Paula at 10:03, just like you told the police, true?

A. That's incorrect.

Q. Oh, so you lied to the police?

A. No.

Q. You have a different story now. It's different now, isn't it?

A. I think it's more accurate now.

Q. It's different, isn't it?

A. Yes.

Q. It's—now you say you didn't get in the Bronco, and drive to Paula's, and call her from the phone, true?

A. That's true.

Q. That's what you now say, true?

A. That's true.

Q. Okay. And you now say that of course after meeting with teams of lawyers and investigators and defense experts and seeing that there are cell phone records at 10:03 putting you in the Bronco, true?

A. True.

Q.   And by the way, at the time you gave your statement to the police, you were not familiar with cell phone records, were you?

A.   I don't understand what you mean.

Q.   Well, you testified in your deposition, at page 2144, that the cell phone bills go to the office and are paid by someone there, meaning Cathy Randa?

A.   Yes.

Q.   Okay.

A.   But I understand cell phone records.

Q.   Now you do?

A.   I always have.

Q.   ... So your story now, then, is that you didn't make this call from the Bronco, right?

A.   That's correct.

Mr. Baker: Objection, argumentative.

.   .   .

The Court: Overruled.

Q.   By Mr. Petrocelli: And your story now, sir, is that, in fact, your cell phone wasn't even in the Bronco at 10:03, right?

A.   That's correct.

Q.   You're now saying that you took it out of the Bronco hours before?

A.   That's correct.

Q.   Let me read what you told to the police about that subject.

(Reading from p. 15 of transcript of police interview):

'... The last thing I did before I left, when I was rushing, was went and got my phone out of the Bronco.' Remember saying that to the police?

A.   I don't think that's complete.

(Counsel hands document to witness).

Q.   By Mr. Petrocelli: Do you remember saying that to the police, yes or no?

A.   I remember saying that and more to the police.

Q.   You think this transcript is wrong, is that what you're saying?

A.   I know it is.

Q.   Had no problem with it on Friday, did you?

Mr. Baker: That's argumentative, Your Honor.

The Court: Sustained.

Q.   By Mr. Petrocelli: You told the police that the last thing
you did, sir, was you, before leaving for the airport, went out
and got your cell phone from the Bronco, because it was in the
Bronco, at 11 o'clock, true?

Mr. Baker: That's argumentative.

A.   It wasn't in the Bronco.

Q.   By Mr. Petrocelli: You don't want it to be there because if
it was there at 11, it was there at 10, and if it's there at 10,
you're in your Bronco and you're not in your home, and it
destroys your alibi?

Mr. Baker: All that is argument. It's great final argument and
great sound bites, Your Honor, but it's not a proper question.

Mr. Petrocelli: No speaking objections.

Mr. Baker: I don't take legal advice from any adversaries.

The Court: Sustained." [Transcript of Nov. 25, 1996, Vol. 22,
pp. 16–23].

6.   COMMENTS AND QUESTIONS

(a) Vincent Bugliosi is highly critical of the prosecutors' decision not to offer Simpson's statement to police detectives during
their case-in-chief:

"There were two fundamental problems with this trial tactic of
the prosecutors. Number one, they were taking an enormous
risk that Simpson would decide not to testify (which, indeed, is
what happened), and at that point it might be too late for the
prosecutors to introduce his statement, since during their
rebuttal, they would be limited to controverting evidence and
testimony offered by the defense during the defense's case. And
if Simpson didn't testify, the defense could argue there would
be no testimony of his to impeach.

Number two—an even more fundamental problem, one
that clearly shows me that these prosecutors knew very little
about prosecuting a criminal case—is that the jury already
knew that Simpson had made the statement. On direct examination of Lange and Vanatter before the jury, the prosecutors
elicited the information that the detectives had taken a statement from Simpson, but then the prosecutors went on to other
matters. At that point, the jurors naturally wondered two
things. One, they wondered what Simpson had told the police,
and two, they undoubtedly wondered why the DA wasn't

offering the statement into evidence for their consideration. This couldn't possibly have been good for the prosecution in the jury's eyes. And as if that weren't bad enough, on cross-examination of prosecution witnesses, whenever the defense alluded to the statement in any of its questions, Clark or another prosecutor would stand up in front of the jury and vigorously object to any reference to the statement. That looked absolutely terrible, and has to have hurt the prosecution's credibility in the jury's eyes. The jurors have to have asked themselves why the prosecution wanted to prevent them from hearing what Simpson had said."

Bugliosi, *Outrage: The Five Reasons Why O.J. Simpson Got Away With Murder,* pp. 106–07 (Norton, 1996).

(b) Marcia Clark explained the prosecution's strategy in withholding the statement in the following terms:

"That fucking statement! How many hours had Hank and Chris and I—in fact, the entire team—spent agonizing over what to do about it? We'd looked at it from every side. There were a couple good arguments for allowing it in. Phil had gotten Simpson to admit that the last time he'd visited Bundy was five days earlier and he told detectives he had not been bleeding at that time. That made it patently absurd for the defense to argue that the blood drops had been left by Simpson on a social visit to Bundy before June 12. But on the other hand, the defense wasn't even thinking about arguing that Simpson had bled there on some other occasion, so we'd gain nothing.

At one point, Simpson had said that the last thing he did before leaving for the airport was to get his cell phone out of the Bronco. That part I liked. When you combined it with the cell phone records showing the call to Paula Barbieri at 10:03, it placed him in the Bronco just before the murders. But the rest of the statement was a disaster for us. Not only were the cops' questions real softballs, but when Phil asked whether Nicole ever got any threatening phone calls, Simpson responded, 'You—you guys haven't told me anything. I—I have no idea what happened. . . . Every time I ask you guys, you say you're going to tell me in a bit.'

Nice bit of sympathy grabbing. The defense was sure to play it for maximum shmaltz: 'Poor Juice. Mean old cops won't tell him anything. Is that any way to treat a grieving man who's had no sleep in the past two days? He's doing everything he can to cooperate. He's giving a statement without an attorney present—surely not the action of a guilty man. And a blood sample? Why, he'd rolled his sleeve right up. Now, I ask you,

ladies and gentlemen of the jury: why would he be so coopera-
tive if he were guilty?'

The only strategy worth considering was whether we
should try and get into evidence that one snippet of tape where
Simpson talked about getting his car phone out of the Bronco
just before he left. That short excerpt would be limited enough
to prevent the defense from getting the rest of the statement
in. Nothing else was needed to explain or qualify it, according
to the evidence code. Of course, the downside to playing one
brief segment was that the jury would naturally wonder why
we didn't want them to hear the rest of the tape.

On the other hand, if we didn't play the statement, we
could still put on the phone records showing that a call had
been made from Simpson's cell phone to Paula at 10:03 p.m. A
reasonable juror would infer that he'd been in the Bronco. The
defense would have no way to counter that but to call Simpson
and get him to try to explain it. That was an idea we all liked.
If we could force Simpson into the blue chair, we just might be
in fat city.''

Clark, *Without A Doubt,* pp. 399–400 (Viking, 1997).

D. FORMER TESTIMONY OF THANO PERATIS

1. THE EVIDENCE

Thano Peratis was a male nurse employed in the jail dispensary at police headquarters in Los Angeles. On June 13, 1994, after
police detectives finished questioning O.J. Simpson, Detective Phil
Vanatter brought him to the dispensary to have blood drawn for
the comparative testing of the blood found at the crime scenes and
in the Bronco. In testimony presented both to the Grand Jury and
at the Preliminary Hearing, Thano Peratis testified that he withdrew approximately 8 C.C.'s of blood:

TRANSCRIPT OF GRAND JURY PROCEEDINGS,
JUNE 22, 1994:

Thano M. Peratis, called as a witness before the Los Angeles
County Grand Jury, was duly sworn and testified as follows:

"Q. Were you requested to remove blood from the arm of a
person by the name of Mr. Orenthal James Simpson?

A. Not quite with that. The initials were O.J. Simpson, yes.

Q. Did you remove a blood sample from that person?

A. Yes, I did.

Q. On June 13?

A.   Yes.

Q.   I will show you People's 23 and you tell me if that's the person you removed blood from.

A.   Yes, it is.

Q.   Can you describe for us what is the method by which you removed blood from Mr. Simpson.

A.   I put a tourniquet on his arm, cleaned the site with aqueous zephrin and put a 10 C.C. syringe with about a No. 20 needle in the vein in his arm and I withdrew about 8 C.C.'s of blood. And then I put the blood into a test tube that had a preservative called E.D.T.A. and then handed it to the officer, to the detective, and then put a dressing on him.

Q.   On the arm?

A.   Yes.

Q.   Approximately how much blood did you remove?

A.   Approximately 8 C.C.'s."

TRANSCRIPT OF PRELIMINARY
HEARING, JULY 7, 1994.

THANO PERATIS, called as a witness by and on behalf of the People, having been duly sworn, was examined and testified as follows:

Cross Examination by Mr. Shapiro:

"Q.   How much blood did you draw from Mr. Simpson?

A.   Approximately 8 C.C.'s.

Q.   When you say 'approximately,' you did not measure the amount?

A.   Well, it could have been 7.9 or it could have been 8.1. I just looked at the syringe and it looked at about 8 C.C.'s. I withdrew the needle from his arm.

Q.   Nobody asked you to take a precise amount of blood.

A.   No.

Q.   And you did not record the amount of blood you took.

A.   No. It's just routinely that's about the amount I usually draw.

Q.   And you do this on a routine basis every day? Do you do this every day in the jail, take blood?

A.   Whenever—not for this sort of thing. It's usually for alcohol, blood alcohol.

Q.   But you do take blood on a regular basis.

A. Yes.

Q. And you take the same amount of blood?

A. Yes."

2. THE TACTICAL CONTEXT

During his opening statement, Johnnie Cochran stated that the evidence would show blood had been "planted" in the case, and that some of the blood taken from O.J. Simpson by Nurse Thano Peratis was "missing." The logs maintained during all testing procedures, recording how much blood was withdrawn from the test tube, together with the amount remaining in the test tube, only accounted for 6.5 C.C.'s of blood. The prosecutors then reinterviewed Thano Peratis, and he allegedly told them he was "mistaken" in his testimony to the Grand Jury and at the Preliminary Hearing. His new "estimate" was that he had withdrawn about 6.5 C.C.'s of blood.

The prosecutors then decided not to call Thano Peratis as a witness. When they rested their case, the defense filed a Motion to Strike all evidence regarding comparisons to purported blood of O.J. Simpson, on the grounds that the People did not offer evidence to show a chain of custody between the blood that was removed from his person and the reference sample that was subsequently analyzed and presented to the jury as the blood of O.J. Simpson. The prosecutors argued that they need not call the nurse who drew the blood to establish the chain of custody. Since Detective Vanatter was present when the blood was drawn, they argued his testimony was sufficient to establish chain of custody, citing *People v. Lewis,* 191 Cal.App.3d 1288 (1987). Judge Ito denied the Motion to Strike. The defense then decided to call Thano Peratis as their own witness. At that point, they discovered Thano Peratis had just undergone triple bypass open heart surgery, and his recuperation would prevent his appearance as a witness. The defense then filed an affidavit from his cardiologist, dated July 16, 1995, concluding:

> "At this point in his recovery, the tension, stress and anxiety that would be produced by any court appearance, much less this one, or even subjecting him to an examination in his own home with court personnel and combative lawyers examining and cross-examining him, would indeed be life threatening. It is my medical opinion that it is impossible for Mr. Peratis to offer testimony under any reasonable condition at any time in the next several months."

The defense then offered the former testimony of Thano Peratis presented to the Grand Jury and at the Preliminary Hearing.

3. DEFENSE ARGUMENT

California Evidence Code Section 1291 provides:

"(a) Evidence of former testimony is not made inadmissible by the hearsay rule if the declarant is unavailable as a witness and:

(1) The former testimony is offered against a person who offered it in evidence in his own behalf on the former occasion or against the successor in interest of such person; or

(2) The party against whom the former testimony is offered was a party to the action or proceeding in which the testimony was given and had the right and opportunity to cross-examine the declarant with an interest and motive similar to that which he has at the hearing."

California Evidence Code Section 240 provides:

"(a) Except as otherwise provided in subdivision (b), 'unavailable as a witness' means that the declarant is any of the following: . . .

(3) dead or unable to testify at the hearing because of then existing physical or mental illness or infirmity."

The leading California case on the admissibility of former testimony offered against a person who offered it in evidence in his own behalf on the former occasion is *People v. Salas*, 58 Cal.App.3d 460 (1976), authored by Justice Bernard Jefferson, the author of the *California Evidence Benchbook*. In *Salas*, the *prosecution* offered the testimony of a witness called by the *defense* at the preliminary hearing, after showing repeated efforts to locate and subpoena him were unsuccessful. The defense argued that the witness had been called as an adverse witness at the preliminary hearing to provide material for subsequent impeachment. The court noted the important difference between subdivision (a)(1) and subdivision (a)(2) of Section 1291:

"... the Former Testimony Exception to the hearsay rule, created by Evidence Code Section 1291, subdivision (a)(1), which makes evidence of former testimony admissible against a party who, as a party to the former proceeding, *offered* the testimony in his own behalf, contains no requirement as to similarity in interest or motive for a party's examination of the declarant between the former proceeding and the current trial."

58 Cal.App.3d at 468. The court then concluded:

"The case at bench is in complete accord with the theory that undergirds and justifies the admissibility of evidence of the former testimony of an unavailable declarant against a party to the current trial who, as a party to the former proceeding, offered such testimony in his own behalf on the former occasion. Under subdivision (a)(1) of the Evidence Code Section 1291, a party's previous *direct* and *redirect* examination of a witness called by him on the previous occasion is justifiably considered to constitute an adequate substitute for such party's present right to cross-examine the declarant."

58 Cal.App.3d at 469.

The unavailability of a witness because of then existing physical or mental illness or infirmity need not be permanent unavailability. As the court noted in *People v. Gomez,* 26 Cal. App.3d 225, 230 (1972):

"In like fashion, the witness presently unavailable because of disabling illness or infirmity ultimately may recover; but if the fact or time of recovery lies only in an uncertain or distant future, no good reason appears for denying the admission of testimony previously given. In recognition of this, Evidence Code Section 240(a), subdivision (3), refers to unavailability 'to testify *at the hearing* because of *then existing* ... illness or infirmity.' (Emphasis added). Such a showing of unavailability seems to have been recognized in California even before adoption of the Evidence Code."

In *People v. Maciole,* 197 Cal.App.3d 262, 282–83 (1987), the court upheld a finding of unavailability of a witness based on medical testimony that she would be "unable to testify without suffering substantial trauma." The doctor described symptoms of extreme stress, including absence of menstruation, water retention, acne, hair loss, chronic gastritis, and hyperventilation syndrome, and concluded that, while the witness might suffer no reaction at all from testifying, "there's maybe a 70% chance that it could—that it would be detrimental to her." In declaring the witness unavailable, the trial court noted,

"And under the Code, I believe that I'm obliged to find that the witness is unavailable and that I can't—it would be improper for me to make—find judgments on how important her testimony is in deciding how much danger to her health we're willing to tolerate."

197 Cal.App.3d at 282.

4. PROSECUTION ARGUMENT

The prosecution did not actively oppose the admission of the former testimony of Thano Peratis. Instead, they prepared to counter it by having him retract it on video tape. On July 27, 1995, during Peratis's recuperation at home, Prosecutor Hank Goldberg, accompanied by District Attorney Investigators Steve Oppler and Teresa Ramirez brought a video camera and recorded an interview in which Peratis demonstrated how he used the syringe with the calibration side down, and simply estimated how much blood was being drawn. He claimed that, after Johnnie Cochran's Opening Statement at the trial, he thought he "screwed up" when he testified he withdrew 8 C.C.'s of blood. He did a "little experiment" by injecting a syringe of water into a vial to the point which he though the Simpson blood vial had been filled. He then discovered the calibration showed 6.5 C.C.'s.

The video tape was offered pursuant to California Evidence Code Section 1202:

"Evidence of a statement or other conduct by a declarant that is inconsistent with a statement by such declarant is not inadmissible for the purpose of attacking the credibility of the declarant though he is not given and has not had an opportunity to deny such inconsistent statement or other conduct. Any other evidence offered to attack or support the credibility of the declarant is admissible if if would have been admissible had the declarant been a witness at the hearing."

The defense objected that Section 1202 could not be applied to recantations subsequent to the prior testimony, and it if were, it denied the defendant of his constitutional right of confrontation and cross-examination. These objections were overruled and the video-tape was played for the jury after editing out the portions deemed to be an out of court "experiment."

5. JUDGES' RULINGS

The former testimony of Thano Peratis was presented through the transcripts and through video tape of his testimony at the Preliminary Hearing, which was televised. Judge Ito instructed the jury that the video tape of his recantation was being admitted for the limited purpose of assessing the credibility of his former testimony. The following instruction was given to the jury at the conclusion of the trial:

"Evidence of the Thano Peratis video taped statement, which is People's Exhibit 615, which may include statements that were consistent or inconsistent with his former testimony presented by reading the transcript of his former testimony given at the preliminary hearing, may be considered by you solely for the purpose of testing the credibility of Mr. Peratis' former testimony."

At the time of the civil trial, Mr. Peratis had recovered and was called as a witness by the Plaintiffs. He testified in accord with his video-taped recantation, that he thought he drew about 6.5 C.C.'s of blood. He was then cross-examined with the inconsistencies in his grand jury and preliminary hearing testimony.

6.   COMMENTS AND QUESTIONS

(a) Consider how the defense might argue to the *jury* that the video taped statement was unfair because it was done without notice to the defense or opportunity to cross-examine. Steve Oppler was called as a witness for the prosecution to authenticate the video tape. During a break in his testimony, defense attorney Peter Neufeld asked to speak to him alone. Mr. Oppler refused, insisting that a prosecutor be present during any attempt to interview him. When he resumed the witness stand, Mr. Neufeld asked him if he had refused to speak to him alone during the recess just concluded. Mr. Oppler conceded that he had:

"Q.   And sir, is that because you felt as a witness that it's important to have both sides present when I interview you?

A.   I—I don't know specifically what I thought. I just—I was in the middle of you questioning me, and to do it off the stand, I did not feel comfortable.

Q.   Well, let me ask you this. Did you think that it would be better practice, sir, that when you went out to Mr. Peratis' to have someone present from the other side as well?

[Objection sustained]."

(b) The video tape was also challenged on the ground that off-screen coaching was taking place. The tape itself had a built in timer, which disclosed a fourteen minute gap during which the video recorder was turned off. The prosecution explained that after concluding the interview, they turned the camera back on for a forgotten follow-up question. Hank Goldberg complains that the attack on this evidence "attempted to imply that Steve Oppler, Teresa Ramirez, and I were part of a cover-up relating to Thano's videotape statement.... Perhaps I was being hypersensitive, for now I was being accused of being a conspirator." Goldberg, *The Prosecution Responds,* p. 280–81 (Birch Lane Press, 1996). Is it unethical for a lawyer to suggest that evidence prepared under the supervision of opposing counsel is unfair or misleading? What precautions can a lawyer take to anticipate and defuse such suggestions?

(c) Justice Jefferson's opinion in *Salas* suggests that Section 1291 (a)(1) only permits a party to offer testimony he elicited on *direct* or *redirect* examination in the prior proceeding. Note that the Peratis Preliminary Hearing testimony that the defense offered was elicited by Mr. Shapiro on *cross-examination.* Should that have precluded its admissibility under the former testimony exception? In *People v. Rice,* 59 Cal.App.3d 998, 1005 (1976), the Court excluded former testimony of an unavailable witness because the proponent elicited it on cross-examination in the prior proceeding. Could the same testimony be offered instead under Section 1291(a)(2), because the party against whom it was offered at the Preliminary Hearing (the prosecution) could have questioned the witness on *redirect* to the same extent they could conduct cross-examination had he been called by the defense? This issue was never raised by the prosecution in the *Simpson* criminal trial. If the defense had been aware of the holding in *People v. Rice,* would they have been obligated to call it to the Court's attention?

(d) The jurors in the criminal trial apparently rejected Thano Peratis' recantation.

> Carrie Bess: "I had a hard time with Mr. Peratis. His first testimony as a witness was okay. But when he had to go back again and indicate he's not sure about how much blood he drew, I had a problem because he's been a nurse for what, twenty, thirty years? He draws blood all the time. I figured if you're doing this on a consistent basis, I have a problem when you state you don't know how much you draw. Because his testimony in the first place was, 'Yes, I did draw 8 C.C.'s. It could have been 7.9 or 8.1 because this is something I do all the time. I would have been either under .1C.C. or over .1 C.C.' But, then all of a sudden, the new testimony is he doesn't know, the syringe was turned a different way and it was a 10 C.C. syringe instead of an 8 C.C. syringe. I had a real problem with that."

> Marsha Rubin–Jackson: "When Mr. Peratis' testimony came up and he had testified before the grand jury, and, I guess, the preliminary hearings, that he had 7.9 or 8 C.C.'s of blood, but then he comes up with maybe it was more like 6.5, then I started to think, *Well* ... That was one of my turnaround points because there was always talk around about how there was blood missing, there was blood missing, there was blood missing. . . . It just started getting sloppy."

Coolely, Bess & Rubin–Jackson, *Madam Foreman: A Rush to Judgment?*, pp. 116–17, 122–23 (Dove, 1995).

Chapter IV

CROSS–EXAMINATION, IMPEACH-MENT AND REHABILITATION OF WITNESSES

A. CROSS–EXAMINATION OF FUHRMAN RE: RACIAL BIAS

1. THE EVIDENCE

In the course of pre-trial discovery and investigation, the defense located three items it hoped to utilize in the cross examination of Detective Mark Fuhrman:

1. A psychiatric evaluation completed in 1981–82, when Fuhrman filed a disability claim for job related stress with the Los Angeles Police Department. In his "Occupational History," the evaluation noted:

> "He was in the Marines from 1970 to 1975. During his last six months, he 'got tired of having a bunch of Mexicans and Niggers that should be in prison, telling (him) they weren't going to do something.' He did not like the voluntary military. He did well in the Marines and was promoted."

The evaluation included numerous descriptions of violent outbursts in which Fuhrman claimed he had beaten and injured suspects:

> "He was in a fight 'at least every other day.' He says, 'They shoot little kids and they shoot other people. We'd catch them and beat them, and we'd get sued or suspended. I had two friends shot by a bunch of those slimes.' He rose a 'beef' for 18 months regarding 'what happened to four guys' that he and his partner caught. He says that he was 'smarter than the people who investigated this incident.' He says, 'You don't see, you don't remember and it didn't happen. Those are the three things you say and you stick to it.' "

The disability claim was denied, based on the psychiatric conclusion that Fuhrman "was deliberately exaggerating his preoccupation with violence in order to make himself appear unsuitable for police work." The report concluded:

> "There is no work-related psychiatric disability. This man has not changed significantly since his Marine days. He has personality problems, but they are long-standing. He is able to work as a police officer, but doesn't want to do so. If he returns to police work his casual attitude toward violence will have to be evaluated by his superiors in terms of assignment, and he might benefit from re-education about the use of violence by the police officer."

2. The defense obtained a sworn declaration from Kathleen Bell, dated August 16, 1994, in which she stated that she met Mark Fuhrman in 1985 or 1986 at a Marine Corps Recruiting Office in the complex where she was employed:

> "I was introduced to Mark Fuhrman by a Marine Corps recruiter. During our initial conversation, Mark Fuhrman told me he was a former Marine and currently a local police officer. During our conversation, Mark Fuhrman stated that he would pull over any vehicle that was occupied by a black man and a white woman. I then asked him, 'What if you didn't have a good reason to pull them over?' Mr. Fuhrman then stated, 'I'd make one up.' I then asked Fuhrman, 'What if two people are in love?' Fuhrman then appeared to get disgusted with me and stated, 'If I had my way, they would take all the niggers, put them in a big group and burn them.' I became visibly upset, began to cry, and left the office."

3. Mark Fuhrman was identified as one of the officers involved in the 1988 shooting and arrest of Joseph Britton, an armed robbery suspect who filed a lawsuit alleging police brutality. He claimed that after he was shot while fleeing an attempted robbery at an automated teller machine, an unidentified officer approached him and said, "you stupid nigger, why did you run." He claimed that a discarded knife was picked up and moved next to him, to justify the shooting. When he asked for some help with his bleeding wounds, an officer said, "Why don't you die and save us the paperwork." He was unable to identify Fuhrman as the arresting officer, but police reports identified Fuhrman as one of the officers who opened fire and as the officer who recovered a butcher's knife adjacent to the suspect's feet.

2. THE TACTICAL CONTEXT

During litigation of the pretrial suppression motions, it became apparent that Detective Mark Fuhrman played a key role in the investigation leading to the arrest of O.J. Simpson, even though Fuhrman had been relieved as a Detective in the case in the early morning hours of June 13, 1994. He guided the detectives from the Bundy crime scene to O.J. Simpson's home, discovered a "blood spot" on the door of the Bronco parked on the street, went over the wall to admit the other detectives to the premises, questioned Kato Kaelin, and then found the "bloody glove" in debris behind the house. The defense focused intense investigative efforts on gathering evidence that might be used to challenge Fuhrman's credibility, but the most important discovery was completely fortuitous and serendipitous. The statement from Kathleen Bell was volunteered after she recognized Fuhrman on television, as he testified during the Preliminary Hearing.

The defense filed a *Pitchess* Motion, seeking discovery of any complaints filed against Detective Fuhrman by others he might have arrested, and any personnel records that would substantiate his racial animosity towards African–Americans. (See *Pitchess v. Superior Court,* 11 Cal.3d 531 (1974); California Evidence Code Sections 1043, 1045). Judge Ito examined the personnel file *in camera*, and concluded no relevant material came within the five-year time limit imposed by statute. The three items of evidence were cited as support for the *Pitchess* Motion. These items were then themselves challenged by the Prosecution in a Motion in Limine, to preclude their use in the cross-examination of Detective Fuhrman at trial.

3. PROSECUTION ARGUMENT

In this motion, we ask the Court to preclude the defense from cross-examining Detective Mark Fuhrman during trial regarding three alleged aspects of his background and from introducing other evidence regarding those aspects. These areas are the detective's 1981–83 Worker's Compensation lawsuit, testimony of a Kathleen Bell regarding an alleged incident in 1985 or 1986, and a civil suit by a man named Joseph Britton regarding an alleged incident in 1988.

Throughout the course of this case, the defense has indicated their intent to delve into these matters at trial. The defense has stated a theory, devoid of evidentiary support, that Det. Fuhrman planted the glove which was recovered from the defendant's Rockingham estate. The claimed reason for the attack on Det. Fuhrman's credibility is to support that theory. However, the inflammatory, remote evidence the defense will seek to admit can offer nothing to support that theory because it was physically impossible for Det. Fuhrman to have planted the glove. Thus, such evidence is rendered devoid of any valid purpose or probative value.

The attempt by the defense to introduce this evidence is analogous to attempts to introduce evidence that a third party, rather than the defendant, committed the crimes because the defense posture is that Det. Fuhrman, rather than the defendant, dropped the glove at Rockingham. Case law is clear that evidence which merely establishes a motive or opportunity in a third party to commit a crime is insufficient to raise a reasonable doubt as to the defendant's guilt and is properly excluded from trial. Our Supreme Court has repeatedly so held in affirming death sentences of convicted murderers. If, as the case law consistently holds, the defense is properly precluded from introducing evidence of a third party's culpability for the crimes themselves, then surely a court can and should properly exclude evidence of the purported "motive" of a third party to act on an alleged bias in which the act alleged was virtually incapable of commission.

The evidence the defense will seek to introduce to discredit Det. Fuhrman should also be excluded under Evidence Code Section 352. As we will demonstrate, the evidence has no probative value. Further, whatever arguable probative value it may have is substantially outweighed by the very real danger of undue prejudice to the prosecution, undue consumption of time in terms of the time it would take to elicit and rebut, as well as its tendency to confuse the true issues in the case and mislead the jury.

a. The Defense Attack on Detective Mark Fuhrman.

The defense opines that Det. Fuhrman saw two gloves at the crime scene, that he removed one of them and planted it in a remote location on the defendant's estate.[17] In propounding their theory, the defense makes the following accusations against Det. Fuhrman: he is a racist, he did not like O.J. Simpson, he disapproved of Simpson's marriage to a caucasian woman and he planted the glove in the hope that the presence of one of the gloves from the crime scene on the defendant's property would cause the defendant to be convicted of double murder.

---

17. Det. Fuhrman testified at the preliminary hearing both on direct and cross exam that he saw a glove. At one point during the latter testimony, when he was consistently testifying as to "the glove," he said he saw "them" at Ronald Goldman's feet, referring, apparently, either to the glove or to the glove and watch cap which was also in the vicinity. He was not questioned about this ambiguity in his answer. The defense, however, used it as an opportunity to deflect attention from the defendant and seized the statement as grounds to launch an attack on Det. Fuhrman.

To state the defense theory is to reveal its total absurdity. Not only is there no evidence to support the defense theory, there can *never* be any evidence to support it, for all of the facts disprove this bizarre "theory."

First, the limousine driver saw Kato holding a flashlight, investigating loud thumps. Simultaneously, he saw the defendant enter the front door of the house. The timing of the loud thumps, Kato's attempt to investigate the noise, and the defendant's entry into his house all coincide perfectly with the defendant being the person who dropped the glove behind Kato's guesthouse. The logical inference under the circumstances is that the defendant dropped the glove. To believe the defense theory would leave no explanation for the "earthquake-like", loud thumps Kato heard against his residence wall approximately an hour and a half before the victim's bodies were discovered.

Second, the photographer who finished photographing the scene before Det. Fuhrman ever arrived, did not see or photograph a second glove anywhere at the crime scene.

Third, the officers and sergeant who were at the scene long before Det. Fuhrman ever arrived did not see a second glove.

Fourth, the officers, sergeant, detective and photographer all saw Detective Fuhrman while he was at the scene and did not see him remove any glove from the scene.

Fifth, Det. Fuhrman went to the scene and was accompanied while there by his partner, Det. Ron Phillips, who did not see him remove or plant any glove.

Sixth, Det. Fuhrman's scrutiny of Kato's shoes at the guesthouse at Rockingham to determine whether Kato might be the murder suspect is inconsistent with a preordained plan to frame the defendant.

Seventh, the defense theory does not account for the forensic evidence in the case which places the defendant at the crime scene.

Eighth, to accept the defense position that Det. Fuhrman removed a glove from the crime scene and planted it at Rockingham, one would have to believe he did so despite his own knowledge that a sergeant and at least five uniformed police officers had been at the crime scene for approximately two hours and none of those people had seen two gloves at the scene. He would also have to have believed that neither Officer Riske nor Det. Ron Phillips had seen two gloves. Further, he would have to have believed that the police photographer, who carefully photographed the scene prior to his arrival, had overlooked one of two gloves. Therefore, not only is there *no evidence* to support the straw-grasping speculation by the defense, their theory is absolutely refuted by the evidence.

b. Mere Evidence of Motive or Opportunity is Insufficient to Warrant the Introduction of Evidence that a Third Party is Culpable, Even if Such Evidence Was Credible.

The sole purpose of the defense attempt to discredit Det. Fuhrman's testimony is to support the speculation that Det. Fuhrman planted the glove. To reach that conclusion, the defense has attempted to characterize Det. Fuhrman as having a motive to want the defendant to be convicted. The defense theory then leaps to two conclusions: (1) if the detective wanted the defendant to be convicted, he would have planted the glove and, therefore, (2) he did indeed plant the glove. This reasoning strains logic, common sense, and is contrary to all of the evidence. As our Supreme Court has explained:

> "Except as otherwise provided by statute, no evidence is admissible except relevant evidence. (Evid. Code § 350). Relevant evidence is evidence 'having any tendency in reason to prove or disprove any disputed fact.... ' (Id., § 210). The trial court is vested with wide discretion in determining the relevance of evidence. [citation]. The court, however, has no discretion to admit irrelevant evidence. (People v. Turner, 37 Cal.3d 302, 321 (1984)). 'Speculative inferences that are derived from evidence cannot be deemed to be relevant to establish the speculatively inferred fact in light of Evidence Code Section 210, which requires that evidence offered to prove or disprove a disputed fact must have a tendency in reason for such purpose.' (citation)."

People v. Babbit, 45 Cal.3d 660, 681–82 (1988)(emphasis added) (affirming conviction and death sentence in upholding trial court's exclusion of evidence of violent nature of movies shown on TV the night of victim's murder which defense claimed was relevant to defendant's state of mind because "the inference which defendant sought to have drawn from the proffered evidence is clearly speculative, and evidence which produces only speculative inferences is irrelevant evidence."). The inferences the defense seeks to draw in order to conclude that Det. Fuhrman planted the glove do not even rise to the level of speculation, for even speculation draws, in part, on reality for its premise. The defense hypothesis is both irrational and illogical in view of the actual evidence in this case.

Essentially, the defense theory is no different than that often used by defendants to demonstrate that some third party had a motive to commit the crime. The defense is not accusing Det. Fuhrman of committing the murders. They are, however, accusing him of an act which the evidence attributes to the defendant, that is, leaving the glove on the defendant's property. Therefore, case law concerning the admissibility of evidence of a third party having a motive to commit the crime is analogous to the instant situation. That case law uniformly holds that evidence of mere motive or opportunity to commit a crime is insufficient to raise a reasonable doubt as to the defendant's guilt. The California Supreme Court has consistently upheld the trial court's preclusion of evidence of third party culpability which had far more probative value than the evidence in this case.

In *People v. Hall,* 41 Cal.3d 826 (1986), the California Supreme Court held that, to be admissible, evidence of third party culpability must be capable of raising a reasonable doubt as to the defendant's guilt. That Court has repeatedly affirmed the exclusion of such evidence by the trial courts due to the defendant's inability to meet that standard. For example, in *People v. Pride,* 3 Cal.4th 195 (1992), the defense complained on appeal that the trial court had erred in disallowing cross-examination that the husband of one of the murder victims received $40,000 in life insurance money and remarried one year after the murder. In affirming the murder conviction and death sentence, the Supreme Court approved the trial court's ruling and held as follows:

> Commonsense relevance limits apply. Evidence of mere motive or opportunity to commit the crime in another person, without more, will not suffice to raise a reasonable doubt about a defendant's guilt; there must be direct or circumstantial evidence linking the third person to the actual perpetration of the crime.

3 Cal.4th at 237–38.... Under this authority, to paraphrase *Hall,* evidence of Det. Fuhrman's motive is inadmissible in the absence of "direct or circumstantial evidence linking him to the actual ..." planting of the glove.

c. The Evidence Should Be Excluded Under Evidence Code Section 352.

... An important consideration in the Court's assessment of the probative value of the evidence is its remoteness. The defense evidence is very old. The Worker's Compensation lawsuit was finished over eleven years ago. The Kathleen Bell incident is alleged to have occurred in 1985 or 1986, which is nine to ten years ago. The Britton incident occurred six years ago, in 1988. The extremely slim probative value to the evidence disappears when its remoteness is considered, and it loses all relevancy.

Under the "Pitchess" statutes, discovery of the evidence at issue would have been barred as too remote to be relevant even for discovery, which carries a much more relaxed standard that that required to introduce evidence at trial. (See Evidence Code Section

832.5(b), requiring police departments to maintain personnel files for only five years.).

. . . Whatever slight probative value the evidence may have is far outweighed by both subsections of Evidence Code Section 352. First, its admission will necessitate undue consumption of time because the prosecution will be entitled to rebut such evidence. With regard to the Worker's Compensation claim, the mere fact that such a claim was filed in 1981 is irrelevant. If any psychiatrist involved in that claim were allowed to give an opinion against Det. Fuhrman, the prosecution would introduce testimony of other psychiatrists in Det. Fuhrman's favor. Regarding the testimony from Kathleen Bell, the prosecution would call in rebuttal several Marines who have stated that Det. Fuhrman made no such remarks. If the defense seeks to admit evidence that Det. Fuhrman planted a weapon on Joseph Britton, the prosecution would impeach Mr. Britton with his televised admission that there were several officers who were present and could have planted the weapon and his further admission that he could not say Det. Fuhrman was the officer who planted it. Further, the prosecution would seek to introduce in rebuttal to any evidence tending to portray Det. Fuhrman as a racist, testimony from the African-American detective with whom he regularly plays basketball as well as other African–American individuals who know him well.

Second, the evidence creates a substantial danger of undue prejudice. . . . In *People v. Von Villas,* 10 Cal.App.4th 201 (1992), the defense sought to introduce the details of the rape of the wife of one of the defendants as a reason for the defendant's purchase of a wig which he claimed was to facilitate his search for the rapist (rather than for use as a disguise when he committed murder). The trial court excluded the evidence under Section 352. The Court of Appeal upheld its exclusion, holding that "the details of the rape would have been highly prejudicial, with little, if any, probative value." *Id.* at 270. The Court explained as follows:

> The assertion that details of the rape would have bolstered Ford's argument is highly speculative. The evidence was thus properly excluded. [citation omitted]. Furthermore, the excluded rape evidence is highly prejudicial. The details of the rape might have engendered a sympathy among the jury for Ford that would have had no bearing on his culpability for the charged crimes.

(*Ibid.*). Here, the defendant is African–American and the victims were Caucasian. In addition, the defendant is already a very sympathetic figure. Therefore, the allegation that Det. Fuhrman is racist is highly inflammatory and particularly prejudicial.

... The evidence would also create substantial danger of confusing the issues and misleading the jury. Although very important evidence, the glove found at Rockingham is not the only critical evidence in this case. This is not a situation where, for example, the uncorroborated testimony of a rape victim is attacked on credibility grounds. It bears emphasis that Det. Fuhrman was not an eyewitness to the murders or any other conduct. He merely found the glove. His credibility is at issue only insofar as the defense seeks to promulgate speculation that he planted the glove. Therefore, allowing the defense to launch an inflammatory, all-out attack on the detective during the trial would not serve to further the ascertainment of the truth, but, rather, has the substantial danger of confusing the issues and misleading the jury. This is particularly true in the area of racism which is an inherently volatile subject in our society. The issue is whether the defendant committed these murders, not whether the detective is a racist. To turn the latter into an issue at trial would only divert the jury's attention from the true issues in the case. Thus, the evidence should be excluded on this ground as well.

Det. Fuhrman has been repeatedly maligned by the defense in this case. Because of the clever defense manipulation of the media, the undue harassment and undue embarrassment he has undergone can never be completely undone. Evidence Code Section 765 provides, in pertinent part, that:

> "The court shall exercise reasonable control over the mode of interrogation of a witness so as to make such interrogation as rapid, as distinct, and as effective for the ascertainment of the truth, as may be, and to protect the witness from undue harassment or embarrassment."

4. DEFENSE ARGUMENT

The People's Motion to Exclude Evidence Regarding the Credibility of L.A.P.D. Detective Mark Fuhrman suffers from four major flaws: First, it is based on an oversimplification and misconception of the defense tactics and strategy. While there is no requirement that the defense reveal their tactics and strategy to the prosecution in advance of trial, it will be readily apparent that the credibility of Detective Mark Fuhrman is an issue that cannot be avoided or suppressed. Second, the motion is based on factual assumptions that have not been established and will be fiercely contested at trial. Third, the motion is supported by no case authority other than a lame attempt to analogize to a rule of evidence that has no application to this situation. Finally, the motion is premature, attempting to limit cross-examination of a witness before the parameters of his direct examination have even been defined.

a. *Relevance of the Credibility of Detective Mark Fuhrman.*

The underlying premise of the People's Motion is that Detective Mark Fuhrman's credibility will be attacked to support a theory that he planted the glove which was recovered from the defendant's Rockingham estate. This oversimplification misconstrues the relevance of Detective Fuhrman's credibility on a wide spectrum of issues, including:

1. The credibility of his account of a 1985 incident in which he allegedly encountered Mr. Simpson and Nicole Brown prior to their marriage.

2. The motivation for and credibility of a letter he wrote in 1989, purporting to describe that encounter in vivid detail.

3. The credibility of his account of the reason detectives went to the home of O.J. Simpson on the morning of June 13, 1994 and his role in that decision and its execution.

4. The credibility of his description of the position of the defendant's Ford Bronco parked in front of the Rockingham residence.

5. The discrepancies between his account of the sequence of events at the Rockingham residence on the morning of June 13, 1994, and the accounts offered by other detectives and witnesses and written records.

6. The credibility of his testimony regarding the discovery of spots resembling blood on the Ford Bronco and in the driveway of the Rockingham residence.

7. The credibility of his account of the interrogation of Kato Kaelin and the search of Kaelin's room.

8. The credibility of his account of his participation in the execution of search warrants at the Rockingham residence.

9. His failure to record any of his activity at the Rockingham premises in any notes or reports or official accounts of the case.

10. His role in and responsibility for the failure of L.A.P.D. officers to follow proper techniques to preserve evidence without contamination.

11. His testimony at the preliminary hearing referring to the gloves at the Bundy crime scene as "them."

California Evidence Code Section 780 provides that "any matter that has a tendency in reason to prove or disprove the truthfulness" of the testimony of a witness may be considered, including:

"(e) his character for honesty or veracity or their opposites;

(f) the existence or nonexistence of a bias, interest or other motive;

(h) a statement made by him which is inconsistent with any part of his testimony at the hearing;

(i) the existence or nonexistence of any fact testified to by him;

(j) his attitude toward the action in which he testifies or toward the giving of testimony."

Relevant evidence is defined in Evidence Code Section 210 to include evidence relevant to the credibility of a witness.

"It follows, therefore, that even though proffered evidence does *not* have any bearing upon a contested fact in the action, if it tends to affect the credibility of a witness it is relevant, and an objection on the ground that the proffered evidence is *collateral* or *irrelevant* should be overruled. The test of relevancy for evidence offered to attack or support the credibility of a witness is *not* whether the evidence will elucidate any of the main issues, but whether it will *aid* the trier of fact in *appraising* the witness' credibility and in *assessing* the probative value of the witness' testimony."

Jefferson, *Synopsis of California Evidence Law,* § 21.9, p. 277 (CEB 1985). The three items challenged by the prosecution include Detective Fuhrman's expressions of intense racial hostility in attempting to qualify for a disability pension shortly before the 1985 incident in which he first encountered O.J. Simpson and Nicole Brown; his expressions of hostility to interracial couples at approximately the same time as the 1985 encounter, and his involvement in physically moving evidence to enhance the case against a suspect he shot at and arrested in 1988. All three of these incidents relate directly to the existence of bias, interest or other motive, as well as his attitude toward this action. While the defense is well aware that evidence of specific instances of conduct relevant only to prove a trait of character are not admissible to attack the credibility of a witness pursuant to Evidence Code Section 787, the relevance of this evidence would not be limited to showing his character for dishonesty; it would be highly relevant to showing his bias and hostility toward the defendant in this case.

b. Inaccurate Factual Assumptions in the People's Motion.

. . . The People attempt to support the arrogant factual conclusion that "there can *never* be any evidence to support" the defense theory. Their "facts", however, include evidence which has never been presented in this case, or tested by cross-examination. Great emphasis is placed upon the allegation that the photographer completed his photography of the scene before Detective Fuhrman arrived. The photographer has never testified in any proceedings in this case, and in fact a "statement" from the photographer was not even produced until December, 1994. The statement is dated November 22, 1994, two months after the trial of this case commenced. The photographer has not even been designated on the prosecution's witness list, so evidently they have no intention of producing him as a witness at trial.

Great reliance is also placed upon factual statements allegedly emanating from Detective Ron Phillips, an unidentified sergeant, and "at least five uniformed police officers" whose identity is known only to God and the prosecution, none of whom have offered sworn testimony in this case. If this motion is to be determined simply on the basis of representations by counsel of what they anticipate the evidence at trial will prove, the defense can unequivocally represent that there will be credible evidence at trial that strongly supports the defense theory, evidence that will come from witnesses called by the prosecution.

c. *Rules of Evidence Regarding the Motive of Third Parties to Commit the Crime Are Inapplicable.*

With a dearth of case authority to support their motion, the People attempt a rather convoluted analogy to cases where the defendant offers evidence that a third person other than the defendant had a motive to commit the crime. This ascribes sinister motives to Detective Fuhrman that cannot be laid at the door of the defense. They suggest the *only* motive for Detective Fuhrman to plant the glove would be because he wanted to 'frame' the defendant and secure his conviction. In fact, if the planting of the glove occurred, it could have been motivated by a number of explanations:

(a) Detective Fuhrman was angry that he had been "kicked off" the case;

(b) Detective Fuhrman wanted to appear as the "hero" who solved the case;

(c) Detective Fuhrman wanted to provide probable cause for a search warrant for Mr. Simpson's home.

Even if the sole motive would be to "frame" the defendant, as the prosecution asserts, the rationale of *People v.Hall,* 41 Cal.3d 826 (1986) offers no support for the exclusion of this evidence. The *Hall* case actually rejected the more restrictive *Mendez-Arline* rule, that required a threshold showing of "competent and substantial proof of probability" that a third party committed the crime before such evidence could be offered. *People v. Mendez,* 193 Cal. 39 (1924); *People v. Arline,* 13 Cal.App.3d 200 (1970).... Neither *Hall* nor the cases it overruled involved attacks on the credibility of a testifying witness. The third party whose culpability was being suggested was neither a party nor a witness in the case.

The standard of admissibility of evidence challenging Detective Fuhrman's credibility is *not* whether the evidence raises a reasonable doubt as to the defendant's guilt. It is whether it has a tendency in reason to disprove the truthfulness of Detective Fuhrman.

d. The Motion Is Premature.

The scope of cross-examination is, of course, greatly influenced by the scope of direct examination. The testimony of Detective Mark Fuhrman will not be limited to the finding of the glove at the Rockingham premises. The Court has not heard, and the defendant has not had an opportunity to cross-examine, many of the witnesses relied upon by the People to support their assertion that "there can *never* be any evidence to support the defense theory." The defense has not had an opportunity to present evidence supporting their theory, and to the extent that evidence will be presented through the cross-examination and impeachment of prosecution witnesses, the defense has no obligation to disclose its "theories" in advance. The most appropriate time to resolve any question of the relevance of attacks on the credibility of Detective Fuhrman is after Detective Fuhrman has testified.

e. The Probative Value of Evidence Challenging the Credibility of Detective Fuhrman Outweighs Any Prejudicial Impact.

The prosecution argument of "remoteness" of the evidence utilizes the event or transaction to which it relates as the murder which occurred on June 12, 1994. This completely ignores the involvement of Detective Fuhrman in events in 1985 that the prosecution proposes to offer as a prior act of misconduct, or in 1989, when Detective Fuhrman wrote a letter purporting to describe the 1985 events. The evidence challenged is closely contemporaneous with these events.

... The suggestion that the challenges to Detective Fuhrman's credibility will inject the issue of racism into this trial is a red herring of rankest odor. If an officer of the Los Angeles Police Department can publicly express attitudes of hostility to interracial couples, yet remain immune from ever being questioned about those attitudes when he testifies against a party to such a marriage, the issue of racism will hardly be submerged. The greatest danger presented here is not that racism will be exposed, but that it will be concealed. Among the many questions to be resolved in this trial is not whether Detective Mark Fuhrman is a racist, but whether he is a liar. Confronting him with his previous conduct and statements will only embarrass him if they are true. To preclude such a confrontation will embarrass justice.

5. ORAL ARGUMENT

The oral arguments on January 13, 1995, on the Prosecution's In Limine Motion with respect to Detective Fuhrman, produced one of the most explosive courtroom exchanges in the entire trial.

"Mr. Darden: Good Morning, Your Honor. Your Honor, I think the best indication, evidence of just how inflammatory the use of this word is, is the fact that it appears that Mr. Cochran and I, the only two black lead lawyers on each side of the counsel table, are somehow dragged into this issue to argue the issue to the court, and I think that may be due in some part to the fact that if anyone should slip and say or utter the word, it is probably better to have a black person do it, because if you have a white person do it, if a white male takes the witness stand and that word is uttered in this courtroom, it will offend every black juror in this case. It will offend me, it will offend Mr. Cochran, it will offend Mr. Simpson, it will offend the African American reporters in this courtroom and it will offend the public and any other African American within earshot of that word. It is a dirty, filthy word. It is not a word that I allow people to use in my household. I'm sure Mr. Cochran doesn't. And the reason we don't is because it is an extremely derogatory and denigrating term because it is so prejudicial and so extremely inflammatory that to use that word in any situation will evoke some type of emotional response from any African American within earshot of that word.

I spoke to Dean Uelmen earlier this morning and I asked him—I said, 'Dean, are you going to use the 'N' word during argument today?' He said, 'Nope, not me.' Well, if Dean Uelmen doesn't want to utter the word and if Cochran doesn't utter the word or allow others to use that word in his household, and I certainly don't, why then should we allow that word in use in this courtroom? Especially in a case like this where it has no probative value. It is completely irrelevant. It was created and designed to do one thing, and that is to demean people, to strip them of their humanity, to evoke an emotional response.

Your Honor, when you use that word you are using fighting words. When you use that word in the presence of an

African American you are asking that African American for a reaction. It is a call to arms. It is a test. It is a test of every African American when they hear that word and the test is where do you stand? On which side of the line do you stand?

Because when that word is used in the presence of an African American, an African American has an obligation to do something about it, to say something. An African American has a duty, in most situations, to confront, to confront the declarant.

It is the filthiest, dirtiest, nastiest word in the English language. It has no place in this case or in this courtroom. It will do nothing to further the court's attempt at seeking the truth in this case. It will do one thing. It will upset the black jurors, it will issue a test, it will give them the test and the test will be whose side are you on? The side of the white prosecutors and the white policemen, or on the side of the black defendant and his very prominent black lawyer? That is what it is going to do. Either you are with the man or you are with the brothers. That is what it does. That is exactly what it does.

No one, no African American can hear that word without getting upset. You hear it in the movies; it upsets you. People don't listen to rap music, black people, because they don't like that word. They don't like the use of that word, and if you search black literature today, black magazines, your will see letters, writers and articles, and people asking why that word is used, why does that word exist? Why would anybody want to use it? Why would anybody want to rap about it? Why would anybody want to write about it? Why would anyone want to repeat it or say it?

The word has no place in the English language. It has no place in this courtroom. You shouldn't let them use it. I'm not going to say the word. We all know what the word is. If Mr. Cochran uses that word today I'm going to be offended, and it is probably the third or fourth time this week that I have been offended, but I can't help but be offended. How can the jury help but be offended?

Detective Fuhrman is going to play a very, very small role in this case. This wasn't his case. He was not the investigating officer or the lead investigating officer in this case. He went to Rockingham with ... three other detectives and he just happened to find an item. Pure happenstance. Pure luck on the part of the police and certainly on the part of the prosecution. He just happened to find a glove. One item.

The man finds one item amongst six or seven or eight hundred other items collected by the police in this case, and now when the man is called to the witness stand we are going to go fifteen years back ... and ask him if he ever made a racial slur, repeated a racial epithet? Why? What is the point of that when the detective is going to play such a small role in this case? There is no legal purpose. There is no valid or legitimate purpose. But Mr. Cochran and the defense, they have a purpose in going into that area and the purpose is to inflame the passions of the jury and to ask them to pick sides not on the basis of the evidence in this case. And the evidence in this case against this defendant is overwhelming. There is a mountain of evidence pointing to this defendant's guilt. But when you mention that word to this jury or to any African American, it blinds people. It will blind the jury, it will blind them to the truth. They won't be able to discern what is true and what is not. It will affect their judgment, it will impair their ability to be fair and impartial. It will cause extreme prejudice to the prosecution's case.

... We have a right to a fair trial just like the defendant has. We are not running around or talking about or seeking to introduce to the jury the notion that this defendant has a fetish for blond-haired white women. That would be inappropriate. That would inflame the passions of the jury. It would be outrageous.

... This isn't a race case. Mr. Cochran wants to play the ace of spades and play the race card, but this isn't a race case. We shouldn't allow him to play that card. We shouldn't allow him to play that card if what we are really interested in is playing by the rules, finding out just what happened at Bundy and if we are really interested in searching for the truth.

Yesterday, I handed to the Court ... Andrew Hacker's *Two Nations,* and if I might, I would like to ... read into the record a particular quote, ... because I think this quote fairly describes the impact and effect the hearing of this word has and will have on any African Americans on the jury:

'When a white person voices it, it becomes a knife with a whetted edge. No black person can hear it with equanimity or ignore it as simply a word. This word has the force to pierce, to wound, to penetrate as no other has. There have of course been terms like "kike" and "spic" and "chink" [and I have used those words and I apologize for using those terms, Your Honor] but these are less frequently heard today and they lack the same emotional impact. Some non-ethnic terms come closer, such as "slut" and "fag" and "cripple." Yet the "N" word stands alone with this power to tear at one's insides. It will reveal that whites have never created so wrenching an epithet for even the most benighted members of their own race. It is a persistent reminder that you are still perceived as a degraded species of humanity, a level to which whites can never descend.'

Mr. Cochran would like to ask a white police officer if he ever used that word and after that white police officer testifies there will be other white male police officers, and by the time those other officers testify ... the jury will have heard this word, they will be upset, they will have become emotional, and as soon as Mr. Cochran works them up into that emotional frenzy he would like to get them into, as soon as he does that and the next white police officer takes the witness stand, the jury is going to paint that white police officer with the same brush Mr. Cochran painted Detective Fuhrman. And there begins the decline of the prosecution's case, a very good case I might add.

... I know the court probably has had its own experience with racial epithets. In my view, and I haven't searched for empirical data on this issue or read any studies on this issue, but I believe and this certainly applies to me and it applies to friends of mine who are also African Americans, ... when we hear this word certain images come to mind.... It always causes me to reflect on the first time I was ever called that word. I remember it today as clear as a bell, and if you read some of the articles I handed the court yesterday, you will see that there are other people who are interviewed and documented in those studies, old people ... and they all remember the day, the first time somebody used that word.

I remember the first time. I'm sure Mr. Cochran remembers the first time. And whenever I reflect back on that experience, I find it extremely upsetting and I probably appear to be getting a little upset right now as I address the court. It is probably the most negative experience I have ever had in my life. And when the jury hears that word from a white police officer, they are going to reflect also, I think, on the most negative experience in their life, ... and I think they are going to become emotional.

Another thing hearing that word causes black people to do, ... it causes you to change your focus. It diverts your attention. If we really want the jury's attention focused on the evidence and on the legal and factual issues, the important legal and factual issues inherent in this case, we shouldn't let them hear this word, because if they hear this word they are going to focus their attention on the issue of race. They are going to be more concerned with whether Mark Fuhrman is a racist than they are with whether there wasn't any way, any possibility, any chance, any theory offered by the defense to establish that Mark Fuhrman planted evidence.

That will be a foregone conclusion. They can just check that one off. He must have done it, he is a racist. That is what Mr. Cochran wants the jury to do, skip the evidence, forget the direct examination and the cross-examination and the real factual points established in the case. The jury is going to find this case on the basis of race. They are all going to be preoccupied with race. After all, Mr. Simpson is an African American and so is Mr. Cochran.

... Now I'm sure Mr. Cochran or Dean Uelmen will step to the podium and they will say, 'Your Honor, you can always issue some limiting instruction. You can say to all the black jurors here, Ladies and Gentlemen, the use of the 'N-word' has been introduced in this case for a limited purpose and this is the purpose and don't consider it for any other reason.' That is pointless. It is a waste of paper and a waste of the court's time because you can't ignore it. Once that word is in front of you, you can't ignore it. I haven't been able to ignore this word over the last week when I suddenly found myself involved in this nasty little issue....

Well, it poses an important moral question for me personally, because my belief is, hey, if you see a racist, let's tatoo it on his forehead so everybody knows when they meet the guy that, hey, he is a racist. And I am not saying Mark Fuhrman is a racist, because I have met Mark Fuhrman and I have talked to Mark Fuhrman. And I have looked at these records, and what I see in the record is that in 1981 and 1982 Mark Fuhrman suffered from stress. He suffered from the same kind of stress that lots of police officers suffer from, not just white police officers, but black police officers as well. I think the records are clear that during those days that Mark Fuhrman had been shot at for no reason other than the fact that he was an L.A.P.D. officer. His friend had been shot at, his colleagues had been killed. People would spit on him just because he wore a blue uniform. People had directed racial epithets toward him. He had just come back from Vietnam when he joined the L.A.P.D. He was suffering from stress and and it has to be stressful to be a police officer in the city of L.A. I mean, geez, the stuff that is going on in this city in the last five to six years, I can't imagine anybody that would want a job like that, but some do and they ought to be commended.

... It is the prosecution's position that if you allow Mr. Cochran to use this word and to play this race card, not only does the direction and the focus of the case change, but the entire complexion of the case changes. It is a race case then. It is white versus black, African American versus Caucasian, us versus them, us versus the system.

. . . Now, the court may well think, well, Mr. Darden, this is an awful extreme argument that you are making, but it is true. That is what this word does, Your Honor. That is what this word does, and to come from a white police officer, that just exacerbates everything.

What happened to Mark Fuhrman fourteen years ago under the conditions in which these statements were allegedly made, while suffering apparently from some form of stress, a post traumatic stress, and after his wife left him, it is unfair. It is unfair to introduce the statements in this case. They are inherently unreliable and it is unfair to allow Mr. Cochran to play the race card and turn these proceedings into a race case.

. . . All the prosecution wants in this case is a fair shot, a fair trial. We just want everybody to play by the rules, and when we don't play by the rules and when there is a perception that we don't play by the rules, the court sanctions us, Dean Uelmen berates us, and we do what we are supposed to do. The rules don't require the court to allow the use of this word in this courtroom or to have this word uttered in this courtroom. We strongly urge the court, and respectfully so, that the court not allow that word, that it not be uttered in this courtroom.

The Court: I was about to say we are going to stand in recess.

Mr. Cochran: I would like to say, or start at this point.

The Court: All right.

Mr. Cochran: Thank you very much, Judge Ito. I have a funeral to attend today, . . . but I would be remiss were I not at this time to take this opportunity to respond to my good friend, Mr. Chris Darden. His remarks this morning are perhaps the most incredible remarks I've heard in a court of law in the 32 years that I have been practicing law. His remarks are demeaning to African Americans as a group. And so I want, before I go to this funeral, to apologize to African Americans across this country. Not every African American feels that way. It is demeaning to our jurors to say that African Americans who have lived under oppression for 200 plus years in this country cannot work within the mainstream, cannot hear these offensive words. African Americans live with offensive words, offensive looks, offensive treatment every day of their lives, but yet they still believe in this country. And to say that our jurors, because they hear this offensive word—to say they can't be fair is absolutely outrageous. For the prosecution to stand here and over the last couple days to present character assassination against this man,[18] unfounded, bogus charges, after charge after charge, then to withdraw seventeen of those charges, for them to have the temerity, the unmitigated gall to come into this courtroom and talk about fairness.

What we are going to be talking about this afternoon, Your Honor, is words out of the mouth of Mark Fuhrman. What I want to share with you are the things this man said, not what we made up. What he said, what he told people. And I am ashamed that Mr. Darden would allow himself to become an apologist for this man, to justify the fact that he is a police officer. Being a police officer is tough. Being a lawyer is tough. Being a judge is tough. That doesn't make you use racism. You can't justify that in a civilized society.

To try and pretend that racism doesn't exist in this country is to bury one's head in the sand. It is the height of naivete. Nobody wants to introduce race into this case, Your Honor, but as Mr. Darden has pointed out, race plays a part of everything in America.

What has happened with African Americans, we have tried to rise above that, because we understand that there are racists in this country, but yet we still love this country because we have helped build this country. So I am proud to be an African American.

But I don't wear that. I am also a lawyer. I am a lawyer who happens to be an African American. But I will not allow myself to be used under these circumstances to become an apologist for people who use racist statements in the past, to malign other African Americans, to say that I'm some expert to come here and testify as an expert as to what Black people think in America.

All across America today, believe me, Black people are offended at this very moment. And so I have to say this was uncalled for, it is unwarranted and most unfortunate for somebody that I have a lot of respect for. Perhaps he has become too emotional about this.

But let's step back and see what we are talking about here. What the prosecution seeks to do, Your Honor, is to prescribe the defense.... We didn't create Mark Fuhrman. We take witnesses the way we find them. We didn't tell him to go to the doctor and say all those things that I will share with you this afternoon. We didn't tell him to say those things in front of

---

18. The reference is to arguments on the admissibility of prior incidents of alleged domestic violence by Mr. Simpson, which immediately preceded the in limine motion regarding Fuhrman's cross-examination.

Kathleen Bell. We didn't tell him to get involved in the shooting with Mr. Britton.

And I want to take this opportunity to put the prosecution on notice that as they are continuing their investigation of Mr. Simpson, we are daily getting additional information about Mr. Fuhrman. And they should be noticed, that if there is additional information coming, we will give it to them as we get it, and they should be very much aware of that.

And so, Your Honor, I hope I have initially expressed how I feel about this. It is hard to remain calm in the face of what we have just heard, especially when one has dedicated one's life trying to rise above racism, to try and act in a professional manner at all times. You are trying not to interject one's personal feelings. And so, when he talks about Mr. Cochran is going to do this, he doesn't know what we are going to do. All we are going to do is conduct this case fairly and honestly.

And the final thing I would like to say before we take our break, Your Honor, it seems to me somebody needs to say to these prosecutors that the fact they are prosecutors doesn't mean they are always right. They don't have any priority on the truth. And the arrogance they have each shown in standing up here and talking about this mountain of evidence, and then come whining back to you saying, well, gee, we can't get a fair trial because jurors are going to be thrown off by one word, how preposterous is that? You will not be swayed by that. And it seems to me that professional lawyers don't talk in terms of 'we've got all this evidence against him.' They withdraw it the next day. They are mouthing.

If they've got so much evidence, let them produce it in court and stop talking about it. And let's all play by the rules, let's play by the fair rules here. And all we want to do is have our fair opportunity. They ... do not have a right to prescribe our cross-examination, and what they would do out of tactics is, Mark Fuhrman has been a central person in this case, but in listening to it this morning, Your Honor, all of a sudden he is a very, very minor player in this case. They wouldn't even call him if they don't want to. They don't want to call Dr. Golden. But, Your Honor, they are left and stuck with these witnesses. We didn't create them. And we have an opportunity and a duty to vigorously cross-examine."

6. JUDGE'S RULING

In a ruling issued January 20, 1995, Judge Lance Ito noted the prosecution's assurances that it intended to limit Fuhrman's testimony in their case in chief to the recovery of the glove and the interview of Kato Kaelin. He then concluded:

"Having placed Fuhrman's role in the appropriate context, the court must then examine the defense offers of proof and determine their relevancy and probative value as to the now defined issues regarding Fuhrman. The appellate courts have wisely held that the trial court must have broad discretion, carefully administered, to preclude impeachment on collateral matters." *People v. Lavergne,* 4 Cal.3d 735, 742 (1971); *Farrell v. Superior Court,* 203 Cal.App.3d 521 (1988).

The 1981 disability litigation file contains doctors' reports wherein Fuhrman is alleged to have made disparaging statements about some members of our nation's volunteer armed forces. It is argued that these comments reflect a racial animus directly bearing upon credibility. The court does not find there to be a direct link between comments made in approximately 1980 and credibility in 1994. What remains is an inference, the probative value of which is lessened by the passage of time and its indirect nature. It would require undue consumption of court time to produce evidence which is at best speculative. The objection under Evidence Code Section 352 is therefore sustained.

The Redondo Beach incident occurred sometime between 1985 and 1986. It is alleged that Fuhrman made a comment from which one might infer racial animus, contempt of interracial couples and the willingness to manufacture probable cause to stop a motor vehicle. It has been agreed by the parties that defendant is African American and victim Nicole Brown Simpson was Caucasian. It would also appear from this record that Fuhrman had met defendant and Nicole Brown Simpson on one memorable prior occasion in 1985. Assuming Bell's statement to be true, a direct inference of a credibility problem is apparent. If the defendant can make an offer of proof as to what evidence they will produce to suggest the moving of evidence and the court is satisfied by that offer of proof, the prosecution's objections will be denied. The court notes here that neither the defendant's response to the prosecution's motion *in limine* nor defense counsel's argument contained the prerequisite offer. The defendant has leave of court to file an offer of proof by 9:00 a.m. on 23 January, 1995, upon condition that they serve a copy upon opposing counsel via facsimile.

The 1988 incident involved the shooting of Joseph Britton. The defendant has alleged that Fuhrman, as one of the officers staking out an automated teller machine, chased and shot Britton, referred to him directly using racial epithets and later moved a knife and placed it at Britton's feet to justify the shooting. The probative value of such allegations appears clear, however the prosecution vigorously challenges the factual accuracy and notes the lack of an acceptable offer of proof. In the excerpt from the transcript of Britton's 1993 deposition in the civil case arising from this incident, Britton describes the officer who shot him and who used racial epithets as a white male with red hair and a mustache. The prosecution argued that Mark Fuhrman does not have red hair and did not have a mustache and this argument was not challenged by the defense. Attachment 5 to the prosecution's reply contains a transcript of a network television news program wherein reporter Reed Galin states that Briton does not accuse Fuhrman of either using racial epithets or moving evidence. The probative value of the alleged incident as portrayed by defendant, without an offer of proof, appears to be highly speculative at the very best. Its presentation would consume an unwarranted amount of court time. The Evidence Code Section 352 objection is sustained.

The prosecution's last request is for an order by this court to prohibit the use in this case of the 'N-word.' The prosecution made an impassioned and heartfelt plea for this court to contemplate and understand the vile, repulsive and explosive nature of that epithet. The prosecution strongly argues that this epithet is so vile that it operates as a divisive demand that those to whom or about whom it is said take some action, and that its use can cloud the operation of good judgment and common sense. Defense counsel, in equally impassioned and heartfelt tones, argues that it gives little credit to jurors in general and African Americans serving as jurors in particular to assert that they will be so inflamed by the use of this epithet that they will ignore their oaths as trial jurors to determine this case based upon the evidence presented and the law as instructed. Both arguments have merit. The racial divisions that exist in this country remain the last great challenge to us as a Nation. How we evolve and hopefully solve the problem will be our memorial in history. When meritorious arguments are raised on both sides, the court must always remember this process is a search for the truth and that it depends upon the sound judgment of our jurors. If the challenged racial epithet was used in a relevant incident, it will be heard in court.''

Based on the defense offer of proof, Judge Ito permitted Fuhrman to be cross-examined about the Kathleen Bell incident. Fuhrman claimed he had no memory of ever meeting Kathleen Bell, and flatly denied ever making the statements she attributed to him. F. Lee Bailey concluded his cross-examination of Detective Fuhrman with a classic example of the way a foundation should be laid for subsequent impeachment of a witness:

"Q.   Do you use the word 'nigger' in describing people?

A.   No, sir.

Q.   Have you ever used that word in the past ten years?

A.   Not that I recall, no.

Q.   You mean if you called someone a nigger you have forgotten it?

A.   I'm not sure I can answer the question the way you phrased it, sir.

Q.   You have difficulty understanding the question?

A.   Yes.

Q.   I will rephrase it. I want you to assume that perhaps at some time since 1985 or 1986, you addressed a member of the African American race as a nigger. Is it possible that have forgotten that act on your part?

A.   No, it is not possible.

Q.   Are you therefore saying that you have not used that word in the past ten years, Detective Fuhrman?

A.   Yes, that is what I am saying.

Q.   And you say under oath that you have not addressed any black person as a nigger or spoken about black people as niggers in the past ten years, Detective Fuhrman?

A.   That's what I'm saying, sir.

Q.   So that anyone who comes into this court and quotes you as using that word in dealing with African Americans would be a liar, would they not, Detective Fuhrman?

A.   Yes, they would.

Q.   All of them, correct?

A.   All of them."

7.   COMMENTS AND QUESTIONS

(a) Both California Evidence Code Section 352 and Federal Rule 403 speak in terms of the danger of prejudice or of misleading *the* jury (not *a* jury). Is it appropriate to address this question with respect to the particular composition of the jury selected to hear the case? Should judges make different rulings on the dangers of prejudice depending on the racial composition of the jury? Their educational backgrounds? Or should rulings be based on an abstract concept of whether the evidence would prejudice a hypothetical *reasonable* jury?

(b) Judge Ito's ruling apparently made it obvious to prosecutors that the question posed by F. Lee Bailey would be asked on cross-examination. Chris Darden arranged a practice examination of Mark Fuhrman in a grand jury room, and elicited Fuhrman's flat denial that he had ever used the "N-word" in the past ten years. Darden then informed Marcia Clark that he would not participate in the direct examination of Fuhrman.

> "I called Chris into my office for a thorough debriefing. 'So what exactly did you ask Fuhrman?' I said. But all Chris could remember for sure was that when he'd asked Fuhrman whether he'd used the slur in the past ten years, Fuhrman had denied it. 'No equivocation? Maybe he just couldn't remember?' I asked hopefully. 'Nope,' Chris assured me. 'He denied it completely and will not budge.'
>
> I found it hard to believe that Mark had never uttered that word. Not after what I'd seen in the disability file. I *did* believe that he'd never said it to an African American, face to face. But *never?* Not over a beer? Not to his buddies? Not in private? That seemed unlikely to me. Could I get him to admit it? Judging from Chris' experience with him, probably not. Perhaps I could get him to soften his denial to 'I don't remember.' But a witness can be pushed only so far.
>
> A prosecutor is in a tough position when she doesn't fully believe her own witness. As I girded up for the encounter with Mark Fuhrman, I made a pact with myself: If I couldn't shake him off his denial about the N-word, then I had an obligation to tell the jury that I had doubts about it. But I'd contrast it with that part of the testimony I was perfectly certain of: that he didn't plant evidence."

Clark, *Without A Doubt,* pp. 342–43 (Viking, 1997). Was Marcia Clark's resolution of her ethical dilemma an appropriate one? Is it *always* unethical to present the testimony of a witness you know is lying, even if you believe the lie relates to a collateral matter and the rest of the testimony is truthful? Consider the risks of waiting until closing argument to "level" with the jury. If the lie has already been exposed by your opponents, will not your concession of having had doubts be seen as disingenuous?

(c) A standard jury instruction, which was given at the conclusion of the O.J. Simpson criminal trial, informs the jury that if they believe a witness lied in any material part of his testimony, the jury may reject all of his testimony. *Falsus in unum est falsus in omnibus.* How might that instruction be utilized by the defense in arguing the credibility of Detective Fuhrman?

(d) Chris Darden's suggestion that black jurors would be blinded by the injection of Fuhrman's racism as an issue in the trial has certainly reverberated since the verdict. Consider the response of juror Carrie Bess:

"The issue that has really bothered us about these accusations is we know about racism. We as African American women have lived in a racist society for a very long time. As I was growing up, I was called a nigger a lot of times. I've gone to places where they wouldn't serve me. I went through Mississippi where they would only serve me through the side window. I was working at this one place and they didn't even allow me to come in the front door. I know what it's like. But I also know black people who are married to white people. We have raised different kids in our family. This is life. You learn. You know it's there. There are so many people who don't know it's there. It doesn't mean you have to be bitter, but you know it's there. When you see it, you know how to get around it unless someone pushes you to the wall and you have to react. But I know it's there. And I will always know it's there.

. . . People are saying Johnnie Cochran played the race card right from the start. I didn't pick up on that at all. I know he just kept saying in his opening statement, 'Pay attention to Detective Fuhrman. He's the one who found all the evidence.' I didn't pick up that Fuhrman was a racist. I just picked up that Fuhrman was lying. He was a liar. I didn't ever put any type of racism to that. So I don't know if that's being naive or if that's just how I perceived it."

Cooley, Bess and Rubin–Jackson, *Madam Foreman: A Rush to Judgment?*, pp. 185–87 (Dove, 1995).

B. IMPEACHMENT OF FUHRMAN BY McKINNEY TAPES

1. THE EVIDENCE

In addition to the eighteen examples of police misconduct offered as "character evidence," considered in Chapter II (B) *supra,* the transcripts of consultations between Detective Mark Fuhrman and Laura Hart McKinney included forty-one examples of Fuhrman uttering the word "nigger" in referring to black persons. The Defense Offer of Proof included the following eight examples:

5. (Commenting on L.A.P.D. politics): "Commander _____, what a dickhead. He should be shot. He did that for one thing. He wants to be Chief, so he wants the city council, and the police commissioner, and all these niggers in L.A. City

Government and all of 'em should be lined up against a wall and fuckin' shot."

6.   (Discussing American aid to drought victims in Ethiopia): "You know these people here, we got all this money going to Ethiopia for what. To feed a bunch of dumb niggers that their own government won't even feed."

7.   (Describing where he grew up in the State of Washington): "People there don't want niggers in their town. People there don't want Mexicans in their town. They don't want anybody but good people in their town, and anyway you can do to get them out of there that's fine with them. We have no niggers where I grew up."

13.   (Discussing where Black Muslims live): "Q. Why do they live in that area? A. That's where niggers live."

19.   (Discussing use of chokehold by L.A.P.D.): "We stopped using the choke because a bunch of niggers have a bunch of these organizations in the south, then, and because all niggers were choked out and killed—twelve in ten years, really extraordinary, isn't it?"

21.   (Directing Ms. McKinney to Wilshire Division): "Go to Wilshire Division. Wilshire Division is all niggers. All niggers, nigger training officers, niggers with three years on the job."

32.   (Describing reaction of rape victim to female officer): "What if I've just been raped by two buck niggers and a female shows up?"

34.   (Describing boredom of working in the San Fernando Valley): "It's pretty clear-cut who the assholes are. You go to Pacoima, you got bikers and niggers."

2.   THE TACTICAL CONTEXT

The prosecution offered to stipulate that the voice on the tapes was Fuhrman's, and argued there was no need to air the tapes in court, seeking to prevent public disclosure of the virulence of Fuhrman's racism. The defense responded that the tone and inflection of his voice were essential considerations in assessing the value of the tapes to impeach his testimony, especially in view of the prosecution's position that Fuhrman was "role-playing." Judge Ito ruled, "I think that there is an overriding public interest in the nature of the offer that you are making, and I don't want this court to ever be in a position where there is any indication that this court would participate in suppressing information that is of vital public interest." With no interruption or explanation, each of the excerpts from the tapes and transcripts was then presented in open court for review by the court and determination of their admissibility.

3. DEFENSE ARGUMENT

California Evidence Code Section 780 provides that "any matter that has a tendency in reason to prove or disprove the truthfulness" of the testimony of a witness may be considered, including:

(e) his character for honesty or veracity or their opposites;

(f) the existence or non-existence of a bias, interest or other motive;

(h) a statement made by him which is inconsistent with any part of his testimony at the hearing;

(i) the existence or non-existence of any fact testified to by him;

(j) his attitude toward the action in which he testifies or toward the giving of testimony.

Particularly with respect to determinations of bias and prejudice, trial courts have been cautioned not to usurp the jury's function of ultimately determining the credibility of witnesses. After outlining a variety of ways in which racial bias might be established, both through cross-examination and by extrinsic evidence, the court in *In Re Anthony P.,* 167 Cal.App.3d 502, 512 (1985) concluded:

"This is not to say proof of any one of these indicia of bias, or even a combination, will necessarily establish a witness is so prejudiced against a given racial group he or she would lodge a false accusation or testify falsely against a defendant who happened to be a member of that race. The judge or jury may well decide the witness is truthful even though racially prejudiced. But this is the inherent nature of any attempt to impugn the credibility of a witness. For instance, the fact-finder may decide to believe in-court testimony even when a cross-examination is able to show several inconsistent statements outside the courtroom. *A trial court could not foreclose the introduction of those prior inconsistent statements merely because it felt the jury would believe the witness' testimony at trial anyway.*"

(Emphasis supplied). The defendant has proffered a very selective and tightly edited array of excerpts from the "Fuhrman Tapes." Although the tapes contain something to offend nearly everyone, only the portions that directly contradict the testimony offered, prove bias or prejudice directly relevant to this case, directly corroborate other witnesses, or demonstrate an attitude toward those directly involved in this case have been selected.

Any risk of undue consumption of time has been minimized, by reducing over sixteen hours of tapes to less than one hour. Any danger of undue prejudice has been minimized by judicious editing. While any decent person would be offended, for example, by Detective Fuhrman's suggestion that American aid was going "to feed a bunch of dumb niggers" in Ethiopia, the diatribe goes on to say, "Let 'em die. Use 'em for fertilizer. I mean, who cares." The object of our offer of proof is not to shock or scandalize the jury by the depths of Detective Fuhrman's callousness, but to present relevant evidence that goes directly to the issues in this case. Detective Fuhrman's central role in the investigation and prosecution of this case requires that the defendant be given wide latitude in challenging his credibility, showing his bias, and demonstrating his motive, intent, plan, custom and habit.

4. PROSECUTION ARGUMENT

The tapes and transcripts made by Laura McKinney between 1985 and 1987 contain the use of numerous utterances of racial epithets by Mark Fuhrman. Although such language is certainly offensive and reprehensible, that observation adds little to the legal considerations necessary to discuss its admissibility. The relevance of racial epithets to a legal proceeding requires a lawyerly analysis that takes into account principles of materiality, probative value and the myriad considerations under Evidence Code Section 352.

For such racial epithets to be admissible, the defense must demonstrate a logical, rational nexus between the use of such epithets and the conduct the defense wishes to attribute to Detective Fuhrman in this case. Otherwise, the admission of such utterances has no probative value and serves only to improperly inflame the passions of this jury, if not the community at large. The misconduct with which the defense charges Detective Fuhrman in this case is, apparently, that he moved one of the Defendant's gloves from the Bundy crime scene to the Defendant's Rockingham residence.

The People fail to see how the utterance of a racial epithet 8 to 10 years ago has any probative value in this regard. The use of the epithet alone unaccompanied by any avowed intent to fabricate evidence against that minority proves absolutely nothing.

To the extent that the defense asserts that the use of the racial epithet 8 to 10 years ago constitutes impeachment of the testimony of Mark Fuhrman, such impeachment is at best collateral. Even that collateral value, already minimal by definition, is substantially reduced to the point of disappearance by the remoteness of those utterances and the fact that they are uttered in a context of no relevance to the issues in this case.

Moreover, when the prejudicial impact is weighed, as it must be, against the non-existent probative value, the inadmissibility of these proffered statements becomes apparent. It is interesting to note that on April 23, 1985, in the very midst of the meetings with Ms. McKinney in which he used racial epithets, Mark Fuhrman met with an African American, an admitted former gang member and then safety on the UCLA football team, James Washington. The meeting was taped by Laura McKinney. The conversation was obviously amicable and Ms. McKinney described their interaction as very warm and cordial. At no time during this meeting did Mark Fuhrman use any racial epithets and indeed professed his admiration for Mr. Washington.

5. JUDGE'S RULING

At the same time he foreclosed any use of the eighteen excerpts relating to police misconduct by Fuhrman, Judge Ito ruled that a very limited use could be made of the racial epithets:

> "On cross-examination the defense was allowed to question Fuhrman as to his biases against African Americans. The defendant now seeks to offer to the jury extrinsic evidence of Fuhrman's racial bias in the form of 41 statements made by Fuhrman to McKinny wherein Fuhrman uses the racial epithet 'nigger' in apparent disparaging references to African Americans. The court has reviewed each of the 41 uses of the racial epithet in question either by reference to the transcripts, audio tapes or both. The court finds that each involves Fuhrman's use of the subject racial epithet in a disparaging manner within the time frame posed by the cross-examination and in contradiction to his testimony before the jury. It is therefore relevant and admissible as impeachment.
>
> Having found Fuhrman's use of the subject racial epithet to be relevant and admissible, the court must then analyze each usage under Evidence Code Section 352: 'The court in its discretion may exclude evidence if its probative value is substantially outweighed by the probability that its admission will (a) necessitate undue consumption of time or (b) create substantial danger of undue prejudice, of confusing the issues, or of misleading the jury.' The specific racial epithet at issue is perhaps the single most insulting, inflammatory and provocative term in use in modern day America. The court's examination of each of these 41 uses reveals not only the racial epithet itself, but a context that only adds to the insulting and inflammatory nature.
>
> ... The probative value of the evidence of Fuhrman's use of racial epithets comes from the fact that he has testified that

he has not used the term in the last ten years, thereby impacting his credibility. Because of Fuhrman's discovery of a bloody glove at the Rockingham residence and its scientific significance, he is a significant although not essential witness against the defendant. As such, the defendant is entitled to effectively cross-examine him. However, as noted above, the court retains some discretion in controlling the inquiry. The defense may present McKinny's testimony as follows:

    a.   Her acquaintenceship with Fuhrman.

    b.   The nature and purpose of their relationship.

    c.   That McKinny has had tape recorded and transcribed conversations with Fuhrman for the nine year period between April of 1985 and July of 1994.

    d.   That during the course of those conversations between 1985 and 1986 Fuhrman used the term 'nigger' in a disparaging manner 41 times.

The defense may play and display the following excerpts as impeachment:

    #8 'We have no niggers where I grew up.'

    #13 Q. 'Why do they live in that area?'

    A.   'That's where niggers live.'

The court finds the probative value of the remaining examples to be substantially and overwhelmingly outweighed by the danger of undue prejudice. Evidence Code Section 352. Just as a defendant with prior felony convictions testifying before a jury is not entitled to a false aura of credibility, neither is Fuhrman. It is apparent by the prosecution's offer to stipulate that Fuhrman had used the subject racial epithet in a disparaging manner within the relevant time period that the prosecution recognizes the danger of presenting what might now appear to be false evidence or perjured testimony. See *In Re Sassounian,* 9 Cal.4th 535 (1995). Having now recognized the problems with presenting Fuhrman as a witness, the concession is appropriate."

Mark Fuhrman was not called as a witness at the civil trial.

6. COMMENTS AND QUESTIONS

(a) Consider the irony implicit in Judge Ito's ruling pointed out in the Defense's Motion for Reconsideration:

    "The only support for ruling that the probative value of the evidence of racial bias and hostility is substantially outweighed by its prejudicial impact is the Court's conclusory characterization that it is 'inflammatory.' Evidence of racial bias will *always* be inflammatory and offensive. Implicit in the Court's characterization is the assumption that the more virulent and disgusting the racial bias is, the less likelihood of its admission. The Court has formulated a rule that turns logic on its head: if a witness is mildly and inoffensively racist, his bias may be proven; but if his racism is virulent and disgusting, it must be concealed from the jury, or at least 'toned down' so it appears mild and inoffensive. The job of assessing the credibility of a witness belongs to the jury, and the jury cannot be deprived of the task of sorting out the offensive racists from the inoffensive ones, to the extent that the *degree* of hate and spitefulness displayed bears any relationship to the *degree* of credibility to be given to the testimony of a witness."

(b) After Judge Ito's ruling was announced, Johnnie Cochran, Jr. called a press conference and made the following statements:

"Today you saw perhaps one of the cruelest, unfair decisions ever rendered in a criminal court in this country. For this judge to rule that only two incidents are admissible is outrageous, specious, and it's unspeakable. To allow the most innocuous areas and he leaves everything else out, that is misleading this jury, it's dishonest, and we don't want to be part of that. O.J. Simpson is a man who has been wrongfully accused and we believe framed and the cover-up continues. We think this jury is much smarter that the Judge gives them credit for. And even though they want to mislead this jury and buy this kind of doctored, tortured decision, we're going to go on with our job and do the right thing."

When, if ever, should a lawyer publicly criticize a judge's rulings during a pending trial? Is this kind of comment protected by the First Amendment? See *Standing Committee v. Yagman*, 55 F.3d 1430 (9th Cir. 1994). Even if a lawyer has a "right" to do it, is it the "right thing" to do?

(c) California Evidence Code Section 412 creates an adverse inference if a party offers "weaker and less satisfactory evidence" when "stronger and more satisfactory evidence" is available. If a judge excludes the "stronger and more satisfactory evidence," is the offering party entitled to an instruction explaining why it was not offered? At the conclusion of the case, the defense proffered the following instruction, which was refused:

"During the testimony of Laura McKinny, you learned of the existence of transcripts and tape recordings of Detective Mark Fuhrman repeatedly using an offensive racial slur. You should not speculate about why you will not have the opportunity to see all of the transcripts or hear all of the tapes. I have ruled that they cannot be admitted in evidence. The court's examination of each of the 41 uses of the insulting and inflammatory term in question reveals not only the racial epithet itself, but a context that only adds to the insulting and inflammatory nature."

(d) Although the prosecutors succeeded in keeping all of the most damaging excerpts of the Fuhrman tapes from the jury, even the minimal portions admitted required a shift in their strategy regarding the other witnesses called to impeach Mark Fuhrman. Rather that the previously planned "slash and burn" attack upon the credibility of Kathleen Bell, Natalie Singer and Roderic Hodge, all of whom testified to hearing Fuhrman use the "N-word," those witnesses were quickly excused after perfunctory cross-examination.

C. THREATS AND PRIOR ERRORS
BY THE CORONER

1. THE EVIDENCE

The following statement was obtained by L.A.P.D. Detective Douglas Raymond from Earl Clark, an investigator with the office of the Los Angeles Coroner:

"I questioned Mr. Clark about the allegations that surfaced regarding Dr. Goldman's possession of a concealable handgun in the workplace and statements he made on the morning of Thursday, July 21, 1994 between 0700 and 0730 hours.

Mr. Clark stated that on that date between 0700 and 0730 hours, he was on the service floor approaching the elevator when he observed Dr. Golden walking in front of him. Dr. Golden was approaching the double doors which led to the autopsy room and was dressed in civilian clothes which included a sports jacket. Mr. Clark stated he heard Dr. Golden call out his first name several times, saying 'Earl, Earl come here, look it,' while pulling on his right shirt sleeve. As Mr. Clark approached Dr. Golden he observed him reach into the right front exterior coat pocket and pull out a handgun. Mr. Clark said he saw Dr. Golden move the gun back and forth as he extended the weapon away from his body. Dr. Golden was holding the weapon in his palm with his index finger alongside the slide mechanism. Mr. Clark then heard Dr. Golden say, 'You know we ought ta go out and kill nine or ten of these attorneys.' Mr. Clark stated that both he and Dr. Golden 'giggled' and then he observed Dr. Golden put the weapon back in his sports coat pocket. Mr. Clark stated he then entered the elevator and left.

Mr. Clark stated he viewed Dr. Golden's actions as more a joke than a serious threat. Mr. Clark described the gun as a multiple grey colored .380 or 9MM automatic. Mr. Clark was unsure of the make or model and would not confirm if, in fact, it was a real handgun. I asked Mr. Clark why he thought Dr. Golden would make such a statement and he stated Dr. Golden told him he was planning a three week vacation out of the state and that the attorneys in several of his current cases told him he could not leave and he should consider himself on call and be available to respond to court. I asked Mr. Clark how the incident involving Dr. Golden was brought to the attention of Supervision at the Coroner's office. Mr. Clark stated that later on in the day he was sharing a cigarette break with his supervisor, Dean Gilmour. In passing, he happened to mention the gun incident involving Dr. Golden. Mr. Clark stated that Mr. Gilmour took the matter very seriously and ultimately disclosed the incident to his supervisor, Craig Harvey. Mr. Clark knew of no reason why Dr. Golden would be armed with a handgun in the workplace and was not sure if Dr. Golden possessed any CCW license. Mr. Clark stated that it is Department of Coroner policy that no one should carry firearms while on duty. Mr. Clark stated that he knew of no classes taught by Dr. Golden in which real firearms were used. Mr. Clark could not recall any other witnesses to this event."

On October 2, 1994, the Los Angeles Times published a profile of Dr. Golden in which they reported that Dr. Golden had been the subject of two prior complaints related to his competency. In a 1990 case, he misidentified entry and exit wounds. He reported that a fatal bullet wound entered in the front and exited in the back. In a subsequent addendum, after his opinion was challenged by another forensic expert, he indicated that he changed his opinion, and now concluded the bullet entered in the back and exited in the front. In another 1990 case, he mischaracterized a contact wound. He said the bullet came from a gunshot several feet from the victim. After another forensic expert examined photos of the wound and stated it was clearly a contact wound, Dr. Golden was directed by his supervisor to make an addendum to his report to acknowledge the error.

2. THE TACTICAL CONTEXT

Dr. Golden testified at the Preliminary Hearing in the *Simpson* case, and was scheduled to again testify at the trial. In his Opening Statement at trial, defense attorney Johnnie Cochran, Jr. suggested the evidence would show significant errors were made in Dr. Golden's autopsies of the victims, most notably in failing to preserve stomach contents (analysis of how far digestion of food had progressed would have helped pinpoint how long after their last meal death occurred), and in failing to take a "rape kit" test of Nicole Brown Simpson, to ascertain if she had engaged in sexual intercourse shortly before her death. As they prepared to present the autopsy evidence, the prosecution had serious second thoughts about putting Dr. Golden on the witness stand. On March 21, 1995, ten weeks after opening statements, the prosecution filed a Motion in Limine "to prohibit cross examination of Dr. Irwin Golden concerning an alleged display of a firearm and errors allegedly made in unrelated autopsies."

3. PROSECUTION ARGUMENT

(A) Display of a toy or real firearm.

Dr. Golden has not been charged with a crime. *A fortiori,* he has been convicted of nothing. Furthermore, Dr. Golden's alleged display of either an imitation or real firearm and stating, "look at this, we should kill nine or ten of those attorneys," does not reflect moral turpitude. Moral turpitude is a readiness to do evil, determined if the least adjudicated elements of the conviction necessarily involve moral turpitude. *People v. Castro,* 38 Cal.3d 301, 314–17 (1985). If no conviction exists, or if the immoral misconduct is not a criminal offense, determining moral turpitude becomes more complicated. *People v. Wheeler,* 4 Cal.4th 284, 297 n.7 (1992). However, convictions and specific acts of conduct which rest on dishonest behavior are more clearly related to credibility than violent or assaultive crimes. See, *People v. Beagle,* 6 Cal. 3d 441, 453 (1972). No California case has held brandishing a real or imitation firearm involves moral turpitude.

Initially, one must note that insufficient evidence has been given to the appropriate prosecuting agency to warrant filing any criminal charge against Dr. Golden. Simply put, the Los Angeles City Attorney's office found insufficient evidence to prove beyond a reasonable doubt the item displayed was a firearm.

Secondly, the alleged conduct neither reflects dishonesty, nor in any way suggests the circumstances were other than jocular in nature. When Dr. Golden displayed the object, there were no attorneys present and the incident was seen as "more of a joke."

Furthermore, the act evidenced neither a readiness to do evil nor a readiness to lie, but simply a frustration with the legal system and lawyers. Though it is unclear whether this frustration stems from the circumstances of this case or an unrelated case, even if the allegations are true, this frustration is not idiosyncratic with Dr. Golden; rather, frustration with attorneys permeates the American population and is the reason lawyers are currently held in such low esteem.[19]

No California case has held a felony brandishing conviction, Penal Code Section 417(c), involves moral turpitude, nor has any case held the specific act of brandishing even a real firearm reflects the required readiness to do evil. Since the Los Angeles City Attorney's office declined to file charges, no conviction exists, and the incident evidences frustration, rather than a readiness to do evil, the court should rule that evidence of this incident does not reflect moral turpitude and preclude cross-examination on this event to avert a mini-trial on collateral credibility issues.

As no charges were ever filed against Dr. Golden and no conviction exists, the circumstances as to what happened are in dispute and would require the examination of multiple witnesses, including Dr. Golden, to determine if the threshold of moral turpitude can be established. Such examination would be a paradigm of unduly consuming the court's time on a clearly collateral issue, a circumstance which Evidence Code Section 352 was established to prevent.

The probative value of the incident is also substantially outweighed by the danger of confusing the issues. A jury should consider "only relevant and competent evidence bearing on the issue of guilt or innocence." *Castro,* 38 Cal. 3d at 313. Dr. Golden's expertise and opinions are relevant to the issues of guilt or innocence. The alleged display of a firearm, however, bears no relevance to Dr. Golden's expertise, opinions or credibility. If the jury is allowed to hear testimony regarding this incident, they will be distracted from the core issues to deciding collateral credibility issues, such as: if the incident occurred; whether a real or imitation firearm was used; if a real firearm was used, whether it was loaded; and whether Dr. Golden intended to harm anyone.

Impeaching Dr. Golden with such conduct also raises other difficult issues. Of course, in any such litigation of the incident, Dr. Golden would have the same Fifth Amendment protection the defendant had when he spoke to police officers before his arrest. Thus, allowing inquiry into this disputed, collateral issue creates the possibility that this court will have to make a determination whether Dr. Golden has Fifth Amendment protection on this issue, whether Dr. Golden should be advised to seek counsel, and if Dr. Golden will exercise any applicable constitutional privilege.

---

19. In a lead article of the Daily Journal dated March 13, 1995, the author noted that a movie theatre crowd clapped and cheered when, in the movie Jurassic Park, a menacing dinosaur ate a lawyer. The article is attached as exhibit "C".

In order to avoid this undue consumption of time, Evidence Code Section 352 empowers courts to prevent criminal trials from degenerating into nitpicking wars of attrition over collateral credibility issues. *Wheeler,* 4 Cal.4th at 296. The court should exercise its discretion in this case to prevent that which Evidence Code Section 352 was designed to prevent.

(B) Errors allegedly made in unrelated autopsies.

Since the June 12, 1994 murders of Mr. Goldman and Ms. Brown, a Los Angeles Times article, written by Ralph Frammolino, was published on October 2, 1994. In that article, allegations were made that Dr. Golden mischaracterized entrance and exit wounds in an October, 1990 autopsy and, in another 1990 autopsy, improperly described the distance from which a gunshot wound was inflicted. In response to a letter of inquiry from Mr. Frammolino, Dr. Lakshmanan Sathyavagiswaran, the Chief Medical Examiner— Coroner for Los Angeles County, addressed the two alleged mischaracterizations. The People submit that evidence of alleged mischaracterizations are inadmissible should the defendant seek to use them for impeachment purposes. Thus, the People hereby move to prevent their introduction.

Prior acts of alleged negligence are inadmissible to prove Dr. Golden was negligent in the autopsies of Mr. Goldman and Ms. Brown. Evidence Code Section 1104 states explicitly:

> "Evidence of a trait of a person's character with respect to care or skill is inadmissible to prove the quality of his conduct on a specified occasion."

It is clear the relevance of these prior mistakes can only be to infer that Dr. Golden failed to exercise the proper care or skill when performing the autopsies of Mr. Goldman and Ms. Brown. Though on two occasions, Dr. Golden appears to have mischaracterized gunshot wounds, the character evidence rule prohibits the introduction of such evidence for the purpose of suggesting he was similarly negligent when characterizing the knife wounds of Mr. Goldman and Ms. Brown.

In an analogous case, *Hinson v. Clairemont Community Hospital,* 218 Cal.App.3d 1110 (1990), the trial court, in a medical malpractice suit, prohibited the plaintiff from cross-examining the defendant, a certified physician, in two areas. One involved the physician's termination for a medical residency program because of inadequate performance, and the second concerned a suspension of hospital staff privileges because the physician performed unnecessary surgeries that endangered the lives of patients. *Hinson,* 218 Cal.App.3d at 1117.

Citing Evidence Code Section 1104, the Appellate Court affirmed the trial court's exclusion of the evidence, ruling "an individual's character as an [in]competent or [un]skilled physician, whether proven by reputation, opinion or specific acts, is not admissible to prove the defendant was negligent on a particular occasion." *Hinson,* 218 Cal. App.3d at 1122. Thus, the doctor could not be impeached with previous failures to show he was negligent on another occasion.

In a similar vein, character evidence involving specific acts of misjudgment is inadmissible to show Dr. Golden lacked the required skill of a physician when autopsying Mr. Goldman and Ms. Brown. Case law is clear that specific acts or opinion evidence is inadmissible to impeach a defendant doctor's general skill as a physician; likewise, a person's character cannot be used to show he or she lacked the requisite skill as a physician on a particular occasion. *Hinson,* 218 Cal.App.3d at 1122. Knowledge and skill, the threshold qualifications for a physician, "generally are evidenced by graduating from medical school, passing the medical boards and receiving certification to practice medicine." *Hinson,* 218 Cal. App.3d at 1120.

Following the rule of *Hinson,* Doctor Golden has clearly satisfied the knowledge and skill requirements of a physician. Dr. Golden graduated from medical school, passed the medical boards, is licensed by the state of California to practice medicine, and has been board certified in forensic pathology since 1981.

Evidence Code Section 1104 and *Hinson* clearly prohibit the use of a character trait, established by prior acts of misjudgment, to prove Dr. Golden was negligent in the autopsies of Mr. Goldman and Ms. Brown, or to establish any lack in Dr. Golden's qualifications as a forensic pathologist. The court should forbid any attempt by the defendant to use such evidence for impeachment purposes.

The probative value of Dr. Golden's two prior mistakes is substantially outweighed by the undue consumption of time necessary to litigate this collateral issue. As noted earlier, Evidence Code 352 enables the court to exclude evidence if its admission will necessitate an undue consumption of time, confuse the issues, or mislead the jury.

Impeaching Dr. Golden with prior mistakes would necessitate an inquiry into the circumstances of each autopsy on which a claim of error is made. Rebuttal inquiry would then be required to show that in the other 6,500 autopsies performed by Dr. Golden during his 15 years as a deputy medical examiner, no mistakes were made.

Along with Evidence Code Section 352, the policy behind Evidence Code Section 1104 applies to the instant case. The Law

Revision Commission's comment to Evidence Code Section 1104 aptly states the purpose of the rule is:

> "to prevent collateral issues from consuming too much time and distracting the attention of the trier of fact from what was actually done on the particular occasion."

Allowing the jury to hear about numerous, unrelated autopsies conducted by Dr. Golden will not only consume precious amounts of the court's time, but distract the jury from what was actually done in the autopsies of Mr. Goldman and Ms. Brown.

Secondly, the probative value of Dr. Golden's two prior mistakes is substantially outweighed by the danger of confusing the issues. Admittedly, Dr. Golden appears to have mischaracterized the entrance and exit gunshot wounds in the October, 1990 autopsy. However, one must nevertheless ask whether mischaracterizing two gunshot wounds, in an unrelated autopsy four years earlier, bears probative value on Dr. Golden's characterizations of knife wounds in the instant case. Are we to litigate the collateral issue of the similarity, or lack of similarity, between the identification of gunshot wounds and knife wounds when no one suggests gunshot wounds play any part in the determination of the cause and manner of death for Mr. Goldman and Ms. Brown? Evidence Code Section 352 suggests otherwise.

Lastly, admitting Dr. Golden's prior mistakes would mislead the jury as to his expertise as a medical examiner, not enlighten them.... Questioning Dr. Golden about two prior mistakes, out of 6,500 autopsies, would only mislead the jury as to his use of care in the autopsies of Mr. Goldman and Ms. Brown. The fact that Dr. Golden may have committed some mistakes in the past does not indicate he was careless in autopsying Mr. Goldman and Ms. Brown. The court should prohibit any such attempt to mislead the jury.

It is clear from defense counsel's opening statement that the defense contends Dr. Golden failed to properly conduct the autopsies of Mr. Goldman and Ms. Brown, thereby leading to the irretrievable loss of valuable evidence to exculpate the defendant. If such is true, defense counsel does not need the 1990 incidents to prove their contention, for the contention is either scientifically valid or invalid. If, as the People will unequivocally demonstrate, counsel's contention that the failures by Dr. Golden led to the the irretrievable loss of valuable exculpatory evidence is scientifically invalid, defense counsel cannot resurrect this strawman by pointing to Dr. Golden's past mistakes.

4. DEFENSE ARGUMENT

(A) Dr. Golden's Alleged Threats to Kill Attorneys.

The unusual solicitude and concern of the prosecution regarding the scope of cross-examination of Dr. Irwin Golden is certainly understandable. Dr. Golden is an essential witness whose testimony will be crucial to the resolution of many of the key issues the jury will have to ultimately resolve:

(1) The time of death of the victims, and the impact of delays in calling the coroner and mistakes made in conducting the autopsies upon the ability to ascertain time of death;

(2) The number of assailants involved in the attack on the victims, in light of Dr. Golden's conclusions that two morphologically different types of stab wounds were inflicted, and that two knives could have produced the injuries on both of the victims, presented at the Preliminary Hearing;

(3) The "rush to judgment" to implicate Mr. Simpson, as exemplified by the presentation of a knife purchased at Ross Cutlery to Dr. Golden by Detective Vanatter.

Dr. Golden's credibility and the weight to be given his opinions will be among the most important issues presented to the jury in this case. California Evidence Code § 721(a) addresses the cross-examination of expert witnesses, defining a permissible scope that both encompasses and surpasses the scope of cross-examination of ordinary witnesses:

"Subject to subdivision (b), a witness testifying as an expert may be cross-examined to the same extent as any other witness and, in addition, may be fully cross-examined as to (1) his qualifications, (2) the subject to which his expert testimony relates, and (3) the matter upon which his opinion is based and the reasons for his opinions."

California courts have frequently restated the rule that "a wide latitude is permitted in the cross-examination of an expert witness in all matters tending to test his credibility so that the jury may determine the weight to be given the testimony." *People v. Tallman,* 27 Cal.2d 209, 214 (1945); *Laird v. T. W. Mather, Inc.,* 51 Cal.2d 210 (1958).

The reports summarizing the internal investigation of the July 21, 1994 incident involving Dr. Golden are guarded and circumspect, but they confirm that on the morning of Thursday, July 21, 1994, Dr. Golden displayed a handgun on the premises of the Los Angeles County Coroner's Office, and said as reported by one witness, "You know we ought to go out and kill nine or ten of those attorneys."

There is ample reason to believe that the targets of Dr. Golden's rancor were the attorneys who are representing Mr. Simpson in this trial. The incident took place shortly after Dr. Golden was subjected to a blistering cross-examination at the Preliminary Hearing of his case. (Dr. Golden's Preliminary Hearing testimony was concluded on July 8, 1994). It was widely reported that the defense team assembled to represent Mr. Simpson included nine or ten attorneys. Dr. Golden's performance in this case had become the object of intense media scrutiny at the same time this incident occurred.

The prosecution's attempt to recast this incident as a display of antipathy for lawyers in general, accompanied by a newspaper clipping reporting theater audiences clapped when a lawyer was consumed by a dinosaur in the movie *Jurassic Park,* is a transparent effort to turn a serious lapse of professional judgment and a potentially dangerous threat to the safety of others into a sick joke. After the tragedy of the assault at Pettit & Martin in San Francisco on July 1, 1993, there is simply nothing funny about a threat to kill nine or ten attorneys, and the report that an Investigator with the Department of the Coroner would "giggle" about it and fail to report a violation of the flat prohibition of firearms in the workplace is itself a rather shocking revelation. Even more shocking is the decision of the City Attorney to dismiss a complaint regarding the incident without making any effort to interview or question Dr. Golden about it.

Equally alarming is the report that Dr. Golden is the registered owner of 22 firearms, and that he admitted to Dr. Rogers that he brought an "unloaded gun" to the workplace, allegedly for a lecture series not scheduled to begin for a month, and in violation of County policy forbidding such use of firearms. In light of these undisputed facts, the Prosecution's repeated description of the incident as involving "a toy or real firearm" is disingenuous.

The relevance of this incident to Dr. Golden's testimony as an expert witness is repeatedly mischaracterized by the prosecution as evidence of "bad character." Its real relevance is to challenge his credibility under California Evidence Code § 780(f), by showing the existence or nonexistence of bias, interest or other motive, and § 780(j), by showing his attitude toward the action in which he testifies or toward the giving of testimony.

In these respects, an expert is subject to the same kind of cross-examination appropriate for any other witness who has expressed hostility or favor to one side or the other, or a general attitude of hostility toward lawyers engaged in examining or cross-examining him. As the Court put it in *Anderson v. Southern Pacific Co.,* 129 Cal.App. 206, 211–12 (1933):

> "This witness having been offered as an expert, respondent had the right to examine fully into his knowledge of the particular matter covering his entire range of experience. More particularly were they entitled to go into the line of examination objected to for the purpose of showing bias or prejudice of the witness."

This Court has already noted the wide scope of inquiry permitted with respect to cross-examination to show bias, relying upon *In Re Anthony P.,* 167 Cal.App.3d 502 (1985). It makes no difference whether a witness' hostility arises from racial animosity or animosity to a particular profession.

The risks of undue consumption of time, confusion of issues or misleading the jury suggested by the prosecution motion are imaginary, conjectural and based upon a misconception of the relevance of this evidence.

The circumstances of what happened as they relate to the issue of bias are not in dispute, nor is a "threshold of moral turpitude" necessary. The evidence goes directly to the credibility of an essential witness. As a leading commentator on the California law of evidence concludes:

> "Section 352 calls for a flexible response tailored by the judge to the circumstances presented by the case being tried. If the witness sought to be impeached on the grounds of bias is a key witness and no other significant ground of impeachment is available, the judge may permit extended inquiry into the existence of, as well as the reasons for, the bias."

Mendez, *California Evidence,* § 15.11, pp. 301–302 (1993).

Any invocation of a Fifth Amendment privilege against self-incrimination by Dr. Golden can be easily overcome by a prosecutorial grant of immunity pursuant to California Penal Code § 1324. The alacrity with which the City Attorney dismissed a complaint in this case suggests little prosecutorial interest in pursuing a criminal prosecution of Dr. Golden.

The constitutional nature of the right to cross-examine witnesses to show bias was recognized by the U.S. Supreme Court in *Davis v. Alaska,* 415 U.S. 308 (1974). Holding that the Sixth Amendment guarantee of the right to be confronted with the witnesses against oneself overcomes even the state interest in protecting the confidentiality of juvenile offender's record, the Court emphasized the importance of cross-examination as "the principle means by which the believability of a witness and the truth of his testimony are tested." More particularly, the Court underscored the relevance of exposing a witness's motivation in testifying:

> "A more particular attack on the witness's credibility is effected by means of cross-examination directed toward revealing possible biases, prejudices or ulterior motives of the witness as they may relate directly to the issues or personalities in the case at hand."

415 U.S. at 316. Counsel conducting such cross-examination must be permitted to elicit the *facts* from which a bias might be inferred even if the witness denies a bias. *Id.* at 318. Thus, preclusion of cross-examination of Dr. Golden regarding his threats to lawyers would not only violate the rights of the defendant under the California Evidence Code, but would also violate his federal and state constitutional rights to confront the witnesses against him.

(B) Previous Mistakes in the Scrutiny of Wounds.

In calling Dr. Golden as an expert witness, the prosecution will seek to quality him as an expert in the analysis of wounds and elicit his opinions as to "whether one or more person or knife could have inflicted all wounds on both victims, the extent of resistance by each victim to the lethal assault, whether any particular wound or injury was inflicted before death (*ante mortem*), around the time of death (*peri mortem*), or after death (*post mortem*) and, in certain situations, whether a wound or injury was inflicted, relatively speaking, earlier or later in the assault." (See Points and Authorities in Support of the Prosecution's Motion to Introduce and Admit Crime Scene and Autopsy Photos of the Victims, p. 12).

Cross-examination regarding Dr. Golden's acknowledged prior mistakes will be highly relevant to the jury's determination of what weight to give his opinions on these issues. While Dr. Golden may offer an explanation that his incompetence in examining wounds is limited to gunshot wounds, and does not carry over to knife wounds, it should be left to the jury whether that is a plausible explanation. The cross-examination clearly comes within the mandate of California Evidence Code § 721 (a), which provides that an expert "may be fully cross-examined as to (1) his qualifications, (2) the subject to which his expert testimony relates, and (3) the matter upon which his opinion is based and the reasons for his opinion."

Once again, the prosecution mischaracterizes the evidence as evidence of "bad character." The relevance of prior mistakes is not to show his conduct of the autopsy was negligent based on prior negligent acts. Its relevancy is to challenge his qualifications to render an expert opinion regarding the character and nature of wounds, and to suggest that such opinions are entitled to little weight or credibility.

The only authority offered by the prosecution to support its argument is completely inapposite. *Hinson v. Clairemont Community Hospital,* 218 Cal. App.3d 1110 (1990) addresses the admissibility of evidence of a physician's failures in training programs to prove his negligence in treating the plaintiff. In fact, the court noted that the same evidence was *not* excluded for impeachment purposes when offered to challenge the testimony of the defendant as an expert. The case simply does not address the question of the relevance of prior mistakes to challenge the qualifications of an expert witness or the credibility and weight to be accorded his opinions.

The courts that *have* addressed this issue have held that the failure to permit cross-examination of expert witnesses regarding prior challenges to their competence is reversible error. In *Navarro de Cosme v. Hospital Pavia,* 922 F.2d 926 (1st Cir. 1991), the court held that the fact that a physician called as an expert witness had previously submitted inflated invoices and was a defendant in three malpractice cases was the type of information that a litigant is "more than entitled to cover" because they "all pertained to his credibility as a witness." 922 F.2d at 933. The Federal Rules of Evidence are analogous to the California Evidence Code with respect to the cross-examination of expert witnesses. Mendez, *California Evidence* § 16.06, p. 327, n.2 (1993). *Accord, Underhill v. Stephenson,* 756 S.W.2d 459 (Kentucky 1988); *Willoughby v. Wilkins,* 310 S.E.2d 90 (No. Carolina 1983).

The fact that Dr. Golden has prepared numerous addendums to the original autopsy report in this case makes the acknowledgement of previous mistakes in addendums to reports highly relevant. The exposed "rate of error" cannot be determined by the gross number of autopsies Dr. Golden has conducted in his entire career, but the number of times he has offered opinions concerning the nature of gunshot or knife wounds. There is no danger the jury will be misled by the acknowledgement of prior mistakes. Even more misleading would be the presentation of Dr. Golden as an expert who has performed thousands of autopsies, without the jury ever knowing that crucial mistakes were made regarding key findings within the expected competency of Dr. Golden in two recent cases.

No question could be more relevant in cross-examining an expert than to ask, "Doctor, have you made mistakes before in rendering an expert opinion regarding wounds?" Ordinarily, the answer to that question would be, "no, not that I'm aware of." In Dr. Golden's case, the answer must be, not once, but twice. The jury that will be instructed to give his opinions the weight they believe they deserve is entitled to hear that answer.

5. JUDGES' RULINGS

Judge Lance Ito granted the prosecution's motion in limine with respect to the gun incident, but denied the motion with respect to prior autopsy mistakes. The prosecution elected not to call Dr. Golden as a witness at the criminal trial, instead relying on the testimony of his superior, Los Angeles County Coroner Dr. Lakshamanan Sathyavageswaran. The plaintiffs in the civil case also relied upon the testimony of Dr. Sathyavageswaran, and did not call Dr. Golden.

6. COMMENTS AND QUESTIONS

(a) If the prosecutors chose to call Dr. Golden, how might they have handled the impeachment with prior autopsies that Judge Ito indicated he would allow? Vincent Bugliosi, who was highly critical of the decision not to call Dr. Golden, offered his own suggestion:

> "Feeling that Dr. Golden would be a liability and an embarrassment on the witness stand, the prosecutors decided not to call him to testify at the trial. Instead, they called Golden's superior, the coroner himself.... Right off the top, this was a very poor strategy. It looked, once again, as if the prosecutors were trying to hide something from the jury, and this fact was spotlighted by the defense when [the coroner] conceded on cross-examination that it was the first time in his career he had ever heard of the DA's calling to the stand a doctor other than the one who had conducted the autopsy relevant to the case.
>
> All prosecutors, all lawyers, in fact, have been confronted many times in their careers with very poor witnesses. But if you prepare them adequately, there's no problem at all. There is no question that Dr. Golden could have been prepared to the point where (apart from his autopsy report, which was water over the dam) he would not have been a further liability. After all, he had been with the coroner's office since 1981, had conducted more than five thousand autopsies, and had testified in close to a thousand cases during his career. The fact that he was still around means that he couldn't have been that bad. If he had been, the DA's office, long ago, would have insisted to the coroner that he not be used on any criminal homicide case. Golden's colleagues, in fact, consider him to be competent. The prosecutor could easily have had Golden himself concede the errors he made in the Simpson case, and that would have been it. Even his mistaking an entrance wound for an exit wound in a previous case is no problem at all.

Suppose it had gone as follows:

'Doctor, in the case of so-and-so, you apparently misidentified an entrance wound as an exit wound, is that correct?'

'Yes.'

'You do, of course, know the difference between an entrance wound and an exit wound?'

'Of course.'

'Would you briefly explain to the jury the differences between the two types of wounds, such as their configuration, the presence or absence of an abrasion collar, and so forth, which a pathologist such a yourself looks to in distinguishing these wounds?'

'Yes.' And the witness does so.

'How many autopsies in your career have you had where you had to determine whether a wound was an entrance or exit wound?'

'Probably five hundred or so.'

'In any of these other five hundred autopsies did you misidentify an entrance wound as an exit wound?'

'No.'

And that would be it."

V. Bugliosi, *Outrage: The Five Reasons Why O.J. Simpson Got Away with Murder,* pp. 120–21 (W.W.Norton & Co., 1996).

(b) The ruling on admissibility of prior autopsy errors may not have been the only reason why the prosecutors decided to keep Dr. Golden off the witness stand. In a pretrial ruling, Judge Ito had revealed to the prosecution the results of a forensic analysis of the stiletto knife O.J. Simpson had purchased at Ross Cutlery two weeks before the murder, showing it could not have been the murder weapon. Detectives had purchased an identical knife from Ross Cutlery, and presented it to Dr. Golden, who rendered an opinion that such a knife could have inflicted all the wounds on both victims. The sealed envelope containing the knife was never opened at the trial. Cross examination of Dr. Golden would have give the defense a "golden opportunity" to dramatically unseal the envelope and expose Dr. Golden's role in the L.A.P.D.'s "rush to judgment." See Uelmen, *Lessons From the Trial: The People v. O.J. Simpson,* p. 17 (Andrews & McMeel, 1996) ("One of the principle reasons the prosecution did not call the coroner who performed the autopsies as a witness at the trial was to avoid the embarrassment of cross-examination about his opinion that the wounds could have been inflicted by the knife that had remained behind Mr. Simpson's bedroom mirror until it was brought to court in a sealed envelope.").

Chapter V

EXPERT WITNESSES

A. LUMINOL TEST RESULTS

1. THE EVIDENCE

On August 30, 1994, O.J. Simpson's Ford Bronco was towed to Keystone Towing in order to conduct "Luminol" testing. The vehicle was placed in a sealed enclosure which could be darkened, and the interior was sprayed with a chemical reagent. The reagent causes a luminescent glow, like a watch dial, when it comes in contact with blood. Photographs were taken to demonstrate that areas of the carpet and upholstery "glowed" after being sprayed with the reagent.

2. THE TACTICAL CONTEXT

An *in limine* motion challenging the admissibility of luminol test results was filed at the same time as the motion challenging the chain of custody of the Bronco. While the luminol tests did not identify the source of any blood stains, the photos had the potential to be very dramatic demonstrative evidence, which the prosecution could have utilized to argue that large quantities of blood stained items, such as a weapon or clothing, had been transported in the Bronco, and that an effort had been made to clean up the Bronco the night of the murders.

3. DEFENSE ARGUMENT

Apart from any Fourth Amendment objections, there are four independent reasons why the results of luminol testing of the Ford Bronco are not admissible in this case:

First, the testing was conducted more than ten weeks after the Bronco was seized. The failure to establish with reasonable certainty that there was no alteration or tampering with the contents of the vehicle as of June 15, 1994 precludes the admission of testing or test results of those contents ten weeks later.

Second, luminol testing is a preliminary, presumptive test which does not even meet the minimum standard of relevancy.

Third, luminol results, even if relevant, should be excluded pursuant to Evidence Code § 352 because they "create a substantial danger of undue prejudice, of confusing the issue, or of misleading the jury."

Finally, and only in the event that the Court rejects all of the first three reasons, the luminol test results must be subjected to a Kelly–Frye hearing, at which it will be established that such tests have not achieved general acceptance in the scientific community to establish the presence of human blood.

While there is no California precedent directly addressing the admissibility of presumptive blood test results to show guilt in a criminal trial, the supreme courts of two different states have recently had occasion to consider their admissibility in criminal cases.

In *Brenk v. State,* 847 S.W.2d 1 (Ark. 1993), the Supreme Court of Arkansas reversed the conviction of a defendant sentenced to death for murdering and dismembering his wife, on the grounds that the results of luminol tests of his trailer and automobile were improperly admitted at his trial.

Noting that Arkansas did not follow the restrictive test of *Frye v. United States,* 293 F. 1013 (D.C.Cir. 1923) in considering scientific evidence, the Court analyzed the admissibility of luminol results under the relevancy standard of the Uniform Rules of Evidence:

> "Under the relevancy approach, reliability is the critical element.... The relevancy approach, unlike the *Frye* standard, permits, but does not require, a referendum by the relevant scientific community to determine the reliability of the technique. Many times that factor alone will determine the issue. One the other hand, courts may look to a number of other factors which bear upon reliability. These include the novelty of the new technique, a relationship to more established modes of scientific analysis, the existence of specialized literature dealing with the technique, the qualifications and professional stature of expert witnesses, and the non-judicial uses to which the scientific techniques are put."

847 S.W.2d at 8. The Court noted that luminol testing is a preliminary test which only indicates the *possible* presence of blood. Among other substances which give positive reactions to the luminol reagents are chemical oxides, nickel salts, copper salts, iodine,

household bleaches, rusts, formalin, horseradish, citrus fruit, watermelon, bananas and numerous other vegetables. Eckert & James, *Interpretation of Bloodstains at the Crime Scene,* p. 122 (1989). The lack of specificity was the key reason for the *Brenk* court's rejection of luminol:

> "Luminol testing is done by spraying a luminol reagent on the item or in the area to be tested. Luminol reacts with certain metals and vegetable matter as well as blood, animal and human, to give off a light blue luminescence similar to a luminescent watch dial. It is impossible to tell without follow-up testing which of the possible reactants is causing the reaction. Further testing is necessary to determine whether what caused the reaction is actually blood and whether, if blood, it is animal or human blood. Luminol testing, without any additional testing, is unreliable to indicate the presence of human blood. Additionally, luminol is not time specific. That is, a reaction will occur even many years after a reacting substance has been in place, so it is impossible to tell how long the substance that is causing the reaction has been in place."

847 S.W. at 9. While leaving the door open to more specific follow-up testing to confirm that blood is human blood related to the alleged crime, the Court concluded that the results of luminol testing itself were not admissible:

> "Given the lack of follow-up testing, the results of the luminol test, which are presumptive only, had no probative value and did nothing to establish the likelihood of the presence of Lou Alice Brenk's blood, or even human blood, in the trailer, the block building, appellant's car, or on any of the other items tested where follow-up testing was not able to confirm the presence of human blood, much less blood of the same blood type as Lou Alice Brenk. *State v. Moody,* 214 Conn. 516, 573 A.2d 716 (1990). Since we have determined that luminol tests done without follow-up procedures are unreliable to prove the presence of human blood or that the substance causing the reaction was related to the alleged crime, we find it was error for the trial court to admit the evidence of luminol testing done by Mr. Smith where there was no follow-up testing done to establish that the substance causing the luminol reaction was, in fact, human blood related to the alleged crime."

847 S.W.2d at 9.

In *State v. Moody,* 573 A.2d 719 (Conn. Sup. Ct. 1990), the Supreme Court of Connecticut reversed the murder conviction of a young man convicted on evidence that he had been cut by the victim and left three "driplets" of blood and the murder scene which matched his blood type. Evidence was also admitted that a stain on the sole of one of defendant's shoes removed from his own apartment gave a positive result to presumptive blood tests. The stain was too small for an actual laboratory test to confirm that it was human blood or identify the type. Thus, only the presumptive test was offered in evidence, along with testimony that the positive result meant it "could be human blood, animal blood, or something other than blood."

The Court concluded:

"In the present case, the result of the 'presumptive test for blood' had no probative value whatsoever. The test result did nothing toward establishing the likelihood of the presence of human blood on the sole of the defendant's shoe. Therefore, we hold that the test result was entirely irrelevant, and thus, the trial court abused its discretion by admitting it into evidence."

573 A.2d at 722. Luminol, of course, is simply a presumptive blood test in a spray can. While the 'glow in the dark' effect lends it a magical element, it adds absolutely nothing to the evidentiary consequence of the results.

The *Moody* court found, in a note from the jury inquiring "what shoe blood found on," that they simply did not understand that the presumptive test was not probative that the stain on the shoe was human blood. 573 A.2d at 723. Thus, it is not appropriate to admit the evidence and leave its inconclusive nature as a matter of weight to be argued to the jury. The danger of misleading the jury is especially great in the presentation of testimony accompanying the test results, in which an 'expert' claims that a pattern of luminol results make it more likely that the positive reaction was caused by human blood. The *Brenk* court addressed this issue directly as an alternative basis for its holding that luminol results were erroneously admitted:

"Additionally, Don Smith was allowed to testify that, in his opinion, the results of the luminol testing were caused by blood, the luminol pictures and testimony by Mr. Smith gave the impression of a bloodbath and cleanup occurring in the trailer and block building behind the trailer that was highly prejudicial. Mr. Smith testified that although he was not aware of any literature dealing with establishing the substance causing the luminol to react based on the type of reaction, he felt he was able to do so. There is no indication in the record that personal observation of the results of the luminol testing is a reliable or accepted way to establish that the reaction was caused by blood and not one of the other substances which react with luminol. We think it was error to allow the photos into evidence and to allow Mr. Smith to testify about the other areas where reactions occurred, but photos were not introduced, and to allow Mr. Smith to testify that he thought that the reactions indicated the presence of blood without adequate follow-up testing having been done to establish that what caused the reaction was, in fact, blood. This was likely to be misleading and confusing to the jury such that even the cross-examination establishing that what caused the reaction in the photos and the areas where no photos were introduced cannot cure the prejudice that certainly resulted."

Luminol results should be excluded from evidence in this case because the tests were performed after a fatal breach in the security of the vehicle, because it is only a presumptive test which is irrelevant to prove the presence of human blood, and because of the substantial danger of undue prejudice, confusing the issues and misleading the jury. Only if all of these objections are rejected will it be necessary to proceed to a *Kelly-Frye* hearing on the degree of acceptance of such tests in the scientific community.

4. THE PROSECUTION ARGUMENT

There is no published opinion in California which addresses the admissibility of evidence of luminol testing. However, in several published cases, it was evident that evidence of luminol testing was indeed admitted at trial, although there was no issue on appeal which dealt with it. *People v. Cooper,* 53 Cal.3d 771, 796 (1991) ("A criminalist from the San Bernardino sheriff's crime laboratory sprayed various areas of the Lease house with luminol, a substance used to detect the presence of blood not visible to the naked eye. A positve reaction consisting of an even 'glow' ranging from about two feet to five feet above the floor was obtained on the shower walls in the Bilbia bathroom. Defendant left his footprint on the sill of this shower. There were also four positive reactions to the luminol on the rug in the hallway leading to the Bilbia bedroom that appeared to be foot impressions. Other positive reactions were obtained in the bedroom closet and bathroom sink. The reactions did not prove the presence of blood, but were 'an indication that it could be blood' "); *Green v. Superior Court,* 40 Cal.3d 126, 130 (1985) ("On February 16, Sitterud [the lead police investigator] arranged with the crime lab to spray the garage with flourinal or luminol, a process which reveals blood traces otherwise not visible"); *People v. Asgari,* 149 Cal.App.3d 107, 109 (1983) ("A luminol test of appellant's truck revealed three spots of blood at the end of the truck bed. Two of the three spots were determined to be human blood samples.").

The Supreme Court of Florida has squarely held that evidence of luminol testing is admissible to the jury and that the value and accuracy of that testing is for the jury to decide, even though there was no confirmatory test done to conclusively establish that the substance revealed by the luminol test was blood. *Johnston v. State of Florida,* 497 So.2d 863, 870 (1986). In *Johnston,* a police officer who performed the luminol testing "demonstrated that he possessed a sufficient working knowledge of luminol testing." The Supreme Court likened his testimony to that in a Florida Court of Appeal case of an officer testifying to his visual comparison of a defendant's automobile's tires with casts of tire prints found on and near the scene of the crime. In affirming the trial court's decision to admit such testimony in that case, the Court of Appeal "stressed the fact that the jury ultimately determines the credence and weight of the testimony." The Florida Supreme Court held:

> "Likewise, in this instance, *the jury properly determined the value and accuracy of the results of the admittedly 'presumptive' Luminol blood test."* 497 So.2d at 870 (emphasis supplied).

The Florida Court of Appeal case of *Florida v. Lewis,* 543 So.2d 760 (1989) is particularly apposite to this case because of a chain of custody issue which was interwoven with the luminol issue in that case, similar to the defense argument in this case with regard to the luminol testing of the interior of the Bronco. In the Florida case the Court of Appeal held that the trial court erred in granting the defendant a new trial based on the admission into evidence of bloodstained carpeting in the house in which the victim was murdered which was revealed by luminol testing. The victim in that case was murdered in the house of her boyfriend, David Mackey. The Court of Appeal explained as follows:

> "Lewis complained of the admission of a video/audio tape of the luminol test made of the carpet and the in-court demonstration of the luminol reaction to blood. John C. Saunders, a fingerprint specialist for the F.B.I., testified that one of the footprints revealed by the luminol test belonged to Lewis. The state theorized that Lewis' footprint was part of a pattern of bloody prints on the hall carpet and showed that Lewis was the perpetrator. Lewis advanced a chain of custody argument asserting that the carpet was not removed from the house for several months after the killing. Although the carpet was not in the continual custody of police, it was in the Mackey house, which was locked after the crime scene was initially investigated and to which access was available only to the owner, Mackey, law enforcement personnel, and the professional carpet cleaners who rolled up the carpet for storage. All of these people were available as witnesses. No evidence of probable tampering was offered, and we think the question of whether various persons' walking on the carpet might affect the luminol test is a matter which goes to the weight, as opposed to the admissibility, of the evidence. (Citation). Therefore, we find

that the trial judge properly admitted the carpet, and this
claim of error by the defense does not support the award of a
new trial."

543 So.2d at 766–67. The Court of Appeal therefore reversed the
order of the trial court granting a new trial. In *State of Nebraska v.
Jones,* 328 N.W.2d 166 (1982), the Supreme Court of Nebraska held
that a forensic serologist properly testified to luminol testing of the
defendant's apartment over the defense objection that she was not
sufficiently qualified as an expert witness. The Court held that
there was no evidence that luminol testing is not in the field of a
professional serologist and there was no abuse of discretion in the
trial court's admission of her expert testimony. 328 N.W.2d at 170.

In this case, the defense seeks to limit the admission of luminol
testing based on Arkansas and Connecticut cases which require the
prosecution to have evidence of follow-up testing that confirmed the
presence of blood before evidence of the luminol presumptive test
for blood can be admitted. There is no indication that the California
Supreme Court would so narrowly proscribe the admission of
luminol testing evidence in this state. The Florida Supreme Court
has declined to do so. We respectfully urge this Court to follow the
lead of the Florida Supreme Court and find that the evidence of
luminol testing should go to the jury for it to determine what
probative value, if any, to assign to it.

5. JUDGES' RULINGS

On November 14, 1994, Judge Lance Ito, in the same order
denying the defense challenge to Bronco evidence based on chain of
custody, ruled that luminol tests results, without follow-up confirmation tests, would not be admitted:

"The defense seeks the exclusion of Luminol testing results on
two additional grounds: 1) that the technique has not passed
the requirements of *People v. Kelly,* and 2) that the technique
is merely a presumptive test and therefore subject to challenge
under Evidence Code Section 352 as evidence whose prejudicial
value outweighs its probative value.

The issue of whether Luminol testing passes *Kelly* muster
is one of apparent first impression in this State. The two
California appellate cases in which the testing technique is
mentioned do not raise the issue of its initial admissibility. The
defense cites two extra-jurisdiction cases, one from the Supreme Court of Arkansas, *Brenk v. State,* 847 S.W.2d 1 (Ark.
1993) and the other from the Supreme Court of Connecticut,
State v. Moody, 214 Conn. 516 (1990). While interesting reading, neither compels the result in this case. Because the tech-

nique involves potential prejudice that outweighs its probative value, an analysis under Evidence Code Section 352, this Court need not determine whether Luminol passes *Kelly* muster.

Luminol is a presumptive test for the presence of blood. For serological evidence to be relevant in this case, it must be of human origin and from a source connected to one of the persons present at the crime scene. Luminol, as a presumptive test for the presence of blood, reacts to human and animal blood, certain metals, the oxidation of certain metals, certain plant enzymes as common as grass, and certain household cleaning products. When done in a properly darkened environment, the luminescent results can be spectacular. Unfortunately, such a spectacular test result has a prejudicial potential which outweighs its probative value. Luminol test results only become relevant after more discerning tests confirm the presence of human blood. Therefore, Luminol test results, without follow-up confirmation tests, will be excluded from this trial."

No luminol test results were admitted in either the civil or the criminal trial.

6. COMMENTS AND QUESTIONS

(a) Compare the admissibility of the results of presumptive tests of substances believed to be drugs. In *Davis v. State,* 217 S.E.2d 343 (Ga. Ct. App. 1975), the court held a 'field test' testing positive for cocaine was sufficient for conviction at trial when accompanied by testimony the defendant called the substance cocaine. In *Curtis v. State,* 548 S.W.2d 57 (Tex. Crim. App. 1977), on the other hand, the court held a "field test" testing positive for heroin was insufficient to even meet the preponderance of evidence standard applied to probation revocation proceedings.

B. WAIVER OF *KELLY–FRYE* HEARING

1. THE PROFFER

After selection of the jury, on the eve of a scheduled hearing of the Defense Motion to Exclude DNA testing results, the Defense filed a "Motion that All Evidence Concerning the Admissibility of Scientific Evidence Pursuant to *People v. Kelly* Be Presented During the Course of Trial in the Jury's Presence and that the Holding of a Separate *Kelly* Hearing Outside the Jury's Presence Be Dispensed With." The Motion was accompanied by the following affidavit of O.J. Simpson:

"I, O.J. Simpson, being duly sworn, declare and say the following:

1. Almost six months ago I was charged with two counts of murder for crimes I did not commit. Since that time I have repeatedly tried to make clear to all who would listen that I am completely innocent of those charges and have repeatedly asked my attorneys to do what they could to get me my day in court before a jury of my peers as soon as humanly possible.

2. My attorneys have told me that the prosecution plans to present DNA evidence at the trial and there is a very good chance that some or all of this evidence may not be legally admissible in California. My attorneys have explained to me that in most cases, people who stand accused of crimes generally have an interest in having the judge decide whether or not this evidence is admissible outside the jury's hearing. They have further explained to me at great length that there are disadvantages to having the jury exposed to this evidence especially if that evidence is ruled inadmissible by the judge.

3. My attorneys have also told me that the hearing on DNA admissibility could last as long as eight weeks. I am not willing to wait that long for my trial to proceed and have been told that I have a constitutional right to a speedy trial. In order to exercise my right to a speedy trial, I am willing to give up my right to have the DNA hearing outside the jury's presence. If the prosecutors present DNA evidence against me that is not legally admissible, I would be satisfied to have the judge instruct the jury to ignore it. I understand that there are legal risks to this approach, but my lawyers have fully and clearly discussed the risks and the benefits and I am prepared to waive any prejudice from the jury's exposure to any DNA evidence which is eventually found to be inadmissible.

5. I have made this decision knowingly and voluntarily because I have absolutely nothing to hide, because I want the whole truth to come out, and because I want the jury to start hearing my case as soon as possible."

2. THE TACTICAL CONTEXT

A hearing of the defense's *Kelly–Frye* motion challenging the admissibility of the expert testimony describing DNA testing results was not scheduled until after jury selection was completed. It would have necessitated a lengthy hearing out of the jury's presence to examine and cross-examine experts regarding the degree of acceptance within the scientific community of DNA testing for forensic purposes. Much of this testimony would then have to be repeated for the jury. The defense decision to waive the hearing came only after carefully weighing the advantages and disadvantages the hearing would present:

"As the time for the *Kelly–Frye* hearing approached, however, we faced a real dilemma. The prosecution had vigorously resisted our efforts to streamline the hearing by limiting the number of witnesses who could be called. The hearing would consume a minimum of two weeks and could easily stretch out to a month. That meant our jury would be kept 'on ice' for a long delay before the first witness was even called for the trial. We began a serious reassessment of what we had to gain and what we had to lose by mounting the *Kelly–Frye* challenge. Judge Ito's other pretrial rulings had convinced us that he would not exclude *any* DNA test results, even PCR. Unless there was clear and unavoidable precedent that compelled him to rule against the prosecution, he gave the prosecutors every benefit the law allowed. While there was no precedent holding PCR was admissible, neither was there any holding it was inadmissible. Judge Ito, we were certain, would let it all come in and leave the precedent-setting to a higher court. If we waived the *Kelly–Frye* hearing, however, we could not even present the issue to a higher court. We might be giving up a strong issue for appeal, to win a reversal if the trial resulted in a conviction.

Some of us on the team considered ourselves primarily 'appellate' lawyers, rather than 'trial' lawyers. We revel in the heady intellectualism of legal arguments to appellate courts, while the 'trial' lawyers grovel in the nitty-gritty of factual issues decided by juries. The appellate lawyers on our team were reluctant to give up an issue for potential appeal that could go either way. The trial lawyers on the team saw lots of advantages to waiving the hearing besides speeding up the trial and avoiding having to put the jury 'on ice.' The strongest evidence we would have to challenge the DNA results would be the sloppy way in which the samples were collected and processed even before the testing was done. Many of the same witnesses we were planning to call for the *Kelly–Frye* hearing would reappear during the trial to support our arguments relating to contamination. Why give the prosecution the advantage of probing our evidence in a 'warm-up' outside the presence of the jury? We would also gain an advantage in compelling the prosecutors to begin presenting their case to the jury sooner than they anticipated. Marcia Clark and Chris Darden were planning on turning over the *Kelly-Frye* hearing to a team of prosecutors with DNA experience assembled from D.A.'s offices all over the state, while they disappeared to prepare their opening statements and their lead-off witnesses so they could start the case with a bang in front of the jury.

We debated the strategy of waiving the *Kelly–Frye* hearing more vigorously than any other tactical call during the entire trial, and ultimately everyone was convinced that the potential advantages of the waiver outweighed the disadvantages. Before agreeing to an outright waiver, however, we decided to propose a compromise. We proposed having the *Kelly–Frye* hearing contemporaneous with the presentation of the evidence to the jury! Usually the hearing is held outside the presence of the jury before the jury hears the evidence in order to avoid prejudicing the jury by exposing them to evidence that may subsequently be excluded. Juries have difficulty putting out of their minds something they have already heard. We argued that that protection is to benefit the defendant. We were prepared to give up that protection. Let the jury hear the DNA evidence, we argued, rather than presenting the same evidence twice, first to the judge, then to the jury. After the evidence came in, Judge Ito could hear any additional evidence that was relevant only for the *Kelly–Frye* determination, and then decide whether it should be struck from the record and the jury instructed to disregard it. This course of action would give us the advantage of preserving the issue for appeal, without the delay of a pretrial hearing and a prosecutorial "preview" of our evidence. Since we anticipated an unfavorable ruling from Judge Ito anyway, we would risk little by allowing the jury to hear the evidence prior to his ruling.

The prosecutorial response to this suggestion was predictable. They squealed like stuck pigs. They did not want us to gain any procedural advantages without paying the price of a complete waiver. The court, however, had nothing to lose and much to gain from our proposal. It would avoid needless duplication, speed up the trial, and preserve the legal issues for orderly review by an appellate court. It was creative and innovative, and soundly based in the law of evidence."

Uelmen, *Lessons From the Trial: People v. O.J. Simpson* (Andrews & McMeel, 1996) at pp. 118–120.

3. DEFENSE ARGUMENT

California Evidence Code Section 402(b) provides:

"The Court *may* hear and determine the question of the admissibility of evidence out of the presence or hearing of the jury, but in a criminal action, the court shall hear and determine the question of the admissibility of a confession or admission of the defendant out of the presence and hearing of the jury if any party so requests."

(Emphasis added). This provision, by *permitting,* but not *requiring* judges to conduct hearings outside the presence or hearing of the jury concerning the admissibility of evidence—including the admissibility of scientific evidence pursuant to the standard set forth in *People v. Kelly,* 17 Cal.3d 24 (1976)—effectively authorizes judges to conduct such hearings in the jury's presence. The clear purpose of this provision is to prevent the party against whom evidence is offered from being prejudiced where that evidence is aired but subsequently ruled inadmissible. Where the party against whom the evidence is offered knowingly and intelligently waives the right to contest any resulting prejudice, the interests of judicial economy strongly militate in favor of providing one single opportunity at the trial for the parties to present the scientific evidence, pro and con, before the admissibility of that evidence is determined by the trial judge pursuant to the standard set forth in *Kelly, supra.*

Under California Evidence Code Section 403, trial judges are expressly authorized "to admit conditionally" evidence where its "*relevance* ... depends on the existence of [a] preliminary fact" which will be "supplied later in the course of the trial."[20] The admissibility of scientific evidence pursuant to *Kelly–Frye* has been expressly recognized by the California Supreme Court to constitute a question of "relevance." *People v. Kelly, supra;* see also, *People v. Leahy,* 8 Cal.4th 587 (1994) (observing that the adoption of the Truth-in-Evidence provision of the California Constitution, Art. I, § 28 (d)—providing that "*relevant evidence* shall not be excluded in any criminal proceeding"—"did not ... abrogate generally accepted rules by which the reliability and thus the relevance of scientific evidence is determined.").

The rationale underlying these provisions was set forth in the Advisory Committee Note to Federal Rule of Evidence 104(c), the federal counterpart of California Evidence Code § 402(b), which explains that the holding of separate hearings on admissibility tends to be "time consuming" and unnecessarily duplicative of evidence eventually presented at the trial:

> "Not infrequently the same evidence which is relevant to the issue of the establishment or fulfillment of a condition precedent to admissibility is also relevant to weight or credibility, and time is saved by taking foundation proof in the presence of the jury. Much evidence on preliminary questions, thought not

---

20. California Evidence Code Section 403 provides in pertinent part that:

(a) The proponent of the proffered evidence has the burden of producing evidence as to the existence of the preliminary fact, and the proffered evidence is inadmissible unless the court finds that there is evidence sufficient to sustain a finding of the existence of the preliminary fact when: (1) [t]he

relevance of the proffered evidence depends on the existence of the preliminary fact....

(b) Subject to Section 702, the court may admit conditionally the proffered evidence under this section, subject to evidence of the preliminary fact being supplied later in the course of the trial.

relevant to jury issues, may be heard by the jury with no adverse effect."

Although the admissibility of scientific evidence is plainly a legal determination for the trial judge and not the jury, see *People v. King,* 266 Cal.App.2d 437 (1968), the courts of this state have never *required* the presentation of *Kelly–Frye* evidence outside the jury's presence over the objection of the party against whom the scientific evidence is offered. There have been, however, a number of cases where the courts have heard testimony about and have ruled upon the admissibility of evidence in the jury's presence during the course of the trial. So, for example, in *Hodo v. Superior Court,* 30 Cal.App.3d 778 (1973), the court, in upholding the admission of voiceprint identification evidence at a probable cause hearing, observed without disapproval that the trial judge found such evidence inadmissible only after both the prosecution and the defense had presented their *Kelly–Frye* evidence *at the trial.* And in the seminal *Frye* case itself, the defense expert on "systolic blood pressure deception test[s]" was "offered" by defense counsel "*in the course of [the] trial,*" where, upon the prosecution's objection, it was ruled inadmissible. *Frye v. United States,* 293 F. 1013, 1014 (D.C. Cir. 1923) (emphasis added). Indeed, it is now a common practice for the courts of this state to hear evidence concerning the second and third prongs of the *Kelly* standard at the trial and in the presence of the jury, even where such courts have chosen to hear evidence concerning the first prong at separate pretrial proceedings.[21]

In numerous other contexts, courts admit evidence provisionally or subject to the laying of a proper foundation. This has even been done in the context of a defendant's confession where the potential for prejudice is enormous. See *People v. Fowler,* 109 Cal.App.3d 557, 564 n.1 (1980) (trial judge's holding of hearing in the presence of the jury on the admissibility of the defendant's confession was not error where the defendant had not moved for an *in camera* hearing); *People v. Perez,* 83 Cal.App.3d 718 (1978) (approving admission of codefendant's statements prior to the receipt of evidence establishing the foundational requirements for co-conspirator hearsay). In those cases where proper foundations were not ultimately established, the courts have simply ruled the

---

21. As the Court stated in *Kelly, supra,* "the admissibility of expert testimony based upon the application of a new scientific technique traditionally involves a two-step process: (1) the *reliability of the method* must be established, usually by expert testimony, and (2) the witness furnishing such testimony must be properly *qualified as an expert to give an opinion* on the subject. . . . Additionally, the proponent of the evidence must demonstrate that correct scientific procedures were used in the particular case." 17 Cal.3d at 28 (italics in original; citations omitted). The latter requirement governing *the scientific procedures used in this particular case* is herein referred to as the "third prong" of the *Kelly* standard.

evidence inadmissible and have issued curative instructions to cure any resulting prejudice. See *United States v. Bagley,* 641 F.2d 1235 (9th Cir. 1981) ("[curative] instructions are generally deemed sufficient as curative of prejudicial impact"). See also California Evidence Code § 403(c).

Where, as here, a criminal defendant has two distinct sets of rights, the right to have potentially prejudicial testimony heard outside the presence of a jury, on the one hand, and the right to a speedy trial, on the other, the defendant must surely be entitled to waive the former in order to vindicate what he believes to be a stronger interest in the latter. In the case at bar, the defendant has been expressly advised by counsel as to the risk and benefits of foregoing a pretrial *Kelly* hearing outside the jury's presence and, in submitting this motion, has knowingly waived the right to claim any prejudice arising from the jury's exposure to potentially inadmissible scientific evidence.[22] See *Affidavit of O.J. Simpson,* p.1.

In so doing, the defendant seeks to exercise his statutory and constitutional right to a speedy trial, Calif. Constitution, Art. I, § 15; U. S. Constitution, amend. VI; Calif. Pen. Code, §§ 686(1), 1050, one of the most "fundamental" rights of those criminally accused. . . . Indeed, the legislature has expressly mandated that "it shall be the duty of all courts and judicial officers and of all counsel . . . to expedite such proceedings to the greatest degree that is consistent with the ends of justice." Calif. Pen. Code § 1050(a). In the instant case, the need for the requested relief in order to preserve Mr. Simpson's right to a speedy trial is particularly compelling given that a separate *Kelly–Frye* hearing would take over five weeks.

In addition, given the extensive and highly prejudicial pretrial publicity which has infected and continues to infect these proceedings, the holding of a separate hearing could cause a delay of as long as eight or more weeks during which jurors and alternates might be exposed to additional highly prejudicial pretrial publicity which would further violate Mr. Simpson's state and federal constitutional rights to due process and to a fair trial before a fair and impartial jury. See *Sheppard v. Maxwell,* 384 U.S. 333 (1966).

Even if the jury is sequestered, there is great risk that the reason for a long delay before opening statements could be the subject of damaging speculation by jurors, and sorely try their patience at the outset of a lengthy and complex trial. An instruction could be fashioned to fully explain to the jury the conditional

---

22. Mr. Simpson is not, however, hereby waiving any claims arising from the court's substantive ruling on the admissibility of the prosecution's scientific evidence, nor is he hereby waiving any claim arising from any improper instructions that may be given to the jury concerning the admissibility or inadmissibility of such evidence.

nature of the DNA evidence, telling them they are not to draw inferences for or against either party if evidence they have heard about is later excluded.

Nor can it be said that dispensing with a separate and duplicative *Kelly–Frye* hearing will in any way prejudice the prosecution which will now be entitled to present relevant testimony supporting the reliability and scientificity of DNA testing before the judge and the jurors during the course of its case in chief. This course of action, moreover, is plainly in the interests of judicial economy and of the California taxpayers who have been patiently footing a multi-million dollar bill for the prosecution of this case.

Because the relief requested is necessary to protect Mr. Simpson's right to a speedy trial before a fair and impartial jury and substantially further the interests of judicial economy without prejudicing the prosecution, all evidence concerning the admissibility of the prosecution's scientific evidence necessary to this Court's determination pursuant to *People v. Kelly, supra,* should be presented during the course of the trial in the jury's presence, the holding of a separate and highly duplicative *Kelly–Frye* hearing outside the jury's presence should be dispensed with, and opening arguments should be scheduled to begin no later than January 4, 1995.

4. PROSECUTION ARGUMENT

Defendant's motion is as beguiling and simple on one level as it is misleading and without legal merit on another level. There is simply no legal authority for Defendant's proposal. In fact, the authorities cited in Defendant's motion demonstrate that the *only* legally appropriate way to litigate the admissibility of new scientific evidence is to conduct a *Kelly–Frye* hearing out of the presence of the jury in this case.

Defendant relies on Evidence Code Section 402(b) for the authority of a trial court to conduct an admissibility hearing regarding new or novel scientific evidence in the presence of the jury. Defendant's reliance is misplaced. Section 402 provides a procedural scheme for the determination of foundational or other facts preliminary to a determination of the admissibility of other evidence. Sections 403 and 405 describe alternative preliminary fact determination procedures, dependent upon the type of evidence sought to be declared admissible.

Defendant assumes a trial court determination of the admissibility of new or novel scientific evidence pursuant to *People v. Kelly,* 17 Cal.3d 24 (1976), and *Frye v. United States,* 293 F. 1013 (D.C. Cir. 1923), to be a section 403 preliminary fact determination.

Specifically, Defendant relies upon section 403(a)(1), requiring the evidence proponent to demonstrate relevance of the proffered evidence—in this case, establishing general acceptance of DNA typing methods as a preliminary fact to allow jury consideration.

The California Supreme Court specifically affirmed the general acceptance standard for the admissibility of new or novel scientific evidence in 1976 in *People v. Kelly, supra.* That standard is the exclusive means in this state for the determination of such admissibility. In fact, the California Supreme Court has specifically repudiated attempts to reject the *Kelly–Frye* standard (*People v. Harris,* 47 Cal.3d 1047 (1989)[based on the adoption of art.I, sec. 28(d) of the California Constitution] and to replace that standard with different guidelines for admissibility. (*People v. Leahy,* 8 Cal.4th 587, 604 (1994) [based on the U.S. Supreme Court rejection of *Frye* in *Daubert v. Merrell Dow Pharmaceuticals, Inc.,* 509 U.S. 579 (1993).

Curiously, Defendant declares that pursuant to Evidence Code Section 403, "trial judges are expressly authorized 'to admit conditionally' evidence where its '*relevance* . . . depends on the existence of [a] preliminary fact' which will be 'supplied later in the course of the trial.' " Defendant is incorrect in his assertion that the admission of new or novel scientific evidence is even governed by section 403.

Were the rule as Defendant advances, Evidence Code Section 403(c)(1) would compel the court on request of a criminal defendant to instruct the jury to disregard the scientific evidence unless the jury determined for itself that the scientific methodology and/or technique were generally accepted. No requirement exists in California that a jury make the same determination as the court renders in its decision of the admissibility of new or novel scientific evidence.

Consequently, no authority exists to support an admissibility hearing conducted in the presence of the jury. The California Supreme Court has repeatedly emphasized the need to insulate the results of new or novel scientific testing from juries absent an *in limine* preliminary showing of general acceptance in the scientific community. (*E.g., People v. Kelly, supra; People v. Leahy, supra.*)

Defendant would have the Court believe that presenting conflicting admissibility testimony before the jury has always occurred and that it is now "common practice" for such testimony to be presented "in the presence of the jury." For example, Defendant would have the Court believe that in *Frye v. United States, supra,* the testimony which was ultimately rejected by the trial court was presented before the jury, simply because the opinion states that the testimony was offered ". . . in the course of the trial." A careful reading of *Frye* does not support that interpretation, but demonstrates that the proffered testimony was debated and ruled inadmissible *outside the presence of the jury.*

The simple historical fact that *Frye* established the legal requirement of such *in limine* hearings also supports the Prosecution's interpretation that the hearing must occur before the trial. If the Court conducts the admissibility hearing before opening statements, as has been the Court's intention, the hearing would occur "... in the course of the trial," just as it did in *Frye.*

... Defendant declares that "[I]t is now common practice for the courts of this state to hear evidence concerning the second and third prongs of the *Kelly* standard at the trial and in the presence of the jury, even where such courts have chosen to hear evidence concerning the first prong at separate pretrial proceedings." Defendant refers to no cases, published or otherwise. The undersigned are actively involved in scientific admissibility litigation in this state and are regularly informed of the progress of such hearings throughout California. As a result of that familiarity, we can knowledgeably assert that Defendant's statement is simply untrue.

Defendant next relies on *People v. Fowler,* 109 Cal.App.3d 557 (1980) to demonstrate an analogous situation wherein a defendant's failure to require a hearing on the admissibility of his confession was not error, apparently to support his position. There is no need for analogy on this point. *People v. Poggi,* 45 Cal. 3d 306, 324 (1988) similarly requires a defendant to object on *Kelly-Frye* grounds or the objection is deemed waived. There is simply no provision in *Poggi* for a defendant's partial waiver of an admissibility hearing, dispensing of the *in limine* portion, but requiring it to be presented and litigated before the jury.

Defendant's earlier estimates of the length of the *Kelly-Frye* hearing seem to have fallen by the wayside, only to be replaced by a new estimate of "... over five weeks." If this recent estimate is correct, the hearing will take the same five weeks whether it occurs before opening statements or during the jury trial. This will mean that if the jury is sequestered—a very real possibility in this case— the defense motion will lengthen the period of their sequestration by at least five weeks. Such an imposition would be unduly burdensome and unfair to the jurors. The duration of the trial will be unaffected by when the *Kelly–Frye* hearing occurs.

Defendant's right to a speedy trial has already been satisfied in this case. Five weeks is five weeks, regardless of when the hearing is scheduled. Defendant gives lip service to the question of jury sequestration and how it relates to this Motion. As noted above, if the hearing is held *in limine,* as California legal authority mandates, there will not be a need to sequester the jury during the estimated five weeks. However, if the hearing is held in the presence of the jury, the jury must be sequestered for five weeks longer than would otherwise be necessary.

Defendant's claim that the Prosecution's case-in-chief trial testimony will be duplicative of the *Kelly–Frye* testimony reveals a basic ignorance of the manner in which DNA evidence is presented in jury trials. The Prosecution's focus at the jury trial will be to present the test results in a clear and meaningful manner. This can be accomplished in relatively short order. Very few of the *Kelly–Frye* witnesses will testify at the trial. The focus of the admissibility hearing is to demonstrate the general acceptance of the methods, a showing which requires hearing from a cross-section of the scientific community. The overall consumption of time will be nearly the same, regardless of when the Court schedules the hearing. The significant difference will be in whether or not the jury must be sequestered for longer than there is a legal necessity that they be sequestered.

. . . A jury confronted with several weeks of unnecessary scientific testimony will be both unduly burdened with irrelevant evidence and forced to forget important facts. Neither Defendant nor the Prosecution should be compelled to abandon the orderly presentation of evidence which an appropriate *in limine* motion regarding DNA evidence will provide.

5. JUDGE'S RULING

On December 18, 1994, Judge Ito denied the defendant's motion without comment, and directed the parties to be prepared to commence the *Kelly* hearing on January 5, 1995. He ordered the jurors to appear on January 18, 1995. The defendant then formally withdrew his motion for a *Kelly–Frye* hearing altogether. All DNA testing results were admitted into evidence at both trials without any challenge to the general acceptance of the testing techniques in the scientific community.

6. COMMENTS AND QUESTIONS

(a) The defense and the prosecution disagree whether the three prongs of the *Kelly–Frye* inquiry, explained in footnote 21, are resolved under California Evidence Code Section 403 or 405. In either event, would not the same evidence heard by the court at the *Kelly–Frye* hearing later be heard by the jury to assess the weight of the evidence?

(b) Would the subsequent withdrawal of the motion waive any error in the Judge's refusal to allow the *Kelly–Frye* hearing to be conducted in the presence of the jury?

Chapter VI

PRIVILEGES

A. JURY INSTRUCTIONS RE: INVOCATION OF THE FIFTH AMENDMENT BY FUHRMAN

1. PROPOSED INSTRUCTION

At the conclusion of Detective Fuhrman's testimony, he was excused subject to recall for further cross-examination. Judge Ito wanted to hear further evidence before he would allow some questions to be put to Fuhrman. After disclosure of the tape recorded conversations with Laura Hart McKinny, Fuhrman was called to the witness stand outside the presence of the jury, and the following testimony was elicited:

"MR. UELMEN: Detective Fuhrman, was the testimony that you gave at the preliminary hearing in this case completely truthful?

DET. FUHRMAN: I wish to assert my Fifth Amendment privilege.

Q: Have you ever falsified a police report?

A: I wish to assert my Fifth Amendment privilege.

Q: Is it your intention to assert your Fifth Amendment privilege with respect to all questions that I ask of you?

A: Yes.

Q: I have only one other question, Your Honor.

Detective Fuhrman, did you plant or manufacture any evidence in this case?

A: I assert my Fifth Amendment privilege."

The defense then requested that the jury be informed that Detective Fuhrman had refused to provide any further testimony in the case on the grounds of his Fifth Amendment privilege. The defense contended the only legitimate basis Fuhrman had to invoke the privilege at this point was fear of a perjury prosecution for the testimony he had previously given in the case. Relying principally upon *People v. Hecker,* 219 Cal.App.3d 1238 (1990), they argued that in the unique circumstance in which a jury may draw an adverse inference against a defendant because of the invocation of privilege by a witness, the claim of privilege may become relevant to an assessment of the witness' credibility. The prosecution argued that California Evidence Code Section 913, *infra,* precluded the jury from drawing any inference from invocation of the privilege. After hearing argument, Judge Ito announced that, while he would not permit any inference to be drawn from invocation of the *privilege,* the invocation of the privilege did render the witness *unavailable,* and the jury could be told that his *unavailability* could be considered by them in assessing his credibility:

"The record in this case indicates in our hearing yesterday outside the presence of the jury—and that was an appropriate procedure to proceed outside the presence of the jury because the counsel for Mr. Fuhrman, Darryl Mounger did advise the Court and Counsel that it was a possibility, in fact, a likelihood that Mr. Fuhrman would in fact seek to exercise his right not to testify under the Fifth Amendment to the United States Constitution.

After we held our hearing yesterday afternoon, the record is also clear that Mr. Fuhrman will refuse to answer any further questions as a witness in this case and he is, therefore, unavailable under the definition of Evidence Code 240.[23]

The record is equally clear that . . . the cross-examination as to Detective Fuhrman was adjourned subject to recall for further cross-examination. The subject matter that Mr. Fuhrman is likely and reasonably and appropriately subject to further cross-examination, we have heard over the last day and half four witnesses who have come in to testify for the specific reason to impeach the testimony of Detective Fuhrman.

Kathleen Bell was called, and this is not a particularly compelling reason for further cross-examination since Detective Fuhrman was in fact asked questions about Miss Bell on direct examination and cross-examination and there was sufficient opportunity since counsel on both sides were aware of the facts and circumstances that led to Miss Bell coming to the attention of counsel on both sides. However, as to Miss Singer, as to Mr. Hodge and as to Miss McKinny, Detective Fuhrman was not direct or cross-examined as

23. California Evidence Code Section 240 (a)(1) defines "unavailable as a witness" to include a declarant who is "exempted or precluded on the ground of privilege from testifying concerning the matter to which his or her statement is relevant."

to any of the statements made by those three witnesses who were called for the specific purpose of impeaching Detective Fuhrman.

The prejudice to the defendant based upon this unique set of circumstances is the inability to further cross-examine as to these three witnesses and the impeachment evidence that they have offered through their testimony, that is Singer, Hodge and McKinny. However, the case law is equally clear to the court that it is not appropriate to call a witness before a jury that counsel knows will invoke the privilege, and that is clearly the fact and circumstance here, and the court will, therefore, deny the request to recall Detective Fuhrman at this time in front of the jury.

The instruction offered as an alternative by the defense ... does have the disability of mentioning the invocation of the right against self-incrimination. Evidence Code Section 913 clearly states that it is not appropriate to comment upon or bring to the finder of fact's attention the invocation of a privilege.

California jury instruction 2.25 ... deals with the situation where a witness in the course of testifying before the jury invokes the privilege and then the jury is instructed not to infer or imply anything from that invocation.[24] Therefore, the court will instruct the jury as follows:

> "Detective Mark Fuhrman is not available for further testimony as a witness in this case. His unavailability for further testimony on cross-examination is a factor you may consider in evaluating his credibility as a witness."

The prosecution immediately sought a writ from the California Court of Appeal, to restrain Judge Ito from giving this proposed instruction. The petition for a writ was filed within five hours after Judge Ito announced that the instruction would be given.

2. THE TACTICAL CONTEXT

The defense sought the instruction to prevent the jury from drawing any *adverse* inference from their failure to recall Detective Fuhrman for further cross examination, since the jury knew he had not been excused. An alternative might have been to move to strike Fuhrman's testimony in its entirety, since his invocation of the

---

24. California Jury Instructions, Criminal (6th Ed. 1997), generally referred to by California lawyers and judges as "CALJIC", contains formula jury instructions for criminal cases which have been approved by a Committee of judges and lawyers. Instruction 2.25 provides:

"When a witness refuses to testify to any matter, relying on the constitutional privilege against self incrimination, you must not draw from the exercise of this privilege any inference as the the believability of the witness [or] [whether the defendant is guilty or not guilty] [or] [any other matter at issue in this trial]."

privilege deprived the defendant of his right to cross-examine, but the defense believed the dramatic evidence now available to impeach Fuhrman and show he committed perjury in his testimony would give the defense a greater advantage than having his testimony struck. The prosecution was concerned that the proposed instruction would invite the jury to speculate on the reasons for Fuhrman's unavailability, and draw inferences adverse to the prosecution. They preferred to have Fuhrman simply disappear from the case without explanation.

The intervention of an appellate court to question a trial judge's ruling on an evidentiary issue while the trial is still in progress is extremely rare, even in California.

3.   PROSECUTION ARGUMENT

A.   MANDATE SHOULD BE AVAILABLE TO THE PEOPLE TO CORRECT AN ERRONEOUS JURY INSTRUCTION THAT, BY THE COURT'S ORDER WILL BE GIVEN, EVEN THOUGH NO APPEAL WOULD LIE.

In *People v. Superior Court (Edmonds)*, 4 Cal.3d 605 (1971), a pretrial motion to suppress evidence was denied and a court trial commenced. At the conclusion of the trial the defendant renewed his motion to suppress evidence. The trial court took the motion under submission. Later, the court granted the renewed suppression motion but did not enter a judgment of dismissal in defendant's favor. The Supreme Court granted a People's petition for writ of mandate, holding that the trial court did not have jurisdiction to entertain the renewed suppression motion during trial. The case was remanded to the trial court for the conclusion of the trial. *Edmonds* demonstrates that a People's petition for a writ of mandate will lie after trial has commenced and prior to judgment. While the trial in that case was a court trial, there is no legal reason why a People's writ would lie in a court trial but not in a jury trial. In the present case, as in *Edmonds,* trial has already commenced but is not complete. Trial can continue pending this court's disposition of this petition. If the evidence portion of the trial concludes before there is a decision on this petition, petitioner will request a stay of trial pending such decision. In the meantime, this court can and should entertain the petition.

Normally, a writ will not lie to direct the trial court to correctly instruct the jury. In *Pryor v. Municipal Court,* 25 Cal.3d 238, 245 (1979), a certain jury instruction was given over the defendant's objection and there was a subsequent mistrial because of a hung jury. Prior to his retrial, the defendant petitioned for writs of mandate and prohibition seeking, inter alia, to prohibit the trial court from again giving the instruction in question. The Supreme

Court stated that 'because the writ of prohibition does not lie to prevent merely anticipated error ... defendant's objection to antici- pated jury instructions states no basis for present relief.

In *Pryor v. Municipal Court, supra,* the defendant's retrial had not yet started, so his petition for a writ to prohibit a repetition of the jury instruction given in the first trial was an effort to "prevent merely anticipated error." In the present case, in contrast, there has not only been a formal decision by the court as to the jury instruction in question but trial has begun and the instruction has been prepared and is ready to be read to the jury. In this situation, the erroneous jury instruction cannot be deemed "merely anticipat- ed error." It is error which has already occurred and must be corrected before the trial is over.... Because jeopardy has attached and no post trial appeal is possible, the only relief available to the People for an erroneous jury instruction is a mid-trial petition for writ of mandate.

Generally, the People may not obtain review by extraordinary writ where there is no statutory right to appeal. There is an exception, however, where the challenged order of the trial court is an act "in excess of jurisdiction," and if the need to correct the judicial error outweighs the conflicting threat of harassment to the defendant. In that situation, the petition may be entertained. *Edmonds, supra; People v. Superior Court (Howard),* 69 Cal.2d 491, 501 (1968). The exception applies to this case. In this case, there can be little, if any, risk of harassment to the accused since there is not danger of further *trial* or *retrial*. Defendant is already in trial, the writ relief sought, correcting the jury instruction which will be given at the next court session and which could be given again at the end of the trial, will not expose him to any *further* trial or *retrial*. Jeopardy has attached and defendant will have no more exposure to further trial than he would be if the writ relief were denied. Thus, there is no danger of harassment of the accused.

B.   RESPONDENT COURT ERRED AS A MATTER OF LAW AND EXCEEDED ITS JURISDICTION IN MAKING AN OR- DER THAT THE JURY BE INSTRUCTED IT MAY CONSID- ER FUHRMAN'S UNAVAILABILITY FOR FURTHER CROSS–EXAMINATION AS A FACTOR IN DETERMINING HIS CREDIBILITY AS A WITNESS.

The facts are not in dispute. Detective Fuhrman, when recalled to the witness stand for further cross-examination, invoked his right against self-incrimination as to each question and indicated he would do the same with each succeeding question. After argu- ment by the parties, respondent court then determined Fuhrman was unavailable as a witness and made its order that the jury be instructed it could consider this in evaluating his credibility. This order was contrary to law and in excess of the court's jurisdiction.

Like any other witness, Detective Fuhrman had the right to invoke his privilege against self-incrimination. (See Evid. Code, § 913; Fifth Amendment, U.S. Constitution.) When he invoked his privilege, certain consequences flowed from this fact. These include that he may not be forced to testify, the invocation may not be held against him, and the jury may not be advised of the invocation or otherwise allowed to evaluate his testimony based on this fact, *i.e.,* the jury is prohibited from drawing any adverse inference from this fact.

Evidence Code Section 913 provides:

"(a) If in the instant proceeding or on a prior occasion a privilege is or was exercised not to testify with respect to any matter, or to refuse to disclose or to prevent another from disclosing any matter, neither the presiding officer nor counsel may comment thereon, no presumption shall arise because of the exercise of the privilege, and the trier of fact may not draw any inference therefrom as to the credibility of the witness or as to any matter at issue in the proceeding.

(b) The court, at the request of a party who may be adversely affected because an unfavorable inference may be drawn by the jury because a privilege has been exercised, shall instruct the jury that no presumption arises because of the exercise of the privilege and that the jury may not draw any inference therefrom as to the credibility of the witness or as to any matter at issue in the proceeding."

Recent California case law has expressly upheld this statute and the procedure set forth therein. (See, *e.g., People v. Cudjo,* 6 Cal.4th 585, 619 (1993); *People v. Fierro,* 1 Cal. 4th 173, 232–233 (1991); *People v. Frierson,* 53 Cal. 3d 730, 743 (1991); *People v. Ford,* 45 Cal. 3d 431, 441 (1988); *People v. Mincey,* 2 Cal. 4th 408, 441 (1992)). As stated in *Mincey,* "A defendant's right to due process and to present a defense do not include a right to present to the jury a speculative, factually unfounded inference." *Ibid.*

In the instant case, the instruction which will be given to the jury is patently in derogation of Evidence Code section 913 and the principles embedded therein. It tells the jury that Fuhrman is unavailable and that they may consider this in determining his credibility. The fact that the court did not permit the invocation itself to occur in front of the jury does not save respondent court from its error because the privilege was invoked and the jury will be instructed they may consider Fuhrman's unavailability in determining his credibility.

Moreover, respondent court's attempt to avoid the prohibition of section 913 yet still give an instruction has exacerbated the problem because the jury is invited to speculate why Fuhrman is unavailable. Assuming arguendo the jury knew and understood the importance of the principle involved, they would at least understand clearly that Furhman's unavailability is the result of his invoking a constitutional privilege. Here, they cannot be sure; they only know he is unavailable. We submit this is not solution to the problem which faced the court. The obvious, correct resolution to the problem raised by the defense was to deny the request and not instruct the jury concerning Fuhrman's invocation of the privilege.

C. ALLOWING THE JURY TO DRAW AN IMPERMISSIBLE INFERENCE FROM THE EXERCISE OF THE CONSTITUTIONAL PRIVILEGE NOT TO INCRIMINATE ONESELF IS NOT AN APPROPRIATE REMEDY FOR THE DEFENDANT'S LOSS OF SOME CROSS–EXAMINATION OF AN ADVERSE WITNESS.

California Criminal Jury Instruction 2.25 and Evidence Code Section 913 state the well-established law that no inference may be drawn for the exercise of the privilege against self-incrimination. Indeed, no inference should be drawn from the exercise of any privilege not to testify. (See California Criminal Jury Instruction 2.26). The public policy in favor of this is obvious: the constitutional privilege is to some extent defeated if its exercise can be considered as an admission. In order to protect the exercise of the constitutional privilege, no inference is to be drawn just because of its invocation.

The rule of Evidence Code Section 913 cannot be avoided by telling the jury they may draw the inference while not telling them about the invocation of the privilege not to testify. It is clear that Detective Fuhrman's unavailability is caused solely by his invocation of the privilege against self-incrimination. That being the case, telling the jury that they "may consider" Fuhrman's *unavailability* in "evaluating his credibility as a witness" is the equivalent of telling them they may draw an inference from his invocation of the privilege. Respondent court's remedy for the defendant's loss of the opportunity to further cross-examine Detective Fuhrman is clearly in violation of Evidence Code Section 913 and CALJIC 2.25 and is therefore an impermissible remedy.

This remedy is unnecessary. It is worth noting that Detective Fuhrman was extensively cross-examined during his earlier testimony during the People's case. Moreover, several defense witnesses have testified in contradiction to statements made in Fuhrman's earlier testimony. The jury has heard damaging tape-recorded out-of-court statements by Fuhrman. Fuhrman's unavailability means that there will be apparently be no rebuttal from him to this impeaching evidence. The jury is clearly going to be told that it may make inferences as to Fuhrman's credibility based on the evidence already offered by the defense on that issue. With the impeaching evidence which has already come in, is it really necessary to unlawfully add to that impeaching evidence by having an inference drawn from the invocation of the privilege against self-incrimination?

The defense has explicitly declined to ask that Detective Fuhrman's testimony be stricken. ("We are not seeking that the testimony be stricken." Daily Transcript 9/7/95, p.67). Why hasn't the defense asked that Fuhrman's testimony be stricken? Perhaps because that would make Detective Fuhrman irrelevant to the case so that all testimony regarding Fuhrman would be stricken and the attention of the jury would be drawn back to the issue of the guilt or innocence of the defendant. No legitimate defense goal is served by attacking a witness' credibility while refusing to ask that his testimony be stricken.

4. JUDGES' RULING

On September 8, 1995, the California Court of Appeal issued an "Alternative Writ of Mandate and Stay Order." The Alternative Writ was issued less than four hours after the Petition of the Prosecution was filed, without inviting or hearing any response from the defense:

"TO THE SUPERIOR COURT OF LOS ANGELES COUNTY:

The petition for writ of mandate, filed September 8, 1995, having been read and considered, and good cause appearing therefor, you are hereby ordered either to:

(a) Vacate your order of September 7, 1995, regarding the proposed jury instruction directed to the unavailability of former Detective Mark Fuhrman to give further testimony as a witness in this case, and whether that unavailability was a factor which the jury could consider in evaluating his credibility as a witness, and enter a new and different order denying any request for a proposed instruction on the issue of former Detective Fuhrman's unavailability to provide further testimony, given the fact that you sustained the claim of privilege asserted by former Detective Fuhrman; or

(b) in the alternative, show cause before this court in its courtroom ... on September 11, 1995 at 9 a.m., why a peremptory writ ordering you to do so should not issue.

... Pending further order of this court, the proposed instruction regarding the unavailability of former Detective Fuhrman is not to be given. You are hereby ordered not to stay any other proceedings in this case."

Judge Ito immediately issued an order vacating his prior ruling, foreclosing the defense from any appearance before the Court of Appeal to show cause why a peremptory writ should not issue:

"The court, having been served with the Alternative Writ of Mandate and Stay Order Concerning the Giving of Proposed Jury Instruction from Division Five of the Second Appellate District of the Court of Appeal of the State of California, hereby vacates its order of September 7, 1995 regarding the court's proposed jury instruction about the unavailability of Mark Fuhrman for further testimony. As directed, the court hereby issues its order denying the defense request for a proposed jury instruction on the issue of former Detective Fuhrman's unavailability to provide further testimony. The court is grateful to the Court of Appeals for the expeditious manner in which this writ was handled."

5. DEFENSE ARGUMENT

On September 11, 1995, the defense filed a "Motion to Strike and Request for Remedies for Denial of Constitutional Right of Confrontation and Cross–Examination." That motion asked Judge Ito to afford the defendant one or more of the following remedies:

(1) The testimony of Detective Mark Fuhrman regarding his discovery of the Rockingham glove should be stricken from the record, and the glove itself should be removed from evidence;

(2) The court should order Detective Mark Fuhrman to testify under a grant of use immunity;

(3) Detective Mark Fuhrman should be recalled to testify to those aspects of cross-examination which are not subject to a valid claim of potential self-incrimination, and the Court should instruct the jury in accordance with CALJIC No. 2.25.

(4) The portions of the "Fuhrman Tapes" and transcripts regarding previous acts of planting or manufacturing evidence should be admitted in evidence as declarations against interest.

The following argument was presented in support of this motion:

"MR. UELMEN: Your Honor, as in so many other points in this trial, we are back to square one on an issue that we thought we had resolved, but we want to make it very clear that square one for us is the constitutional right to confront and cross-examine the witnesses against the defendant. And that right is so fundamental that no trial can be called a fair trial where that right has been denied. And the defendant will not waive that right by resting his case without some remedy that avoids an unfavorable inference from his unexplained failure to recall Detective Mark Fuhrman in the presence of the jury. Saying nothing and doing nothing actually prejudices the defendant because the jury is aware that he was subject to recall. In light of the evidence that has been presented, the failure to recall him or explain why we were not doing so can only result in an inference unfavorable to the defendant.

THE COURT: If you recollect that my ruling indicated that I felt ... that some instruction was appropriate because Mr. Fuhrman had not been subjected to cross-examination with regards to Singer, Hodge and McKinny.

MR. UELMEN: Yes, Your Honor. We would add Rokahr to that list.[25] ... What we have proposed, Your Honor, are three alternatives that this court has not previously considered, and we have renewed our request for a fourth alternative. We believe that any one of these four alternatives would be a satisfactory resolution of the problem, but no less than one of these is absolutely necessary.

The first alternative we propose is moving to strike the portion of the testimony of Detective Fuhrman that dealt with the discovery of the Rockingham glove and to strike the glove itself from evidence.

As we noted in our moving papers, we have not previously moved to strike any of Detective Fuhrman's testimony because we intend to rely on some of that testimony and we have a right to rely on it to put in evidence some very important issues from the defense perspective. We believe that as to some of the evidence provided by Detective Fuhrman, it is favorable to the defense or it contradicts other witnesses for the prosecution and can be used to challenge their credibility. It is a question of either Fuhrman is lying or one of these other witnesses is lying, and we believe we can argue, based on Detective Fuhrman's testimony, that perhaps other witnesses have perjured themselves in this trial as well.

I have delineated in the moving papers the areas in which we believe we are entitled to rely on the testimony of Detective Fuhrman.

---

25. Subsequent to Fuhrman's testimony that he did not physically approach the evidence at the Bundy crime scene before he accompanied other Detectives to Mr. Simpson's Rockingham residence, and that a photo of him kneeling and pointing to the Bundy glove was taken at 7:00 a.m. after his return from the Rockingham location, Police Photographer Rokahr was called and testified that the photograph was taken at night, and its sequence placed it among the photographs taken before Detectives departed for the Rockingham residence.

THE COURT: You are asking me to strike specific testimony. You want some, but you want some left in and you want some taken out, so I need to know specifically what it is that you are asking me to strike?

MR. UELMEN: Well, what we are asking be stricken is the only portion of Detective Fuhrman's testimony where the denial of cross-examination has seriously prejudiced us the most, and that is with respect to the discovery of the glove.

We would like stricken all of his testimony with respect to his discovery of the glove behind the residence at Rockingham and the glove itself, that they be stricken from evidence and the jury just simply be told to disregard that, don't rely on Detective Fuhrman's testimony with respect to finding that glove and ignore the glove in your deliberations.

We have been prejudiced in terms of cross-examination on whatever motives he might have had to plant that evidence. We have been precluded from confronting him with the testimony of the witnesses McKinny, Hodge, Singer and Rokahr with respect to the motives and opportunity in that respect. And we believe the appropriate remedy is simply tell the jury disregard it, forget it happened.

Our second alternative is closely related to the first, because it really points out the unfairness and the injustice of the prosecution putting a witness on the stand and getting the benefit of his direct testimony and relying on that testimony to prove their case without taking the lumps that come along with cross-examination, because of the invocation of the Fifth Amendment. The prosecution really has it within their control to eliminate that obstacle to cross-examination by the grant of immunity to the witness.

What we have proposed is that the court actually take judicial authority to grant use immunity to Detective Fuhrman. Under these circumstances to say to Detective Fuhrman none of the testimony you present on cross examination by the defense at this point will be used against you in a future prosecution, and thereby make his testimony on cross-examination available to the defense. We believe the prosecution should be estopped from objecting to that kind of a grant of use immunity because of their past reliance and their future intended reliance on Detective Fuhrman's testimony.

The strongest authority for that proposition comes from a case in which the Court of Appeal actually said that the prosecution could be compelled to grant statutory immunity under Section 1324 of the Penal Code under circumstances very similar to what we are presented with here. That case has not been previously called to the court's attention, and it was not even called to the attention of the

Court of Appeals in the petition for a writ that was filed by the People last week. We have ended up with a very curious situation where we have a controlling precedent from the Second District Court of Appeal that apparently was not considered by the court in issuing its alternative writ last week, nor has it yet been considered by this Court. That is the case of *People v. Garner*, 207 Cal.App.3d 935 (1989), where a very analogous situation is presented....[26]

[*Garner*] points out the irony of the prosecution's position if they are actually going to oppose the grant of use immunity to Detective Fuhrman, because the use immunity issue only comes up in the context in which he can legitimately claim the Fifth Amendment, if at all, and that is because he faces the risk of prosecution for perjury in the testimony he presented in this case to this jury. For the prosecution to come into this court and say we want to rely on that perjured testimony, we want to use it to convict this defendant and send him to prison for the rest of his life, and we don't want to immunize this witness from subsequently being prosecuted by us for perjury. Well, you can't have it both ways. And that's essentially the ruling that the court handed down in *Garner*.

So what the court is saying is, okay, it is your choice. If you are not going to accept immunity, then you have to accept striking the testimony. You can't have it both ways. And that is precisely the situation we have here. The invocation of the privilege is apparently based on a fear of prosecution of perjury, and the People intend to rely on this perjured testimony in making out their case in chief and arguing that the jury should consider this evidence of Detective Fuhrman finding this glove and the evidence of the glove itself.

The third alternative that we propose would involve the court making a much more specific determination of the availability of the privilege against self-incrimination by the witness Mark Fuhrman.

What Detective Fuhrman did in his brief appearance on the stand is to sweepingly invoke the privilege as to all future questions, and we believe that may be an inappropriate invocation of the Fifth Amendment, if the only concern is potential prosecution for perjury. Even with respect to potential prosecution for perjury, if in fact he assumes the risk by getting on the witness stand and in direct testimony willfully and knowingly presents perjured testimony, we believe that itself may have been a waiver of the Fifth Amendment privilege. Now, we recognize Your Honor's prior deter-

---

26. The moving papers also cited a New York case holding that if a prosecutor opts to use the testimony of a witness who invokes the Fifth Amendment based on claimed fear of a perjury prosecution for previous testimony, the use of the previous testimony can be conditioned upon the prosecutor's grant of immunity to the witness to permit full cross examination. *People v. Priester*, 470 N.Y.S.2d 478 (1983).

mination of the appropriateness of the invocation of the Fifth Amendment should be done out of the presence of the jury, but that can be accomplished in a Section 402 hearing at which Detective Fuhrman is subjected to question-by-question cross examination and the court makes a ruling in the context of that examination whether he can appropriately invoke the Fifth Amendment privilege. But bear in mind the burden is on him. Under Section 404 of the Evidence Code it is the witness who invokes the Fifth Amendment privilege who bears the burden of showing that his invocation of that privilege is appropriate.

Now, once the court has made such a determination, we can then proceed to cross examination of Detective Fuhrman in the presence of the jury with respect to the issues where the court has determined he has waived his Fifth Amendment privilege and he may not rely upon the privilege against self-incrimination in declining to testify. That, however, does not eliminate the need for some sort of instruction to the jury, because if we cross examine on very limited areas where he has not appropriately invoked the Fifth Amendment and are precluded from cross examining in those areas where the court has determined his invocation of the privilege is appropriate, we are left with the same problem. The jury will infer from our failure to cross examine in certain areas that we are conceding the credibility of his testimony when in fact the reason we are precluded from asking questions in those areas is because of his facing a realistic risk of a perjury prosecution for that testimony, so just the opposite inference should be drawn.

The *Garner* court addressed that problem. In fact, the *Garner* court very specifically said under these circumstances the jury should know that he has invoked the Fifth and they should invoke an adverse inference against him because the only basis for his invocation of the privilege is the risk of a perjury prosecution.

Recognizing that the court has already ruled on that issue, we want to emphasize that we are not waiving our objection to that ruling. But we are saying under those circumstances, the most appropriate instruction to give the jury now would be the 2.25 instruction of CALJIC. And it is important to note that the CALJIC Use Note itself indicates that this instruction, as slightly modified, can be given where the invocation of the Fifth Amendment is taken out of the presence of the jury. And what we have proposed is a slight modification of 2.25. So if we are permitted to cross-examine Detective Fuhrman in the areas where the court has indicated he may not invoke the privilege, the court should instruct the jury with respect to specific questions his invocation of the privilege has been upheld and they should not infer anything from that invocation of the privilege one way or the other.

The final alternative that we propose is one that we have proposed before, that in lieu of cross-examination we be allowed to present additional excerpts from the McKinny tapes and transcripts as declarations against interest.

[The invocation of the Fifth Amendment privilege has made Detective Fuhrman unavailable for cross-examination about the prior incidents of planting or destroying evidence. Those prior statements now qualify as declarations against interest as an exception to the hearsay rule.... In fact, they really present us with almost textbook examples of declarations against interest. Your Honor will recall that California Evidence Code Section 1230 provides that:

> "Evidence of a statement by a declarant having sufficient knowledge of the subject is not made inadmissible by the hearsay rule if the declarant is unavailable as a witness, and the statement, when made, was so far contrary to the declarant's pecuniary or proprietary interest or so far subjected him to the risk of civil or criminal liability or so far tended to render invalid a claim by him against another or created such a risk of making him an object of hatred, ridicule or social disgrace in the community."

I can't imagine any statements that could have more subjected a person to the kind of hatred, ridicule and social disgrace in the community that Detective Fuhrman now faces, than the kind of statements he made in those taped conversations with Miss McKinny. And the community that we are talking about of course is Los Angeles, not Sandpoint, Idaho.

THE COURT: Well, Counsel, let's not cast aspersions of the State of Idaho gratuitously.

MR. UELMEN: I don't intend to, Your Honor. What I'm saying is that under this exception to the hearsay rule, the social disgrace that the witness, at the time he makes the statements, may be subjected to is a social disgrace in the City of Los Angeles, and that is where these statements were made and that is the degree of social disgrace that we are looking at. And this exception to the hearsay rule really adds a new dimension to the probative weight that Your Honor must balance under 352.]

One of these four alternatives is going to be necessary in terms of the balance that the court must strike. We would contend that when a conflict arises between the fundamental right of the defendant to confront and cross-examine the witnesses against him, and the right of a witness to invoke the Fifth Amendment privilege, it is the Sixth Amendment right of confrontation that must prevail. We have proposed four very reasonable alternatives that would accommodate Mr. Simpson's right to confront and cross-examine Detective Fuhrman and still respect the valid assertion of a privilege against self-incrimination."

6. FINAL RULING OF THE COURT

Following argument by the prosecution opposing each of the four alternatives proposed by the the the defense, Judge Ito announced the following ruling:

> "With respect to the first request to strike the testimony of Detective Fuhrman as it relates to his discovery of the Rockingham glove, I find that prior to the submission of the arguments concerning the request for a jury instruction that that request was waived. Notwithstanding the waiver, assuming the defendant has the right to renew the request subsequent to the action by the Court of Appeal, I find that with regard to the issue presented and most forcefully argued, that is regarding the issue of the discovery of the glove, that Mr. Fuhrman was in fact cross-examined with regard to that specific issue, there was a full opportunity to cross-examine him over six days.
>
> ... As to the request that the court order the prosecution to grant use immunity, the court finds that the facts and circumstances in *Garner* are very unlike the facts and circumstances in this case. In that case, the sole evidence that was presented of the defendant's guilt was the preliminary hearing testimony that was presented because the witness was no longer available, having claimed the Fifth Amendment privilege. Here, the situation is that Mr. Fuhrman was subjected to direct and cross-examination over a six day period. His testimony encompasses six full volumes of this court's transcripts. He was ably examined and cross-examined. *Garner* is distinguishable.
>
> The court finds no other authority for the proposition that this court can either on its own grant immunity or direct the prosecuting agency to do so.
>
> With regards to the request to recall Detective Fuhrman, the court has previously ruled on that issue. The ruling will stand.
>
> The court has previously ruled on giving a jury instruction. This court's ruling was overturned by the Court of Appeal. I have no authority to go beyond that.
>
> And with regard to the declarations against interest, that is a renewal of that request and the court's previous ruling will stand for the reasons previously stated."

7. COMMENTS AND QUESTIONS

(a) In a post trial interview, three of the jurors were asked by Court TV anchor Rikki Klieman: *Did any of you ever learn that Mark Fuhrman took the Fifth Amendment before you reached a verdict? What did you think when Fuhrman was not recalled to the witness stand?*

Armanda Cooley: "No, I never heard that. At first, I didn't really think anything, because there were still certain other witnesses who I was waiting to hear from, like Faye Resnick, Al Cowlings— you know, people they had mentioned in the beginning in the opening statements. But my first impression about Mr. Fuhrman was that he was lying from the beginning and I just didn't have any faith in his testimony from jump street, so I didn't think it was necessary for me to even hear from him again. When he walked on the stand immediately I knew that the man was a snake. It's just something that hit me. I'm saying, 'Don't prejudge the man, Armanda. Give him an opportunity.' But they tell you over and over again, as jurors, do not leave your common sense out the door. Use your gut feeling."

Marsha Rubin–Jackson: "It didn't matter. In fact, I really didn't think anything of it at all when Fuhrman was not recalled. Because once they brought the tapes out, there was no need for him to even come back up there—we knew the man had lied. . . . His getting up there and saying he had never said nigger and I'm thinking, 'Oh, come on now, I know you're lying about that.' It didn't discredit his whole testimony to me. But after they had validated the tapes and the court had confirmed they were his tapes, there was no need for them to bring him back."

Carrie Bess: "Up until they brought the tapes out, I thought O.J. was gone. Because I really had not discredited Fuhrman, I really hadn't. I just figured here's a sharp cop. This guy was really on it and he was just lucky enough to find every damn thing when it came to the evidence. I'm just figuring that he's one of those lucky cops . . . that he must have been a hell of a detective, and then I come to find out he was a, you know. . . . "

Cooley, Bess & Rubin–Jackson, *Madam Foreman: A Rush to Judgment?*, pp.199–200 (Dove, 1995).

(b) The "alternative writ" procedure was not an actual ruling on the merits of Judge Ito's proposed instruction, but simply an order to withdraw it or have counsel appear before the Court of Appeal to defend it. The defense was surprised and disappointed by Judge Ito's decision to simply withdraw it:

"With the assistance of Dennis Fischer, one of the best appellate lawyers in California, we prepared to appear in the Court of Appeal to defend Judge Ito's ruling. Without notice or hearing, however, Judge Ito promptly withdrew his ruling. The process of review was somewhat bizarre. Completely ignoring precedent from another division of the same Court of Appeal, and without any opportunity for the defendant to be heard, the California Court of Appeal had injected itself into an ongoing trial to reverse a trial court's ruling. Judge Ito's conduct was equally bizarre. Apparently, he didn't have enough confidence in his ruling to let it stand long enough so we could go to the Court of Appeal on Monday and defend it."

Uelmen, *Lessons From the Trial: People v. O.J. Simpson,* p. 162 (Andrews & McMeel, 1996). The defense subsequently sought review of the Court of Appeal ruling in the California Supreme Court, which was denied.

(c) Marcia Clark describes the decision to seek a writ in terms of a personal vendetta:

"For me, this was the final straw. Ito's ruling was a direct violation of the Constitution, which says you can't sanction anyone for taking the Fifth. If the ruling stood, the jury could reasonably assume that *all* of Mark's testimony was bogus— and more easily accept the conspiracy theory the defense thrust in their faces day after day. I was prepared to fight like an alley cat for this one. I told Ito that I would be taking the matter over his head. I was going to file a writ with the Court of Appeals and try to get him overruled. Ito was livid with anger. Whatever fragile truce had existed between us after the recusal incident was now broken. But I really didn't care. Seven months earlier, when he issued his disastrous ruling on allowing the N-word in, I'd agonized over whether to try and get him overruled on appeal. I'd decided against it, so as not to prejudice him hopelessly against our side. I'd been wrong. He'd shafted us anyway. And I'd foregone a shot—admittedly a long shot—at keeping the trial on track. To this day, my personal failure of nerve in not appealing the N-word from the start remains my biggest regret. I would not compound my error by repeating it."

Marcia Clark, *Without a Doubt,* p. 454 (Viking, 1997).

(d) Why was Judge Ito's ruling on the proposed jury instruction "in excess of jurisdiction"? Are all evidentiary rulings against the prosecution reviewable by writ in the midst of a criminal trial? Which ones are "in excess of jurisdiction" and which ones are not?

B. INVOCATION OF CLERGYMAN–PENITENT PRIVILEGE BY ROSIE GRIER

1. THE EVIDENCE

While O.J. Simpson was in custody awaiting trial in the Los Angeles County Jail, he was frequently visited by his friend Roosevelt Grier, former N.F.L. football player-turned-minister, who brought along a bible for bible reading and counseling. In late November, 1994, in the midst of jury selection, counsel for both sides were notified that the Court had received a sealed document from the Los Angeles County Sheriff's Department, which supervised the jail, accompanied by the following affidavit:

"I, Jeff Stuart, declare:

On November 13, 1994, I was supervising the visiting area at a time Mr. Simpson and Mr. Roosevelt Greer [sic] were visiting in the area adjacent to the control booth.

At one point during the conversation, both Mr. Simpson and Mr. Greer spoke in raised voices which were discernible from within the control booth. I did not try to overhear the conversation. However, I was able to discern a portion of the conversation.

... This memorandum submitted under seal reflects a true and correct account of the statements made by Mr. Simpson and Mr. Greer which I overheard."

Judge Ito announced the memorandum would remain under seal until he determined whether it was protected by privilege. The defense immediately filed a claim of privilege pursuant to California Evidence Code Sections 1030–1034,[27] accompanied by the following affidavit:

27. California Evidence Code Section 1030 defines "clergyman" as "a priest, minister, religious practitioner, or similar functionary of a church or of a religious denomination or religious organization," and Section 1031 defines a "penitent" as "a person who has made a pentitential communication to a clergyman." A "penitential communication" is defined by Section 1032 as "a communication made in confidence, in the presence of no third person so far as the penitent is aware, to a clergyman who, in the course of the discipline or practice of his church, denomination or organization, is authorized to accustomed to hear such communication and, under the dis-

cipline or tenets of his church, denomination or organization, has a duty to keep such communications secret." The California Evidence Code then recognizes two separate claims of privilege:

"Section 1033. Privilege of penitent. Subject to Section 912, a penitent, whether or not a party, has a privilege to refuse to disclose, and to prevent another from disclosing, a penitential communication if he claims the privilege."

"Section 1034. Privilege of clergymen. Subject to Section 912, a clergyman, whether or not a party, has a privilege to refuse to disclose a peni-

"I, ROOSEVELT GRIER, declare and say as follows:

1.   I was ordained as a Minister by Dr. Frederick K.C. Price of the Crenshaw Christian Center, Los Angeles, California. I am engaged full time in the work of my ministry to the poor and needy, which is supported by "Are You Committed," a religious organization registered under Section 501(c)(3) of the Internal Revenue Code of the United States.

2.   Since his confinement in the Los Angeles County Jail in June, 1994, I have visited O.J. Simpson on a regular basis to provide spiritual counseling as part of my ministry. Before visiting him, I met with Chaplain Dickinson of the Los Angeles County Jail, and provided to him a copy of my ordination papers and a letter from my church. I attempt to meet with Mr. Simpson each Thursday and Sunday that I am in the Los Angeles area, and prior to each visit, I call the Watch Commander's office to let them know I am coming and the purpose of my visit.

3.   I assumed that all of my meetings with Mr. Simpson were private, and was never aware of any third persons listening to our private conversations.

4.   I am authorized and accustomed by my ministry and the practice of my church to hear penitential communications, and have a duty to keep such communications secret. This authorization and duty includes all of my communications with Mr. Simpson since his confinement.

5.   I hereby claim and assert my privilege under California Evidence Code 1034 to refuse to disclose any of the penitential communications I received from O.J. Simpson at the Los Angeles County Jail."

2.   TACTICAL CONTEXT

The prosecution was, of course, anxious to offer any statement of O.J. Simpson that could possibly be construed to be an admission. Such evidence would serve two purposes. First, it might itself convince a jury that Simpson was the perpetrator of the murders. Even if it didn't, however, it could put real pressure on Simpson to take the witness stand and explain or deny the alleged admission.

---

tential communication if he claims the privilege."

Section 912 of the California Evidence Code provides that a privilege is waived "with respect to a communication protected by such privilege if any holder of the privilege, without coercion, has disclosed a significant part of the communication or has consented to such disclosure made by anyone. Consent to disclosure is manifested by any statement or other conduct of the holder of the privilege indicating consent to the disclosure, including failure to claim the privilege in any proceeding in which the holder has the legal standing and opportunity to claim the privilege."

In this respect, the evidence was similar to the "dream" elicited from witness Ron Shipp. (*Supra,* Chapter I(B)). The possibility of having such evidence provided by a Sheriff's Deputy was especially attractive, since the L.A. County Sheriff's Department had no role in the investigation of the case, and would be outside the ambit of any "conspiracy to frame" that the defense might suggest.

For the defense, the Deputy's claim of overhearing a portion of the conversation was a nightmare which haunts every criminal defense lawyer. Jails are full of snitches and guards who have much to gain by becoming important witnesses. Every good defense lawyer repeatedly cautions a client in custody to exercise extreme caution in *all* conversations with *anyone* while in custody. In O.J.'s case, the defense went to great lengths to insure that the arrangements for visits and consultations were secure and private. The defense was confident that there had been no confession or admission. The risk remained, however, that any fragmentary conversation that the Deputy claimed to have overheard would be construed or interpreted to be some sort of admission, and would then have to be explained or denied by Simpson or Grier. The defense, like the prosecution, had no idea what the Deputy claimed to have overheard.

3. PROSECUTION ARGUMENT

The authorities cited herein make it clear that the People are entitled to know the content of defendant's statement in order to fully litigate whether it is privileged. The People request this court not to rule on the issue of privilege until the statement is turned over to the People. If the Court decides to rule now, based on the uncontradicted information, defendant's statement is not privileged. The reason is that none of the elements of the clergyman-penitent privilege have been established. Moreover, even if the privilege were established, defendant has waived the privilege.

A. THE DEFENDANT'S CONVERSATION WITH MR. GRIER IS NOT PRIVILEGED.

For the clergyman-penitent privilege to apply, the following elements must be established: (1) the communication was made in confidence; (2) it was made while no third parties were present; (3) it was made to a clergyman; and (4) the communication is a "penitential communication." Evidence Code Sections 1030–33. These four elements cannot be established.

(1) The communication was not made in confidence.

The circumstances of this case reveal that the communication was not confidential as a matter of law. The reason is that it was made in a jail setting under circumstances which did not lull defendant into a false sense of privacy. The United States Supreme Court has held that "given the realities of institutional confinement, any reasonable expectation of privacy that a detainee retained necessarily would be of a diminished scope." *Bell v. Wolfish,* 441 U.S. 520, 557 (1979). An inmate does have a right to privacy "insofar as concerns consultation with his attorney in a room designated for that purpose...." *People v. Lopez,* 60 Cal.2d 223, 248 (1963).

In *North v. Superior Court,* 8 Cal.3d 301 (1972), a detective allowed a suspect and his wife to have a conversation in the detective's office. The detective exited the office and shut the door leaving them entirely alone before the conversation. The detective surreptitiously recorded the conversation. The court held:

> "In view of the general rule that an inmate of a jail or prison has no reasonable expectation of privacy, it would follow that an ordinary jailhouse conversation between spouses could not be deemed to have been 'made in confidence' as required by Evidence Code Section 980 to establish the privilege."

However, because the detective had lulled defendant into a false expectation that the conversation was private, the statement was ruled to be privileged. *Id.* at 310. *North* stands for the proposition that an otherwise privileged communication (other than the attorney-client privilege) is not protected in a jail setting unless the police lulled defendant into a false expectation of privacy; see also, *People v. Burns,* 196 Cal.App.3d 1440, 1454 (1987) (defendant had no reasonable expectation of privacy in communication with other inmate); *People v. Hammons,* 235 Cal.App.3d 1710, 1716–17 (1991) (although there is generally no expectation of privacy in jail, "an expectation of privacy based upon express representations by police officers, even in a jailhouse setting, is one which society is prepared to recognize as reasonable.") In our case, the Sheriff did nothing to create a false expectation that defendant's conversation would be private. Hence, the general rule that defendant does not have a reasonable expectation of privacy in communications in jail applies.

"[T]he fact that a communication is made under circumstances where others could easily overhear is a strong indication that the communication was not intended to be confidential and is, therefore, unprivileged." Evidence Code Section 917, comment. In *People v. Von Villas,* 11 Cal.App.4th 175 (1992), the defendant and his wife were communicating in a jail visiting room. Because the telephone system in the facility was not working, they had to speak in raised voices through a plexiglass partition. Part of the conversation was heard by a deputy sheriff who was visually monitoring their visit from a control booth. Distinguishing *North,* the court found that the deputy had done nothing to lull the couple into a false sense of privacy. *Id.* At 222–23. The court ruled that "no valid assertion of the marital privilege can be successfully made ... because there was no justifiable expectation of privacy and no intent of nondisclosure as to their conversation. *Id.* At 223. *Von Villas* is on all fours with our case. Here, defendant was talking much louder than normal. He was talking under circumstances where the likelihood of being overheard was obvious. Both the fact that it was made in a jail setting, and that it was made under circumstances where it was likely to be overheard, demonstrate that the communication was not confidential.

(2) A third party was present.

The privilege by its express terms requires that a third party not be present insofar as the pentitent is aware. Evidence Code Section 1032. Here, it would have been apparent to defendant that a third party was in earshot. This defeats any claim of privilege.

(3) There is no showing that Mr. Grier is a clergyman.

A clergyman is a "priest, minister, religious practitioner, or similar functionary of a church or of a religious denomination or religious organization." Evidence Code Section 1030. However, for the privilege to apply, this person must be authorized under the discipline or tenets of his church to keep penitential communications secret. *Id.* At 1032; *People v. Thompson,* 133 Cal.App.3d 419 (1982) (church of scientology ethics officer was not a clergyman for purposes of privilege). Defendant may, in fact, be able to establish this element of the privilege. The point is that he has not yet done so.

(4) There is no showing that the communication is a "penitential communication."

To constitute a privileged "penitential communication," the communication must be made to a clergyman "who, in the course of the discipline or practice of his church, denomination or organization, is authorized or accustomed to hear such communications and, under the discipline or tenets of his church, denomination, or organization has a duty to keep such communications secret." Evidence Code Section 1032. Of the small number of cases on this issue, *People v. Edwards,* 203 Cal.App.3d 1358 (1988) contains the most detailed discussion of what constitutes a "penitential communication." There, the defendant confessed to the rector of her church that she had written bad checks. She requested his help in preventing the checks from bouncing. The rector testified that he believed that the conversation was in the nature of a secular request for counseling and not absolution. The defendant, on the other hand, characterized the communication as penitential. Despite the conflicting evidence, the appellate court upheld the trial court's determination "that the questioned statement was not a penitential communication within legal contemplation...." *Id.* at 1365. "Where such determination is supported by substantial, credible evidence, as shown, we are duty bound to uphold it." *Id.*

The teaching of *Edwards* is that a communication which bears none of the ear marks of a religious confession, but rather is simply an inculpatory statement that happens to have been addressed to a clergyman should properly be deemed non-privileged. See also, *People v. Thompson, supra,* 133 Cal.App.3d at 427 (confession not privileged where it was 'not to confess to a flawed act and to receive religious consolation and guidance'); *People v. Johnson,* 270 Cal. App.3d 204, 207 (1969) (where semi-exculpatory statement defendant made while fleeing from police to a minister he happened upon, statement was not made 'in the course of' the clergyman-penitent relationship); *Simrin v. Simrin,* 233 Cal.App.2d 90 (1965) (statements to rabbi performing as a marriage counselor and not a spiritual advisor were not protected under the clergyman-pentitent privilege).

In our case, we do not know the substance of the statement in question. *Edwards* demonstrates that the People must be aware of the content of the statement in order to fully litigate whether it is confidential. The content may demonstrate that it was in the nature of a non-privileged secular conversation, not a request for absolution.

B. ASSUMING THAT DEFENDANT'S CONVERSATION WAS PRIVILEGED, THE PRIVILEGE WAS WAIVED.

The privilege is "waived with respect to a communication protected by such privilege if any holder of the privilege, without coercion, has disclosed a significant part of the communication or has consented to such disclosure made by anyone." Evidence Code Section 954. That the conversation took place under circumstances where it was likely to be overheard clearly demonstrates a waiver. See *People v. Poulin,* 27 Cal.App.3d 54, 64 (1972) (holding that courtroom conversations between a defendant and his attorney are not privileged when conducted in the presence of a bailiff); *People v. Castiel,* 153 Cal.App.2d 653, 659 (1957) (court reporter overheard conversation between attorney and his client during a recess).

4. DEFENSE ARGUMENT

The broad protection afforded to penitential communications by California law extends to all communications between Mr. Grier, a clergyman within the meaning of California Evidence Code § 1030, and Mr. Simpson, a penitent within the meaning of § 1031, even if such communications are overheard by an eavesdropper. At no time did Mr. Grier or Mr. Simpson manifest an intention to have any third persons listen to their communications, and there is no evidence either of them were aware of any reasonable possibility that third persons could hear their communications. Under California law, such communications are presumed to be confidential.

A. DISCLOSURE OF ANY STATEMENT PENDING DETERMINATION OF PRIVILEGE IS PRECLUDED; THE PEOPLE MUST BE EXCLUDED FROM ANY FURTHER PROCEEDINGS.

The prosecution has requested the Court "not to rule on the issue of privilege until the statement is turned over to the People." Any such disclosure is prohibited by California Evidence Code § 915, which provides:

"(a) Subject to subdivision (b), the presiding officer may not require disclosure of information claimed to be privileged under this division in order to rule on the claim of privilege; provided, however, that in any hearing conducted pursuant to subdivision (c) of section 1524 of the Penal Code in which a claim of privilege is made and the court determines that there is no other feasible means to rule on the validity of such claim other than to require disclosure, the court shall proceed in accordance with subdivision (b)."

Penal Code § 1524(c) relates to items seized pursuant to search warrants for the offices of lawyers, physicians, psychotherapists and clergymen. Evidence Code § 915(b) relates to claims of privilege for official information, identity of informers, and trade secrets. Thus, there are no relevant exceptions to the broad prohibition of disclosure pending a ruling on a claim of privilege. The comment of the Law Revision Commission to Section 915 notes "the general rule that revelation of the information asserted to be privileged may not be compelled in order to determine whether or not it is privileged. This codifies existing law."

The appropriate course of proceeding to determine the claim of privilege is carefully laid out by the California Supreme Court in its recent opinion in *Menendez v. Superior Court*, 3 Cal.4th 435 (1992), determining the applicability of the psychotherapist-patient privilege to tape recorded consultations with Erik and Lyle Menendez seized from the office of Dr. Leon Jerome Oziel. As noted in the Supreme Court's opinion:

"For the most part, on the Menendezes' motion pursuant to Evidence Code Section 915 and over the People's opposition, the superior court held the proceedings in camera in the presence of the brothers and their respective counsel without the People's representatives. At the hearing in camera, Dr.

Oziel and Smyth were among those who testified. Exhibits submitted included the three audiotape cassettes as well as the transcripts of their contents made at the direction of the Menendezes' counsel. The people filed a list of questions they they requested the court to ask Dr. Oziel. They also filed a request for a statement of decision, including resolution of certain specified issues."

3 Cal.4th at 443. The record of the *in camera* hearing remained sealed, and even pending the hearing before the California Supreme Court, the People's request to unseal it was denied. This procedure was explicitly approved over a number of procedural and constitutional objections presented by the People. 3 Cal.4th at 456, n.18.

B. THE CLERGYMAN–PENITENT PRIVILEGE IS APPLICABLE TO COMMUNICATIONS BETWEEN ROOSEVELT GRIER AND O.J. SIMPSON AT THE LOS ANGELES COUNTY JAIL.

California recognizes a broad privilege which can be asserted by a penitent to refuse to disclose, and *to prevent another from disclosing* a penitential communication. California Evidence Code § 1033. A separate privilege is provided to the clergyman in his own right, which may be claimed even if the penitent has waived the privilege granted him by Section 1033. California Evidence Code § 1034. The penitential communication is broadly defined to *expand* prior protection which was limited to "confessions." The Law Revision Commission Comment to Section 1032 notes the expansive nature of the definition of "penitential communications":

"Under existing law, the communication must be a 'confession.' Code Civ. Proc. § 1881(3) (superseded by the Evidence Code). Section 1032 extends the protection that traditionally has been provided only to those persons whose religious practice involves 'confessions.'"

As the Declaration of Roosevelt Grier demonstrates, the communications between himself and Mr. Simpson at the Los Angeles County Jail were 'penitential communications' between a clergyman and a penitent.

C. THE CLERGYMAN–PENITENT PRIVILEGE PROTECTS AGAINST DISCLOSURE BY EAVESDROPPERS.

The extent of the protection of the clergyman-penitent privilege against disclosure by eavesdroppers is clearly spelled out in the Comment of the Law Revision Commission to Section 1033 of the Evidence Code:

"Section 1033 also protects against disclosure by eavesdroppers. In this respect, the section provides the same scope of protection that is provided by the other confidential communication privileges. See the Comment to Section 954."

The comment to Section 954, which defines the lawyer-client privilege, addresses the problem of "eavesdroppers" in some detail:

"*Eavesdroppers.* Under Section 954, the lawyer-client privilege can be asserted to prevent *anyone* from testifying to a confidential communication. Thus, clients are protected against the risk of disclosure by eavesdroppers and other wrongful interceptors of confidential communications between lawyer and client. Probably no such protection was provided prior to the enactment of Penal Code Sections 653i and 653j. See *People v. Castiel,* 153 Cal.App.2d 653 (1957). See also Attorney–Client Privilege in California, 10 Stan.L.Rev. 297, 310–312 (1958), and cases there cited in note 84.

Penal Code Section 653j makes evidence obtained by *electronic* eavesdropping or recording in violation of the section inadmissible in "any judicial, administrative, legislative, or other proceeding." The section also provides a criminal penalty and contains definitions and exceptions. Penal Code Section 653i makes it a felony to eavesdrop by an electronic or other device upon a conversation between a person in custody of a public officer or on public property and that person's lawyer, religious advisor or physician.

Section 954 is consistent with Penal Code Section 653i and 653j but provides broader protection, for it protects against disclosure of confidential communications by anyone who obtained knowledge of the communication without the client's consent. See also Evidence Code § 912 (when disclosure with client's consent constitutes a waiver of the privilege). The use of the privilege to prevent testimony by eavesdroppers and those to whom the communication was wrongfully disclosed does not, however, affect the rule that the making of the communication under circumstances where others could easily overhear it is evidence that the client did not intend the communication to be confidential. See *Sharon v. Sharon,* 79 Cal.633, 677 (1889)."

The rule regarding communications "under circumstances where others could easily overhear it" has to application to the circumstances here. All of the cases cited by the People involve conversations where no arrangement for private consultations had been sought. In *People v. Von Villas,* 11 Cal.App.4th 175, 221 (1992), a husband and wife were "in a regular jail visiting room speaking loudly to each other through the plexiglass with knowledge that a guard was watching them. Their conduct clearly indicated there was no expectation of privacy during the conversation. Further,

their conduct demonstrated that they did not intend nondisclosure...." In *People v. Poulin,* 27 Cal.App.3d 54, 65 (1972), a bailiff
testified, without objection, to observations of a defendant's ges-
tures to counsel in open court while a trial was in session. In *People
v. Castiel,* 153 Cal.App.2d 653, 659 (1957), a court reporter testified
to a conversation between defendant and counsel during a recess in
a trial. "The reporter testified that he was in plain sight and no
question of surreptitious eavesdropping is presented."

California Evidence Code § 917 provides:

"Whenever a privilege is claimed on the ground that the
matter sought to be disclosed is a communication made in
confidence in the course of the ... clergyman-penitent ...
relationship, the communication is presumed to have been
made in confidence and the opponent of the privilege has the
burden of proof to establish that the communication was not
confidential."

The Comment of the Assembly Committee on Judiciary to Section
917 notes that, "if the privilege claimant were required to show
that the communication was made in confidence, he would be
compelled, in many cases, to reveal the subject matter of the
communication in order to establish his right to the privilege."

5. JUDGE'S RULING

After personally visiting and inspecting the area where the
conversation was allegedly overheard, Judge Lance Ito issued the
following order on December 18, 1994:

"The Court has before it a statement allegedly made by
defendant Simpson to Roosevelt Grier in the Module 8000
attorney/inmate visiting area on Sunday afternoon, November
13, 1994. The prosecution seeks discovery of the written report
of this statement prepared by Los Angeles County Deputy
Sheriff Jeff Stuart.

As a general proposition, there is no reasonable expectation of privacy in a jail facility. *Lanza v. New York,* 370 U.S.
139 (1961); *Donaldson v. Superior Court,* 35 Cal.3d 24 (1983);
People v. Von Villas, 11 Cal.App.4th 175, 212–213 (1992). Also
as a general proposition, penitential communications between a
clergyperson and penitent are privileged. Evidence Code Sections 1032–1034. Eavesdropping upon a conversation between a
person held in custody and that person's religious advisor is a
serious crime in California. Penal Code Section 636. *In Re
Arias,* 42 Cal.3d 667, 679–83 (1986).

The record before this Court indicates that Roosevelt Grier
meets the definition of a clergyperson as that term is defined

by Evidence Code Section 1030. The record also supports the finding that Grier and Simpson were engaged in a penitential communication as that term is defined by Evidence Code Section 1032. The issue presented to the Court is whether the conduct of Simpson and Grier, i.e. yelling at each other through the sealed plexiglass partition separating them, operated as a waiver of the clergy/penitent privilege. Key here is the Evidence Code Section 1032 requirement that the subject statement be made '... in the presence of no third person so far as the penitent is aware ...' It is clear that Simpson and his visitors, including Grier, were aware of the nearby presence of Deputy Sheriffs operating the control booth. It is the duty and obligation of the deputies assigned to the control booth to keep inmates and visitors under observation to maintain the security of the jail facility. At the time of the subject statement Stuart was attending to paperwork in the control booth, approximately ten feet away from Simpson, separated by the scaled glass wall of the control booth and the sealed plexiglass wall between the inmate and visitor sections of the Module 8000 visiting area.

On 29 November 1994, the Court, along with counsel from the prosecution and defense, examined the Module 8000 visiting area and control booth. From inside the control booth the Court was able to hear snatches of loud/normal conversation [conversation that is loud, but still within the range of normal speech, as distinguished from shouting or yelling] from the attorney/clergy side of the visiting area. The Court was unable to clearly hear similar loud/normal conversation emanating from the inmate side of the visiting area. Shouting could be heard from the inmate side. The glass wall between the control booth and the attorney/clergy side is heavily tinted, giving it an effect similar to a one-way mirror. From both the attorney/clergy side and the inmate side it is possible to see occasional shadow-like movements within the control booth. From inside the control booth is it easy to see into the inmate and attorney/clergy sides of the visiting area. The view from inside the control booth is similar to wearing dark sunglasses in a relatively well lit indoor room.

At this point, were this the complete factual record, the prosecution would prevail in its discovery demand because clergy/penitent communications must be made in confidence. Yelling defeats this purpose and renders the privilege waived, especially where it is apparent there are third persons nearby whose job requires them to pay attention to any behavior that is out of the ordinary.

Within the complete factual record, it must be noted that
the construction of the attorney/inmate visiting area in Module
8000 was done at the direction of this Court with the coopera-
tion of the Los Angeles County Sheriff's Department. For
budgetary reasons, the normal first floor attorney/client visiting room, including booths where an inmate may visit with
multiple persons at the same time, is open Mondays through
Thursdays, from 10:00 a.m. to 8:00 p.m. Counsel for Simpson
have complained to this Court and to the Sheriff's Department
that they have been engaged in trial fulltime since 12 September 1994, Mondays through Fridays, and that because of the
complexities of this case, it is necessary to meet and confer
with Simpson on Fridays, Saturdays and Sundays. For security
reasons, Simpson is housed in a one-man cell in Module 8000.
Counsel for Simpson objected to conferring with Simpson in
the regular Module 8000 visiting area because of concerns
regarding confidentiality of their communications with
Simpson. This was brought to the Court's attention with the
request that this Court order the Sheriff's Department to open
the regular first floor attorney/inmate visiting room on Fridays,
Saturdays and Sundays. Simpson at one point offered to pay
for any overtime expenses incurred by the Sheriff's Department. At the request of defense counsel, the Court met and
conferred with Captain Albert A. Scaduto, the commanding
officer of the Men's Central Jail. The Court examined the
Module 8000 visiting area in the company of Scaduto. Rather
than ordering the Sheriff's Department to open the first floor
attorney/inmate visiting room on Fridays, Saturdays and Sundays, the Court accepted the Sheriff's Department's proposal to
make certain modifications to the Module 8000 visiting area to
separate it from the regular visiting area and to make it
acceptable for attorney/client conferences.[28] Counsel for
Simpson were assured that the proposed modifications would
make a portion of the Module 8000 visiting area suitable for
attorneys to confer in a confidential manner with their inmate
clients. Counsel for Simpson now argue Simpson was lulled
into a false sense of security in regard to the confidentiality of
his communication in the Module 8000 visiting area. Under the
highly unusual and apparently unique factual setting in this
case, with regard to this single incident, the argument is well
taken. The demand for discovery is therefore denied."

---

28. The Court notes that attor-
ney/client communications can often be
boisterous in nature. See our high
court's similar observations re penitential communications in *In Re Arias, supra.*

6. COMMENTS AND QUESTIONS

(a) Does Judge Ito's ruling conclude there *was* a waiver but the state is somehow estopped from taking advantage of it, or that under the unique circumstances, yelling would *not* constitute a waiver because even yelling would not be overheard if the regular visiting facilities had been made available? Vincent Bugliosi argues:

"The only problem was that if there was a waiver, as Ito virtually had to rule there was, there was no *legal* basis for excluding the statement. If one were to accept Ito's nonlegal justification for excluding the statement, I guess it wouldn't have made any difference how loudly or how often Simpson shouted out his confession or incriminating statement, it would be inadmissible because he had been 'lulled into a false sense of security.' "

Bugliosi, *Outrage: The Five Reasons Why O.J. Simpson Got Away Wilth Murder,* p. 77 (1996).

(b) The prosecutor's never conceded Roosevelt Grier was a *bona fide* clergyman. Even in her book two years later, Marcia Clark refers to Grier as "purportedly now a minister", and sneers, "For all we knew, Grier had gotten his credentials through a diploma mill." Clark, *Without A Doubt,* p. 251 (Viking, 1997). From a tactical standpoint, was that a wise position to take?

(c) Would it be ethical for the prosecutors to seek to persuade Deputy Sheriffs to tell them what they overheard "off the record"? In her book, Marcia Clark complains:

"Ito had ordered the sheriffs not to say anything, and they were so scared of bad press they wouldn't even tell us on the QT.... And so we found ourselves in a ridiculous position: the Sheriff's Department, the judge, and the defense team all knew what Simpson had said—but we didn't."

Clark, *Without A Doubt,* p. 251 (Viking, 1997).

(d) Several tabloids claimed that unidentified sources reported Simpson said to Grier, "I did it." Although Vincent Bugliosi and Marcia Clark were occasionally critical of the coverage of the trial (and themselves) by sleazy tabloids, they both quoted tabloid reports in their books as authoritative accounts of what Simpson allegedly said. Do lawyers have any ethical obligation to respect the invocation of a privilege that has been sustained in their public commentary?

See Bugliosi, *supra* at 77 (quoting *Globe*) and Clark, *supra* at 251(quoting *National Enquirer*).

C. ATTORNEY–CLIENT PRIVILEGE
AND POLYGRAPH EVIDENCE

1. THE EVIDENCE

When Detectives Phil Vanatter and Tom Lange questioned O.J. Simpson on June 13, 1994, they asked him whether he was willing to take a polygraph examination. Two days later, on June 15, 1994, Attorney Robert Shapiro faxed a letter to Vanatter and Lange, with copies to the district attorney's office and the coroner's office, in which he offered the assistance of defense experts Dr. Michael Baden and Dr. Henry Lee to assist in the investigation, requested that a second autopsy be done before the bodies were interred, and responded to the detective's request for a polygraph:

"Mr. Simpson will be willing to consider a polygraph examination, with the stipulation that the results would be admissible in any potential investigation."

Apparently, Shapiro fully anticipated this offer would be refused. As he explains in his book, *The Search for Justice,* pp.26–27 (Warner Books, 1996):

"The use of the lie detector, or polygraph, in the criminal justice system is full of inconsistencies.... The test results create charts that can be interpreted and reinterpreted by experts, and challenged on the basis that the operator asked the wrong questions, framed them the wrong way, or misinterpreted the data. Because the results are open to such wide interpretation, prosecutors have traditionally been averse to use polygraphy, especially in the courtroom. In fact, in California, polygraph tests are specifically precluded by law unless both sides stipulate that the results will be admissible. At that time, Marcia Clark, an assistant to William Hodgman (the head of L.A.'s Special Trials Unit) and David Conn had been assigned by the district attorney to prosecute the case. They responded that the D.A.'s office would allow O.J. to be tested, but they would not stipulate that the results would be admissible. I wasn't surprised at their answer, but I wanted it on the record."

The only mention of polygraphs during the criminal trial occurred in the testimony of Ron Shipp concerning the "dream," considered in Chapter I (B) *supra.* After the trial, Lawrence Schiller and James Willwerth published a book entitled, *American Tragedy: The Uncensored Story of the Simpson Defense* (Random House, 1996). Although Robert Kardashian, one of Simpson's lawyers throughout the trial, was not identified as an author, he was acknowledged as the source of much of the information in the book. The book publicly alleged, for the first time, that on June 14, 1994, Shapiro and Kardashian accompanied O.J. Simpson to the office of polygraph examiner Edward Gelb, and Simpson was attached to a polygraph and questioned. The book quotes the examiner as reporting a result of minus 22, meaning "Simpson failed virtually all of the questions about the murders." The book suggests Shapiro and the examiner were in agreement that O.J.'s "intense emotional level" so soon after the death of his ex-wife might have affected the validity of any results, and concludes with everyone agreeing to wait a week and try the test again. Shapiro is quoted as cautioning Kardashian, "This is only between us."

O.J. Simpson did not consent to the publication of *American Tragedy,* and protested its publication because it violated his attorney-client privilege. Prior to the book's publication, Simpson wrote a letter to all member of his defense team, as follows:

> "I require that all information you have gained in the course of our professional relationship be held inviolate. Unless and until you receive express and written permission from me, any written authorization shall be limited to specific communications described in the authorization and shall not be construed as a broad or blanket authorization or waiver; therefore, it is essential that any draft manuscript be reviewed by me before it is shared with others."

2. THE TACTICAL CONTEXT

The lawyers representing the Brown and Goldman families in the civil lawsuit against O.J. Simpson learned of the disclosures in *American Tragedy* after they had concluded their depositions of O.J. Simpson. They were, of course, looking for an "opening" at trial that would allow them to get the alleged negative polygraph results before the jury. The opening may have been presented in Opening Statements at the beginning of the civil trial. In the course of a lengthy chronology of the entire investigation, Robert Baker, representing O.J. Simpson, recounted the sending of the Shapiro letter to the homicide detectives to suggest that there was no "consciousness of guilt" on Simpson's part, then briefly returned to the subject with this comment:

> "In fact, ladies and gentlemen, I want to talk to you a little bit about the glasses, because as I mentioned a little earlier, Mr. Simpson, through his attorneys, offered the services of some forensic scientists, including Michael Baden and Barbara Wolf. It was refused. He offered to take a polygraph. It was refused. On the day of June 22, I believe, Dr. Baden, Dr. Wolf are examining evidence...."

There was no objection.

During the plaintiff's case in chief, O.J. Simpson was called to the witness stand for cross examination. His lawyer then interposed the following objection:

"Mr. Blasier: ... As the Court is aware, Lawrence Schiller has written a book that purports to contain a great deal of information provided to him by Robert Kardashian, who is one of Mr. Simpson's attorneys. Much of that material concerns privileged communications between various members of the defense team and Mr. Simpson. In November—November 28 of 1995, Mr. Simpson wrote a letter to all members of the defense team. [The above letter requiring written permission for disclosures and advance review of manuscripts was read]. This was not complied with with respect to that particular book. My motion [is] that the plaintiffs be precluded from asking questions about excluded material in this book, as Mr. Simpson does not waive, has not waived his attorney-client privilege. To do so— to ask such questions in front of a jury would be improper, require him to assert privilege in front of the jury."

The motion elicited the following ruling from Judge Hiroshi Fujisaki:

"The rest of it is denied without prejudice. I don't see any basis on which I should grant a motion at this late stage. There was ample opportunity to exercise that privilege at the time the book was published. Your should have had a motion at that time.

Mr. Blasier: Mr. Simpson wasn't planning to testify at that time. He's now testifying. He's making the motion. We are not waiving the privilege. He should not be asked questions to assert it in front of a jury.

The Court: He has testified at the time of the deposition—

Mr. Blasier: No problem with anything he testified at deposition. We're talking about this material in the book he has not already testified to.

The Court: As far as I'm concerned, he's already published it; I think he's waived it.

Mr. Blasier: He didn't publish anything, Your Honor.

The Court: He didn't bring any action to suppress it at that time.

Mr. Blasier: That's being considered at this time.

The Court: It's a little bit late."

3. EXAMINATION OF O.J. SIMPSON

"Q. By Mr. Petrocelli: You got to Rockingham. You were then taken down to the police station?

A. That's correct.

Q. And you met at the police station with Detective Lange and Detective Vanatter and you gave a statement, correct?

A. That's correct.

Q. Okay. Now in this statement, in regard to the question of a polygraph test, you told the police that you had some weird thoughts. Remember that?

A. That's correct.

Q. They had asked you about taking a polygraph test and you said, 'Wait a minute. I've got some weird thoughts, you know, about Nicole.' Do you recall that?

A. I think I said, yeah, I've had some pretty weird thoughts, yes.

Q. And you were concerned about taking the polygraph test because of those weird thoughts, correct?

A. I think my biggest concern was, I was really tired. I didn't understand what a polygraph was, and I just wanted to make sure that it focused on that it was, this particular crime, and not on other things that may be in your mind.

Q. And those weird thoughts that you had in your mind when they chatted with you about this, had to do with violence towards Nicole, true?

A. No, that's not correct.

Q. They had to do with violence, true?

A. I would think in one instance it was violence, that Nicole hit my housekeeper and I wished that my housekeeper would have called the police on her.

Another instance when she was doing drugs with Faye Resnick, they crashed into a car an old man and kid was in, they lied to the police as to who was driving, and I honestly—and I think I said this to her parents, I honestly wish she would have got caught, and, you know, I just felt the things she was doing in those months leading up to this—

Q. Excuse me. Can you stick with the question?

A. That's my answer.

Q. Now, when you were asked about the weird thoughts, it is your testimony that you had in mind an act of violence against Nicole, true?

A.   No, more an act of violence from Nicole hitting my housekeeper, that my housekeeper would have called the police, and on another occasion, as I just explained—

Q.   Well, let's stick with the housekeeper situation.

A.   Yes.

Q.   You had in mind an act of violence involving Nicole, true?

A.   An act of violence by Nicole.

Q.   An act of violence by Nicole against your housekeeper of a number of years, a woman named Michelle, right?

A.   . . . Yes.

Q.   And you did not have in mind, sir, any kind of thoughts in your own thinking, about violence by you against Nicole, true?

A.   That's correct.

Q.   So you were concerned that you might not pass this polygraph test because this idea of Nicole's striking your housekeeper might somehow enter into your thinking, and for that reason you might fail the test, true?

Mr. Baker: Objection, there's no foundation for that, it's argumentative, Your Honor.

The Court: Overruled.

By Mr. Petrocelli: Is that true, sir?

A.   No.

Q.   And in fact, what you said at your deposition is that what you were thinking about was Nicole hitting your housekeeper, Michelle?

A.   Yes.

Q.   In talking about this question of weird thoughts that you had about Nicole, you said, "I kind of at one point thought it would have been nice if Michelle, when Nicole punched her, who was my housekeeper, if Michelle would have punched her back."

Do you recall giving that testimony?

A.   Yeah, part of that. But Michelle would have got beaten up. Michelle couldn't beat up Nicole.

Q.   Excuse me. Do you recall giving that testimony?

A.   Yes.

Q.   So hours after your wife's murder, when you're questioned about this subject, the thoughts that you had in your mind about Nicole had to do with Nicole hitting your housekeeper and how you hoped that your housekeeper would have punched Nicole back, is that true, sir?

A.   That's not true.

Q.   That's what you said sir, correct?

A.   That's not what I said hours after. I think what my process was is that I had a lot of weird thoughts about those type of things, I wanted to know just how true-blue it was, and eventually I told them I would—I would do one after I had got some sleep and stuff. As a matter of fact, that was something that they were concerned about too.

Q.   And you did take the test, and you failed it, didn't you?

Mr. Baker: Objection.

A.   That's not correct.

Q.   You failed it, true?

Mr. Baker: Objection.

A.   No, that's not correct.

Q.   You got a minus 22?

Mr. Baker: Your Honor, I'm going to object to this.

Mr. Petrocelli: Your Honor—

Mr. Baker: I want to approach. This is an outrage.

The Court: Approach the bench.

[The following proceedings were held at the bench].

Mr. Petrocelli: First of all, the witness himself just volunteered himself how he, you know, wanted to take a lie detector test. It was refused. Trying to argue that he had taken what he would have asked, and that's exactly what Mr. Baker argued to the jury in his opening statement, that he had no reason to say what he said here other than to suggest that Mr. Simpson was totally innocent, and had he taken the test, which he was happy to do, he would have passed it.

And he has absolutely opened the door on that issue, and I am entitled to follow up, to demonstrate not only did he—did he take it, but he failed it, Your Honor.

Mr. Baker: Well, two things: One, he never took a lie detector test. Two, he didn't fail a lie detector test. And three, a letter sent to Vanatter and Lange, as well as also the DA's office, indicating that there was a lie—they would offer for him to take a lie detector test at the same time they offered the services of Baden, and he offered the services of Lee, and let the chips fall where they may, the LAPD refused all of that. Now, to infer that he has taken a lie test and failed it is absolutely false.

Mr. Petrocelli: I've not inferred he—I'm asking the question. He opened the door. I have the right to ask him.

Mr. Baker: No.

Mr. Petrocelli: We know he went to take the test the 14th, 15th at the offices of Edward Gelb. It's all outlined in the book. I'm going to ask him about it, Your Honor, particularly since he opened the door wide open.

Mr. Baker: No, no. There's a couple things—and I want to make a record relative to the Court's ruling that you say that that book—because we have not filed a lawsuit, we have waived any attorney-client privilege. That is, to me, absolutely without foundation. And the—in the law anywhere, we have never waived any attorney-client privilege. The fact that somebody else attempts to waive an attorney-client privilege for Mr. Simpson does not waive it for him at all. And he has never waived it. And I think the Court's ruling is improper.

And I think for them to bring this up is terribly improper. That is all because Kardashian waives the attorney-client privilege, or does whatever he does and gives an interview for a book because he gets 40 percent of the proceeds. And it's my understanding, presently he's under investigation by the state bar over exactly this. That doesn't waive his privilege. Only the holder of the privilege can waive it. The holder is O.J. Simpson.

Mr. Petrocelli: We've heard, Your Honor, one month ago, when this book came out, counsel of record in this case, F. Lee Bailey, Mr. Leonard's partner, went on national television on the Larry King Show, and spoke openly about this test, openly. Notwithstanding the Court's gag order, he talked about how Mr. Simpson went there, and he didn't think they asked all the right control questions, and on and on. And the point is, basically, this—not only did the witness get it out to the jury, but Mr. Baker, in opening statement—we didn't utter a word about polygraph tests, and he opened that door. And he cannot have it both ways.

The Court: Are you going to address the issue of the book once more?

Mr. Petrocelli: The book—this book was put out by Simpson's colleague, Schiller, who wrote his first book with him. He, in consultation not only with Kardashian, but with all of Mr. Simpson's lawyers, all of them, Dershowitz and Cochran and—what's that other guy—Scheck, and Neufeld and on and on. This book has been in the works for a long time. They never once filed any action to enjoin it. They never ever tried to stop the publication of it. You can't simply allow material to go out there and then claim it's privileged without doing anything to stop the publication of it. That is an absolute waiver. A waiver doesn't have to be in writing. Waivers are frequently implications and acquiescence.

The Court: Okay.

Mr. Baker: Wait a second. That is not true. His representations are absolutely false. And that's why he's making a bunch of accusations he has no foundation to make. Peter Neufeld wrote every lawyer in this case, as Mr. Simpson's lawyer, he wrote Random House, he wrote Schiller, and he said, if you do what you say you're going to do, there's going to be a lawsuit and there is going to be a lawsuit. And for him to say we have acquiesced and waived it is absolutely an absolute bold-faced lie.

. . .

The Court: I think you better lower your voice.

Mr. Baker: I think it's an outrage. Simpson has done everything possible to stop that book. We represented to the Court and read portions of a letter to this Court, November 28 letter, and there has been at least four or five more pieces of communication to Schiller, to Random House, and to all of his lawyers, that they have not—that he has not waived the attorney-client privilege. Now, to say that he's waived it by acquiescence is a bold-faced lie. It hasn't happened. He has never waived it.

The Court: When did Mr. Simpson first get notice that it was going to be published?

Mr. Baker: About mid-September. I had a conversation with Mr. Scheck in early September, when they[Schiller and Kardashian] indicated that they were going to publish this book. And there was a plethora of communications back and forth ordering them not to.

The Court: Was there any effort to file a—file for an injunction?

Mr. Baker: My understanding is they got a representation that the book wasn't going to be published. And they, it was published. And that's why there was no injunction filed for it. But Mr. Neufeld—we'll get the communications, and he can wait on this until we get the communications. I will get the communications from Peter Neufeld and have them faxed.

Mr. Petrocelli: This tells the tale.(Indicating to transcript). This is a red herring about what—Mr. Simpson sat for interviews for this book. He gave all the tapes up. That's how—they gave the tapes—he gave his notes up, too.

Mr. Baker: That's absolutely not true.

Mr. Petrocelli: Why does Mr. Baker tell the jury that Mr. Simpson was more than happy to take a lie detector test, but they refused, other than to suggest that he was innocent and would have passed the test? This—that's the only inference he wanted the jury to draw.

The Court: Okay. I'll stand on my ruling. Overruled.

(The following proceedings were held in the presence of the jury):

Q. By Mr. Petrocelli: Mr. Simpson, you were testifying a few moments ago about how you were, once you understood the process, happy to take a lie detector test, but it was refused. Do you recall that?

A. Yes.

Q. Now, in fact, Mr. Simpson, before you communicated that position to the DA's office, you went to the office of Dr. Edward Gelb on June 15, did you not?

A. I don't know.

Q. You went to the office of some person on Wilshire Boulevard and sat down and were wired up for a lie detector test, true?

A. That's not true. I mean that's not true in totality.

Q. Well, what do you mean, "in totality?"

A. We didn't take a lie detector test. What I was asking him is how did it work, and I wanted to understand it. And he sort of gave me an example of how it—

Q. And he hooked you up to the process and started asking you questions about Nicole, and Nicole's death and whether you were responsible for it, true?

A. I don't know if he went that far with it.

Q. Okay. At the end of that process, you scored a minus 22, true?

A. I don't know what the score was.

Q. And you understood that was a polygraph test, right?

A. I understood that once I finished, and I understood it, that I was willing to do one for the police.

Q. And you understood that what you were doing that day was a polygraph test, on June 15; true or untrue?

A. Not the way they explained it to me, no.

Q. You were wired up to a polygraph machine, were you not?

A. They wired me up to something and they—the guy started to explain to me about how it works, and we went through it once for my understanding. Once I understood how it worked, I told my lawyers, let's do it. And we wanted it to be in evidence.

Q. And the minus 22, by the way, is a score indicating extreme deception, true?

A. I don't—

Mr. Baker: Your Honor, I object to that.

The Court: Sustained.

Mr. Baker: There's no foundation for that at all.

Q. By Mr. Petrocelli: Now, you went to this polygraph examiner's office on Tuesday, June 14, true?

A. I don't know.

Q. It was that time frame, right?

A. I believe it was that week; it was—that week is kind of fuzzy for me.

Q. And I asked you in your deposition in January: (Reading)

"Question: Have you ever taken a polygraph test?

A. No.

Q. I was going to say, since Nicole's death, have you taken a polygraph test?

A. No."

That was untrue, wasn't it, sir?

A. As far as I know, I didn't take a polygraph test.

Q. You did, in fact, sit for that test, didn't you?

A. That's incorrect.

Q. When you returned from the police station, you went back to your office in Brentwood, right?

A. Yes.

Q. And then you went back to your house and had some people over that night, right?

A. That—there was a lot of people there coming in and out.

Q. And you had a conversation with a fellow named Ron Shipp that night?

A. I don't recall having a conversation with Ron.

Q. And the subject of a polygraph test was on your mind because the police had mentioned it to you earlier in the day, true?

A. No.

Q. And you asked—Mr. Shipp is a—was a friend of yours, right?

A. We were friendly, yes.

Q. And he had been a member of the police department for a number of years, right?

A. That's correct.

Q. And you understood that he knew about such things as blood tests, and DNA tests, and polygraph tests?

A.   I don't think I ever thought about that.

Q.   And you only had some close friends and relatives over to your house that night, correct?

A.   No. All types of people that I knew casually, people that I knew well; people were coming in and out.

Q.   Mr. Kardashian was there, right?

A.   Yes.

Q.   Your long-time friend, Joe Delaney, right?

A.   Joe came at one point.

Q.   Your children, Jason and Arnelle?

A.   And friends of theirs.

Q.   Your mother's two sisters, brother-in-law, and your assistant, Cathy Randa, they were up there?

A.   Among all the many people coming in and out, yes.

Q.   At some point in the evening, I think you had a private conversation with Mr. Shipp, true?

A.   No, I never had a private conversation.

Q.   And you asked—

Mr. Baker: Excuse me. I'm going to object.... There's no foundation. It's totally argumentative.

Mr. Petrocelli: I don't have to accept that answer.

The Court: All right. Overruled as admission of party, if you can prove it up. Otherwise, it's going to be stricken.

Mr. Petrocelli: Absolutely, your honor.

The Court: Okay.

Q.   By Mr. Petrocelli: You had a conversation with a man named Ron Shipp, and the subject matter was polygraph tests, right?

A.   That's incorrect.

Q.   And you asked Mr. Shipp what,—in effect, what would happen if you took a polygraph test, and you had dreams of killing Nicole, would that somehow interfere with the test and cause you to fail it, true?

A.   That's absolutely wrong.

Q.   And you asked Mr. Shipp how long it took for DNA tests to come back, true?

A.   No.''

4. RECONSIDERATION OF RULING

Two weeks after O.J. Simpson left the witness stand at his civil trial, Judge Hiroshi Fujisaki revisited the admissibility of the polygraph results, after the letter from Robert Shapiro to the detectives offering to take a polygraph was read into the record during the examination of Detective Vanatter:

"Okay. It's my opinion that this is probably the most troublesome aspect of this case, that has been brought about by the reference of the defense of the polygraph, the failure of the plaintiff to object at the time, and we are in a state of the case wherein references to the polygraph have been made. The Court is satisfied that the state of the law is, polygraphic evidence is not admissible by statute, as well as by case law in this state. And the Court is inclined to not permit the evidence in this regard.

Before counsel may be permitted to make any argument in closing argument in this regard, I will visit this issue again and allow counsel to submit points and authorities in that regard. My inclination is not to permit at this point any further comment on the polygraph, because to permit comment on it, it would appear to me, it would be to permit a contention that the polygraph has probative value as to truthfulness or untruthfulness, there being no evidence received in that regard. Number one.

Number two, the Court, having the understanding that it's not admissible evidence statutorily or by case law, that such comments should not be permitted, possibly with the exception of a stipulation by counsel that it were to be considered and there not be any such stipulation, the Court, the same preclude any reference to polygraphs pending further points and authorities on that issue.

Mr. Petrocelli: For the record, I want to object to the Court's ruling. He opened the door once in opening, after your Court's limiting instruction, to which I objected because of the scope of it. He then opened it up a second time on this witness's examination. He elicited that Mr. Simpson, once again, wanted to take one. The implication being if he had taken one, he would have passed. The implication being that it was trustworthy and reliable as a scientific device. And I don't see how I could possibly be precluded at this time, after he elicited this testimony, from me responding to it.

The Court: Mr Petrocelli, so far as I've seen, this far, based upon all of your papers, your points and authorities, there is no admissible evidence in that regard that you can offer.

Mr. Petrocelli: Mr. Simpson testified that he was hooked up to a polygraph operator. And I can produce a witness that can say he did take a test, irrespective of the outcome of the test. But it's unfair for him to keep throwing this up to the jury and we can't respond to it.

The Court: You have a witness that was present at the event?

Mr. Petrocelli: We have Robert Kardashian; we have the polygraph operator, and we have whoever else was there. I'll serve a subpoena on them and bring them in. He keeps saying that Mr. Simpson would gladly and happily have taken a test. The fact is, he did take a test.

The Court: Well, how do you get around work product and privilege?

Mr. Petrocelli: How does he—How does he get around opening up a subject matter that, at the same time, he claims is work product and privilege and then bars us—

The Court: ... At this point, I'm going to stand on what I said today. I'm not permitting any further movement on this issue, and I'm not going to permit defense to argue this.

Mr. Petrocelli: He's precluded from asking any further evidence— questions about this?

The Court: At this point. You show me some points and authorities that allows you to do that.

Mr. Baker: For the record, I, first of all, have disagreed with the Court's opinion relative to the fact that—that I opened the door in opening statement. As this Court is well aware, an opening statement is not evidence, number one. Number two, the incident of this letter and the incident that he's talking about are totally separate and apart. Mr. Brewer gets up and announces to the jury in opening statement, the title of my remarks is The Presumption of Guilt, Consciousness of Guilt. This goes to the consciousness of innocence that was opened by them. And I objected to the—any going into the polygraph test by Mr. Petrocelli. We had a side-bar. I was totally overruled. And I've also moved for mistrial on that basis.

And he opened the door and represented to the jury what a purported score was, what it meant, and that Mr. Simpson took a test without any good-faith belief in any of the above.

The Court: I've ruled on those issues already.

Mr. Petrocelli: Well, for the record I did have a good-faith basis.

The Court: Okay.''

5. INSTRUCTIONS TO JURY

On December 3, 1996, Judge Fujisaki gave the following instruction to the jurors:

"Ladies and gentlemen, the Court at this time will give you specific instructions regarding the plaintiff's examination of Mr. Simpson which was just completed, concerning lie detectors. I want you to listen very closely.

All communications between an attorney and his client are absolutely privileged. This means that such communications cannot be used by anyone for any purpose except with the permission of the client. Mr. Simpson cannot be asked any questions about any communications with his attorneys. Further, there is no evidence that Mr. Simpson consented to the publication of any of his communications with his attorney.

You will recall, Mr. Simpson's attorney, Mr. Baker, in his opening statement to you, spoke on the subject of a lie-detector test. By this opening statement, Mr. Simpson opened the subject of lie detectors to examination by the plaintiff. This, however, did not open the subject of any communication on this matter between Mr. Simpson and his attorneys, or persons acting for the attorneys for any purpose.

In this trial, Mr. Petrocelli questioned Mr. Simpson whether he took a lie-detector test, any score and meaning thereof. I instruct you that his questions do not and cannot establish that Mr. Simpson took a lie detector test, a score and meaning thereof. Statements of counsel, that is, the statements or questions of Mr. Petrocelli, are not evidence and may not be considered by you for any purpose. The references or statements regarding a lie detector test and Mr. Petrocelli's questions are not evidence unless they were adopted by Mr. Simpson in his answers. A question by itself is not evidence. You may consider questions only to the extent the content of the questions are adopted by the answer. Mr. Simpson's answer to the question of whether he took a lie detector test was that he was given an explanation of how the test worked and that he did not take the test.

There is no other evidence before you that Mr. Simpson took a lie detector test, and the plaintiff is bound by Mr. Simpson's response. Likewise, when Mr. Petrocelli asked Mr. Simpson whether he knew what the score on the test was, whether it was a minus 22, or whether it indicated extreme deception, these were questions by an attorney and do not constitute evidence. Mr. Simpson denied any test score or any knowledge of what test scores meant, and there is no evidence before you of any test score or what a score means. There was only Mr. Petrocelli's questions which were not adopted by an answer. Plaintiff is bound by Mr. Simpson's response.

Therefore, there is no evidence before you that Mr. Simpson took a lie detector test, no evidence about any score on such a test, nor any evidence of what any score means. You must totally disregard the questions about taking lie detector tests, test scores and their meanings, and treat the subject as though you had never heard of it.

Do all of the jurors understand these instructions?

Jurors: Yes.

The Court: Do any of the jurors have any questions about these instructions?

Jurors: (Nod negatively).

The Court: Okay. Thank you. Plaintiffs may call their next witness."

6. MOTION FOR MISTRIAL

The defendants made a motion for a mistrial, which was denied. The motion was renewed at the conclusion of the trial, and again denied:

Defendant Orenthal James Simpson hereby submits this Memorandum ... to augment the record regarding Mr. Simpson's Motion for Mistrial based upon the erroneous admission of evidence. On November 25, 1996, plaintiff's counsel was allowed, over objections, to question Mr. Simpson regarding a purported polygraph test and numbers claimed to be the results of a test taken on June 14, 1994 in a recently published book. The admission of such evidence over objection by defense counsel was contrary to law, an abuse of discretion and irreparably prejudicial to Mr. Simpson. Moreover, the instruction given to the jury on December 3, 1996 in no way cured the error.

a. *Reference to Taking a Purported Polygraph Examination.*

More than thirty years ago in *People v. Jones*, 52 Cal.2d 635, 653 (1959), the California Supreme Court stated that polygraph test results "do not scientifically prove the truth or falsity of the answers given during such test." In *People v. Thorton*, 11 Cal.3d 738, 763–64 (1974), the Supreme Court affirmed the general rule that because the results of polygraph examinations lack the requisite level of scientific acceptance and thus are of questionable probative value, a stipulation among the parties is required for such evidence to be admissible. In 1983, the Legislature enacted Evidence Code § 351.1, codifying the long-standing rule.[29] It is generally held that admission of such evidence is prejudicial error and that such error is not cured by a warning instruction. *People v. Wochnick,* 98 Cal. App.2d 124 (1950). A similar rule regarding the admission of polygraph tests and results per stipulation has been applied in the civil context. *See Robinson v. Wilson,* 44 Cal.App.3d 92 (1974).

Although Section 351.1 refers to criminal proceedings, it has been broadened to encompass non-criminal matters. "While Section 351.1 applies only to criminal proceedings specifically, its enactment by the Legislature nullifying the *Weatherspoon* decision reflects a continuing doubt in the law about the reliability of polygraph examination results." *Arden v. State Bar,* 43 Cal.3d 713, 723–24 (1987). "Absent an offer of proof that the polygraph is now accepted in the scientific community as a reliable technique, the evidence was presumptively unreliable and inadmissible." *People v. Harris,* 47 Cal.3d 1047, 1094–95 (1989).

In this case, there was no stipulation between the parties agreeing to admit evidence of a purported polygraph test or the alleged results thereof. In fact, defense counsel voiced strenuous objections to the line of questioning by plaintiff. Moreover, there was no proper offer of proof that the test is accepted in the scientific community as a reliable technique thereby making the evidence presumptively unreliable and inadmissible.

Nor did defense counsel "open the door" in Opening Statement to allow questioning of a purported polygraph test or the numbers claimed to be the results. As the Reporter's Transcript on October 24, 1996 will reflect (p.110), defense counsel made one brief comment of an offer by Mr. Simpson to take a polygraph. . . . There was no objection by plaintiff's counsel and if those comments were inappropriate any objection was waived. During the questioning of defendant, plaintiff's counsel inquired as to the interview of Mr. Simpson by Detectives Lange and Vanatter on June 13, 1994, regarding the taking of a polygraph test. . . . Mr. Simpson testified that he told the detectives he would do one after he got some sleep. However, plaintiff's counsel, with obvious intent to mislead the jury, then questioned Mr. Simpson about a purported polygraph test referenced in Lawrence Schiller's book *American Tragedy, The Uncensored Story of the Simpson Defense,* a wholly different situation from that which was commented on in Opening Statement and questioning of Mr. Simpson initially.

29. See fn. 2, *supra,* for full text of California Evidence Code § 351.1.

... Plaintiff's counsel acknowledged that the information regarding the purported polygraph test came from Mr. Schiller's book which is clearly hearsay and lacks foundation. The admission of such evidence is all the more egregious and prejudicial to the defendant in light of the fact that there was no evidence that Mr. Simpson was ever asked questions regarding the homicide, much less failed the alleged test. In fact, Laurence Schiller admitted on television on November 25, 1996 that he had no idea whether any of the questions that were supposedly asked of Mr. Simpson had anything to do with the crime.[30] There was absolutely no good faith factual basis for the questions plaintiff's counsel asked. Rather, this was an intentional act by plaintiff's counsel to deliberately implant in the minds of the jury that defendant failed the purported test. Actions such as plaintiff's counsel's have been assigned as misconduct, highly prejudicial and prejudicial error.

In the case of *People v. Aragon,* 154 Cal.App.2d 646 (1957), the Deputy District Attorney in his Opening Statement referred to a conversation in which defendant asked and was told that he failed the lie detector test; defendant's objection was overruled and the jury was admonished that they were not to take into consideration that this was any evidence as to the efficacy of the lie detector test. During the trial, over the defendant's objection, the conversation was repeated and the jury was again admonished that "you are to disregard any portion of the conversation which relates to the outcome of the lie detector test, or its efficacy as evidence." On cross-examination of the defendant, the prosecutor asked about the conversation drawing objections from defense counsel on the ground that it was improper cross-examination, stating, "This man has never denied that conversation or any part of it." The objection was sustained and the court added, "any reference to the lie detector test, it's out, or results." *Id.* at 657.

In holding that the prosecutor's misconduct constituted prejudicial error, and the admonitions to the jury [were] ineffective, the court held that his good faith and intentions were immaterial, and noted there was no evidence to establish what kind of lie detector test was given, if any; no evidence of the accuracy of the test, the skill of the operator or that the test has received scientific recognition; no foundation; and no stipulation for its admission. The court wrote:

> "It is not at all unlikely that a popular belief has been formed from press, radio, television, stage and screen that the lie detector is an accomplishment of modern science the results of which are as reliable as those of fingerprinting, blood tests and

30. A transcript of Mr. Schiller's appearance on *Internight with Jack Ford* on the MSNBC Network on November 25, 1996 was attached as an exhibit.

ballistics. However, this is not correct. It is general knowledge among those familiar with the lie detector machines that the results are greatly dependent upon the training, experience and skill of the operators and that the results vary with different types of subjects.... If the result of the lie detector test is inadmissible in the first instance, surely no one would contend that the results can be cloaked in the raiment of an accusatory statement and then slipped into evidence. If we were to hold that such a course is proper we would have sanctioned the receipt of damaging evidence which, but for such masking, could not be heard by the jury. We believe that the prosecution should not be permitted to introduce into evidence by indirection what would be highly improper if done directly. Our system of jurisprudence is not constructed upon such a foundation. Moreover, it would be hard to believe that the jury here considered the statements solely as accusatory statements. Obviously, the statements with reference to the lie detector test as introduced in this case were highly prejudicial and in our opinion constituted prejudicial error."

Id. at 658–59. The *Aragon* case [was] cited in *People v. Schiers,* 19 Cal.App.3d 102 (1970), [which] likewise found that the admission of the polygraph evidence was prejudicial error, compelling a reversal of judgment against the defendant. The *Schiers* court found that it was unlikely that the judge's admonition had operated as an effective cure for the prejudicial inference left with the jury:

"The court struck out the objectionable statement of the officer but the damage had been done and could not have been cured by the court's admonition. The mere direction that the testimony should be disregarded was no antidote for the poison that had been injected into the minds of the jurors."

Id. at 114. In the case at bar, the damage had been done and no admonition could "unring the bell...."

b. Admission of the Purported Polygraph Test Violated the Attorney–Client Privilege.

Apparently the Court is of the impression that because the purported polygraph was written about in a book recently published by Lawrence Schiller, that Mr. Simpson has somehow waived his attorney-client privilege by not seeking to enjoin publication of the book. Nothing can be further from the truth.

The holder of the attorney-client privilege is Mr. Simpson. California Evidence Code § 954(a). Only the client, in this case Mr. Simpson, may waive the privilege. Evidence Code Section 912 provides in pertinent part:

"(a) Except as otherwise provided in this section, the right of any person to claim a privilege provided by Section 954 ... is waived with respect to a communication protected by such privilege if any holder of the privilege, without coercion, has disclosed a significant part of the communication or has consented to such disclosure made by anyone. Consent to disclosure is manifested by any statement or other conduct of the holder or the privilege indicating consent to the disclosure, including failure to claim the privilege in any proceeding in which the holder has the legal standing and opportunity to claim the privilege."

At no time has Mr. Simpson waived the attorney-client privilege, either expressly or by implication. Nor does the claimed absence of an injunctive challenge by Mr. Simpson to the publication of Mr. Schiller's book constitute a waiver of the attorney-client privilege or somehow extinguish the right to assert the privilege. As the Declaration of Peter Neufeld, counsel for Mr. Simpson, attached hereto, establishes, Mr. Simpson has expressed in writing to members of his defense team, including Mr. Kardashian, who collaborated with Mr. Schiller for his book, that "all communications have been and continue to be privileged." Mr. Simpson further expressed in writing that any such authorization to disclose confidential communications must be in writing signed by Mr. Simpson. In fact, Messrs. Schiller and Kardashian's requests for a written waiver have been rejected by Mr. Simpson. From October 2, 1995 to the present, Mr. Simpson has never provided the required written waiver to any member of the defense team.

Moreover, following the request by Messrs. Schiller and Kardashian for waivers, Mr. Simpson in writing again reiterated to all counsel the obligations contained in his previous correspondence and further explained in greater detail that the prohibition against disclosure extended beyond privileged communications to include, among other things, all information gained through discussions with other attorneys, witnesses, friends and family.

As Mr. Neufeld declares, he personally informed Random House, Messrs. Schiller and Kardashian in wiriting that Mr. Simpson has refused to waive the attorney-client privilege and that he objected to the anticipated publication of the manuscript to the extent that it included privileged or confidential material.

Under Evidence Code Section 912, no act or purported failure to act on behalf of Mr. Simpson can be construed as a waiver of the attorney-client privilege. There was certainly no "proceeding" against Random House and Messrs. Schiller and Kardashian pending wherein Mr. Simpson could assert the privilege. Nor is there any principle in law requiring Mr. Simpson to seek injunctive relief.

Moreover, the type of relief sought would constitute a prior restraint on a publication protected by the fortress of the First Amendment. It would be extremely burdensome and oppressive for a client to have to go to the lengths of obtaining an injunction to prevent his lawyer from disclosing confidential communications which the lawyer is duty-bound to protect, or risk losing the privilege he holds by a 'waiver' if he does not do so.

7. COMMENTS AND QUESTIONS

(a) Examine Judge Fujisaki's corrective instruction with care. Does he instruct the jury to disregard the polygraph results because they are privileged, because they were never admitted in evidence, or because polygraphs are unreliable? Does it make any difference?

(b) Did Judge Fujisaki's ruling simply exclude the references to the purported polygraph test described in the Schiller book, or all references to polygraph tests? What about Simpson's offer to take a polygraph test contained in the Shapiro letter? What about Simpson's testimony that he received an explanation of how the test works and did not take a test? Is the rule of exclusion mandated for criminal cases in Evidence Code Section 351.1 *broader* than the rule of exclusion propounded in the cases cited by the defense?

(c) Is Judge Fujisaki "commenting" on the defendant's invocation of the attorney-client privilege? If so, is the comment allowed under California Evidence Code Section 913, which precluded any mention of Detective Fuhrman's invocation of the Fifth Amendment privilege in the criminal trial?

(d) If polygraphs are not reliable, why do police and prosecutors employ them so frequently in internal investigations? At one point in the criminal trial, Marcia Clark expressed the wish that potential jurors could be put on polygraphs to ensure their truthfulness in the *voir dire* examination for selection as jurors. When the content of the rehearsal of Detective Fuhrman's testimony in a grand jury room was leaked to the press, Chris Darden demanded that every person on the prosecution team take a polygraph. Clark, *Without A Doubt,* pp. 209, 340 (Viking, 1997).

(e) Marcia Clark, assuming the accuracy of the Schiller disclosure, comments:

"Polygraphs are risky. A subject can dope himself up to pass, which is why cops don't like to administer the test unless they've had the suspect in custody for a while. (Unbeknownst to me or the cops, Simpson had *already* taken a polygraph test and scored a minus 22, meaning he failed every single question about the murder.[31] I did not learn this until well after the verdict. Then I shook my head in amazement. It's hard to imagine that a lawyer would be stupid enough to offer his client up for a second poly after he'd failed the first time."

Clark, *Without A Doubt,* p. 40 (Viking, 1997). Apart from "stupidity", what other explanations might there be for Shapiro's offer? When, if ever, should a lawyer offer to stipulate to the admission of polygraph results?

(f) If a defendant successfully passes a polygraph, and then testifies at his trial, should the polygraph examiner be allowed to offer opinion testimony that the defendant is being truthful? Even if the defendant does not testify, should the testimony of the polygraph examiner be admissible as evidence of "consciousness of *innocence*"? See Imwinkelried & McCall, *Issues Once Moot: The Other Evidentiary Objections to the Admission of Exculpatory Polygraph Examinations,* 32 Wake Forest L.Rev. (1997). Many federal courts are reassessing the admissibility of polygraph evidence after the U.S. Supreme Court's abandonment of the *Frye* rule in *Daubert v. Merrell Dow Pharmaceuticals, Inc.,* 509 U.S. 579 (1993). See McCall, *Misconceptions and Reevaluation—Polygraph Admissibility After Rock and Daubert,* 1996 U.Ill.L.Rev. 363 (1996).

---

31. In the Motion for Mistrial filed by the defense, Schiller is quoted as admitting he had no knowledge whether Simpson was even asked any questions about the murder.

†